Unorthodox Lawmaking

New Legislative Processes in the U.S. Congress

Fourth Edition

Barbara Sinclair
University of California, Los Angeles

Los Angeles | London | New Delhi
Singapore | Washington DC

CQ Press
2300 N Street, NW, Suite 800
Washington, D.C. 20037

Phone: 202-729-1900; toll-free, 1-866-4CQ-PRESS (1-866-427-7737)

Web: www.cqpress.com

Cover design: Auburn Associates, Inc.
Composition: C&M Digitals (P) Ltd.

♾ The paper used in this publication exceeds the requirements of the American National Standard for Information Sciences—Permanence of Paper for Printed Library Materials, ANSI Z39.48-1992.

Printed and bound in the United States of America

15   14   13   2   3   4   5

Library of Congress Cataloging-in-Publication Data

Sinclair, Barbara.
    Unorthodox lawmaking : new legislative processes in the U.S. Congress / Barbara Sinclair. — 4th ed.
        p. cm.
    Includes bibliographical references and index.
    ISBN 978-1-60871-236-6
    1. Legislation—United States. 2. United States—Politics and government—2001-2009. I. Title.

    KF4945.S58 2011
    328.73'077—dc22

                                        2011007491

To
Dick Fenno,
teacher, mentor, friend

Contents

List of Tables and Figures

Tables

Figures

Preface

DURING MY FIRST TWENTY YEARS of doing research on Congress and teaching courses about the institution, the gap between the legislative process that I observe on Capitol Hill and the legislative process described in U.S. government textbooks became a chasm. Like most teachers, I tried to give my students a sense of the contemporary legislative process in all its variety while still presenting the "textbook" model as the standard. That approach, I came to believe, was no longer adequate or accurate.

The reception the earlier editions of this book received from my colleagues persuaded me that most share my perception; thus another edition.

This book describes how the legislative process in the U.S. Congress really works today. In it I show how the process has changed, explore the reasons for the change, and examine its consequences. Although based on original research, the book is written with the nonspecialist in mind. No extensive knowledge of Congress is presupposed. I believe that it will help prepare readers to pursue further studies of Congress if they so choose, but my primary aim is to enable them to make sense of congressional politics and to judge claims about congressional performance.

I refer to the contemporary legislative process as "unorthodox lawmaking" to distinguish frequently employed contemporary procedures and practices from what is still often presented in textbooks as the standard process. The term emphasizes the extent of change and gives me a handy way of referring to a set of procedures and practices that are either new or much more frequently employed than they used to be. In fact, the legislative process for major legislation is now less likely to conform to the textbook model than to unorthodox lawmaking.

This new edition is similar to the previous ones in intent, in organization, and mostly in argument. I have updated the data series through the end of the 111th Congress (2009–2010), have substituted more current examples for many of the older ones, and have replaced most of the case studies with new ones. I have also brought the examination of changes and trends up to date, especially by discussing heightened partisanship and its consequences. I retain some of the examples from the earlier editions because I believe they help to illuminate how unorthodox lawmaking works in a variety of political contexts.

The book begins with two short case studies that provide a vivid example of how much the legislative process changed in the two decades between 1970 and 1990. Chapter 1 describes the passage of clean air legislation in those two years and then, through a comparison of the process on the two bills, introduces unorthodox lawmaking and the questions it raises. Chapters 2–5 explain the procedures and practices that make up the new legislative process. Chapter 2 begins with the introduction of a bill and proceeds step by step through the process in the House, at each stage examining and illustrating frequently used procedures. Chapter 3 traces the path a bill takes through the Senate. Before 1970 one could speak of a standard legislative process that most major legislation traversed, but as these chapters show, there are now many routes from introduction to enactment. Once the House and Senate have passed legislation, the two different versions must be reconciled, as I explain in Chapter 4. In recent years, how the chambers reconcile their differences on major legislation has changed in significant ways, as that chapter describes. Chapter 5 addresses omnibus legislation, the budget process, and legislative-executive summits. Chapter 6 explores the historical origins of the procedures and practices that characterize contemporary lawmaking and documents the change over time in their frequency. Chapters 7–9 analyze unorthodox lawmaking through a series of case studies. Case studies of the 2008 and 2009 economic stimulus bills and the health reform bill in 2009–2010 illustrate the range and variability of the contemporary legislative process. The account of the enactment of President George W. Bush's tax cuts—and the use of the budget process in the course of enacting the health care bill—shows how the budget process works and demonstrates its contemporary use as an instrument of comprehensive policy change. Chapter 10 examines the influence that the changes in procedures and practices have had on legislative outcomes and on how Congress functions.

I chose to describe the contemporary legislative process early in the book, in Chapters 2–5, followed by a chapter that analyzes the trajectory of change and the reasons for it. For those who prefer their history first, the order of those chapters can be reversed, with Chapter 6 read before Chapters 2–5. Chapter 7, the case study of the two stimulus bills, could easily be read after Chapters 2–4 and before Chapter 5, which deals with the budget process.

In addition to the quantitative analysis of the process on major legislation described in Chapter 1, this book is based on my observations and experiences as an American Political Science Association congressional fellow in the office of the House majority leader in 1978–1979, in the office of the Speaker in 1987–1988 on an informal basis, and on interviews with members of Congress, their staffs, and informed observers over the course of more years than I am now willing to admit. I owe Jim Wright, Speaker of the House from 1987 to 1989, and his staff an enormous debt for giving me the opportunity to observe the legislative process from the inside. I am also grateful to all of those very busy people who made time to talk with me over the years and from whom I learned so much. All unattributed quotations are from interviews I conducted.

I would especially like to thank Peter Robinson, formerly of the House Parliamentarian's Office and of Speaker Wright's staff and now of the Senate Parliamentarian's Office; Stanley Bach, Richard Beth, Walter Oleszek, Elizabeth Rybicki, and Valerie Heitshusen of the Congressional Research Service; and Robert Dove, formerly Senate parliamentarian. All are incredibly knowledgeable and extremely generous in sharing their expertise. Stan Bach, Michael Kraft, and Sandy Maisel read the first-edition manuscript and gave me invaluable comments and advice. I want them to know how much I appreciate their detailed and thoughtful reviews; they significantly improved the manuscript. Robin Kolodny, Bruce Oppenheimer, and Steve Smith, who read the proposal and much of an early draft, provided perceptive and helpful advice. Cary R. Covington, Rebekah Herrick, and David Menefee-Libey reviewed the first edition and provided me with many useful suggestions for improving the second. I'd also like to thank the following reviewers for their suggestions for the fourth edition: Douglas Harris, Loyola College; Wesley Hussey, UCLA; Henry Kim, University of Arizona; Marvin Overby, University of Missouri; Brian Reed, Montana State University-Billings; and Keith W. Smith, University of the Pacific.

Stan Bach read the new case studies for the second edition and the entire third edition with his discerning eye and commented on them with his combination of great knowledge and common sense. Bruce Oppenheimer and Allen Shick also reviewed the third edition and gave me numerous useful suggestions. James Wallner read Chapter 3 of the fourth edition and provided valuable information and suggestions. I am truly grateful. Over the years, David Jones, Gregory Koger, and Alan Rozzi provided superb research assistance. Much of the quantitative material has been presented in papers at professional meetings; I thank the many colleagues who commented on those papers. I continue to learn from my colleagues in the congressional scholarly community; there are too many to list here, but I thank them all. Of course, none of these people is responsible for any remaining errors. Finally, thanks to Janine Stanley-Dunham, copy editor extraordinaire, and to Brenda Carter, Charisse Kiino, and Laura Stewart of CQ Press. They have been great to work with.

Clean Air: An Introduction to How the Legislative Process Has Changed

In 1970 CONGRESS PASSED A PATH-BREAKING Clean Air Act, legislation Congressional Quarterly called "the most comprehensive air pollution control bill in U.S. history" (*Congressional Quarterly Almanac* 1970, 472).

Reported by the House Interstate and Foreign Commerce Committee, the bill was considered on the House floor under an open rule allowing all germane amendments. Of the nine amendments offered, eight were defeated, most on voice votes; only one technical amendment was accepted. The bill passed the House 375–1.

In the Senate the Public Works Committee reported a bill stronger than the House legislation or the administration's draft. After two days of floor debate, during which ten amendments were accepted by voice vote and two rejected by roll calls, the Senate voted 73–0 to pass the strong bill. The conference committee, consisting of five members of the House committee and nine senators, came to an agreement on a bill much closer to the Senate's stringent version than to the House's milder bill, and both chambers approved the conferees' version by voice vote.

Although the bill was far stronger than the legislation he had initially proposed, President Richard Nixon signed the Clean Air Act, "one of the most far-reaching laws ever passed by Congress to regulate the domestic economy," in the words of a prominent journalist. The act set auto emission standards so stringent that it forced the development of new technology, and it directed the Environmental Protection Agency to establish national air quality standards (Cohen 1992, 13).

* * *

1

By 1989, when the 101st Congress began work on a major revision of the Clean Air Act, the political and institutional environment had changed, and the path the legislation traversed to enactment was very different from that of its 1970 predecessor. In the Senate the slightly renamed Public Works and Environment Committee again reported a strong bill. The bill was considered on the Senate floor for six days, but the majority leader, George Mitchell, D-ME, could not muster the sixty votes needed to overcome a threatened filibuster. To construct a bill that could pass the chamber, the majority leader began negotiations with the administration and with a large and shifting group of senators. Members of the Environment Committee participated on a continuous basis, but many other senators with an interest in specific issues also took part. After a month of talks, an agreement was reached. To guard against any unraveling of the compromise, Mitchell and President George H. W. Bush pledged to oppose floor amendments, even those that reflected their policy preferences.

Mitchell offered the compromise worked out in the talks as a substitute amendment to the bill the Environment Committee had reported. He negotiated a complex unanimous consent agreement (UCA) for considering the bill on the floor. That UCA did not limit either debate or amendments; it simply required senators to put the amendments they wished to offer on a list. This provided a modicum of order to floor consideration of the bill. After ten days' debate over a month's time, the Senate passed the bill 89–11. Of about 250 amendments on the list, 25 were offered and pushed to a roll call vote; 9 of these passed. None was a "deal breaker."

In the House the legislation was referred to three committees, rather than just one as the 1970 bill had been. The Energy and Commerce Committee, successor to the Interstate and Foreign Commerce Committee, was the lead committee, and after protracted internal negotiations it reported legislation that represented a compromise among its factions. One key issue, however, had been decided by extremely close votes in both the subcommittee and the full committee, and Speaker Tom Foley, D-WA, was concerned that the issue might well lead to a bitter party-splitting battle on the floor. He thus instructed the lead representatives of the two Democratic factions, Henry Waxman of California, chair of the subcommittee, and John Dingell of Michigan, chair of the full committee, to work out a compromise. In order to pressure them to act expeditiously, Foley set a deadline for floor action on the legislation. The Speaker and his aides then worked with Waxman and Dingell to help them come to an agreement. The other committees, also under Speaker-imposed deadlines, reported their legislative language.

Unlike its 1970 predecessor, the 1990 clean air legislation went to the floor under a rule that restricted amendments to the nineteen listed in the Rules Committee report and that carefully structured how these amendments would be considered. The crucial Waxman-Dingell deal was offered as an amendment on the floor and approved 405–15. In all, six amendments were pushed to a roll call vote and five passed; none of these threatened the key compromises. The House then approved the bill 401–21.

Speaker Foley chose 130 conferees to represent the seven committees with some jurisdiction over the bill's subject matter. Nine members from two committees represented the Senate. Protracted negotiations produced a bill that passed both chambers easily. A dramatic expansion of the Clean Air Act, the 1990 bill for the first time set up a program for controlling acid rain, established a stringent new program to control emissions of toxic air pollutants, and set new standards and timetables for improving urban air quality (*Congress and the Nation* 1993, 469, 473–474). Although it was considerably stronger than the draft he had proposed, President Bush signed the legislation.

* * *

These examples illustrate how greatly the legislative process on major legislation has changed since the early 1970s.[1] The legislative process on the 1970 Clean Air Act perfectly fits the bill-becomes-a-law diagram that is still a staple of American politics and legislative process textbooks (see Table 1.1). The 1970 bill was considered by a single committee in each chamber. It came to the House floor as drafted and approved by the committee, and it was considered there under an open rule allowing all germane amendments. The Senate also considered the bill as drafted by its committee; no senator mounted a filibuster, and no amending marathon occurred. After both chambers had passed the bill, a small group of senior members of the two committees got together in conference and worked out a compromise between the House and Senate versions.

The process on the 1990 bill, by contrast, was much more complex and not amenable to a nice, neat diagram. The legislation was considered by several committees in the House, and in both chambers compromises arrived at through informal processes altered the bills after the committees reported their legislation. Floor procedures were complex and tailored to the specific bill at issue. In the Senate the real possibility of a filibuster shaped the process, making it necessary for Majority Leader Mitchell to build through negotiations an oversized coalition. The final

---

1. These accounts are based largely on primary documents, interviews (in the case of the 1990 act), and the following secondary sources: Congressional Quarterly's accounts, Cohen (1992), and Smith (1995, chap. 12).

TABLE 1.1   The 1970 Clean Air Act as an Example of the Textbook Legislative Process

Action	House	Senate
Committee	HR 17255 referred to the Committee on Interstate and Foreign Commerce Hearings held March 16–21 and April 14, 1970 Bill marked up Bill reported June 3, 1970 Rules Committee grants open rule	S 4358 referred to the Senate Public Works Committee Hearings held March 16–20, March 23–26, and April 17, 1970 Bill marked up Bill reported September 17, 1970
Floor	Considered in Committee of the Whole and passed June 10, 1970	Debated on the floor September 21–22 and passed September 22, 1970
Conference	Conferees appointed Conference meets Conference agreement reached Conferees file report December 17, 1970	
Floor	House approves conference report December 18, 1970	Senate approves conference report December 18, 1970
Presidential	Sent to the president. President signs December 31, 1970	

conference agreement was worked out by a much larger and more diverse group of members than in 1970.

In the contemporary Congress the textbook diagram describes the legislative process for few major bills. The seemingly unorthodox legislative process on the 1990 Clean Air Act is actually more characteristic of contemporary major legislation than the supposedly standard textbook process that the 1970 Clean Air Act went through. To be sure, even during the textbook era not all legislation followed the relatively simple, straightforward process depicted by Table 1.1; there always have been alternative paths. Their use, however, was extraordinary, not ordinary; most major legislation followed the textbook process.[2]

---

2. Shortcut processes to handle noncontroversial legislation did and have continued to exist.

Today the bill that, like the 1970 Clean Air Act, is reported by a single committee and considered on the floor under a rule that allows all germane amendments is rare. In fact, the legislative process is now bifurcated to a considerable extent. Most bills are passed through shortcut procedures—suspension of the rules in the House (see Chapter 2) and unanimous consent during the end-of-the-day "wrap-up" in the Senate (see Chapter 3). These, however, are not major bills; they are neither controversial nor far reaching in impact. In contrast, the legislative process on major legislation is now regularly characterized by a variety of what were once unorthodox practices and procedures.

Rather than being sent to one committee in each chamber, many measures are considered by several committees, especially in the House, while some measures bypass committee altogether. Not infrequently, after a bill has been reported—but before it reaches the floor—major substantive changes are worked out via informal processes. Omnibus measures of great scope are a regular part of the legislative scene, and formal executive-congressional summits to work out deals on legislation are no longer considered extraordinary. On the House floor most major measures are considered under complex and usually restrictive rules often tailored to deal with problems specific to the bill at issue. In the Senate, bills are regularly subject to large numbers of floor amendments that are not necessarily germane; filibuster threats are an everyday fact of life, affecting all aspects of the legislative process and making cloture votes a routine part of the process. This book explores how and why the legislative process in the U.S. Congress has changed since the 1970s and examines the consequences of those changes.

Although the changes in the legislative process in the past several decades that I focus on here were preceded by a long period of stability, they are by no means unique. The Constitution does not specify how Congress is to carry out its core task of lawmaking; beyond a few basic requirements, it allows each house to determine its own rules and procedures. During its history of more than two hundred years, the Congress has altered its legislative process a number of times.

In the very early years the legislative process in both the House and Senate emphasized the full membership's responsibility for lawmaking. The full membership debated a subject on the floor, decided whether legislation was warranted, and, if it was, laid out substantive guidelines. Then a special or select committee was appointed to draft legislation according to those guidelines (Cooper and Young 1989; Risjord 1994).

Even in the early decades not all business could be given so much time and attention; minor business was sent first to small committees. The House then began to create standing—that is, permanent—committees to handle recurrent complex issues, and the Senate began to send to a particular select committee all matters relating to the subject for which the committee had been initially created. During the second decade of the 1800s in the House and not much later in the Senate, standing committees became predominant. The committees did the initial work on legislation; only after they were finished did the rest of the membership have their say.

Floor procedure, too, has changed over time. In the early years both chambers' floor proceedings were relatively fluid and unstructured; even the House placed few limits on members' debate time (Binder 1996). Considering bills in the order they were introduced, the House was able to dispose of all of its business. Soon, however, House floor procedures became problematic. In 1811 the House adopted its first significant restrictions on floor debate, and throughout the nineteenth century the chamber struggled to develop a fair and efficient way of setting and ordering its floor agenda. Not until the 1880s and 1890s did the House develop its premier device for floor scheduling of major legislation: special rules from the Rules Committee (Oppenheimer 1994). Special rules, which required a simple majority of the House membership for approval, allowed legislation to be taken up out of order; this innovation made it possible for the majority party and its leaders, if they controlled the Rules Committee in fact as well as in form, to control the House schedule.

Senate floor procedure changed in much less basic ways over the course of its history (Bach 1994). The chamber's lack of limits on debate, initially the result of no considered decision, became over time a revered defining characteristic (Binder 1997). In the early years the Senate's small size made it unnecessary to limit the time members could debate an issue. Eventually, however, senators' extended debate prerogative became a problem. By then, the prerogative was well entrenched; the formidable barrier the rules themselves erected against change was fortified by the widely accepted myth that extended debate reflected the framers' intent (Binder and Smith 1997). Under extraordinary pressure from the president and the public, the Senate in 1917 for the first time changed its rules in such a way as to make cutting off debate possible. The resulting cloture procedure, however, was cumbersome and required a two-thirds vote for success.

Why has the legislative process changed over time? The long evolution of the legislative process is far too complex to review here, and scholars do not agree about just why things happened as they did (Cooper 1981; Gamm and Shepsle 1989). Certainly increases in workload, alterations in the political and social environment, and the strategic behavior of parties and of members as individuals were important determinants. For example, increases in the congressional workload and in the size of its own membership put pressure on the House to modify procedures that had adequately served a smaller, less busy legislature. Majorities, especially partisan majorities, found their legislative goals stymied by chamber rules that facilitated minority obstructionism. These majorities were able to change such rules in the House but were largely blocked in the Senate. On a more abstract, theoretical level, changes in the legislative process can be seen as the responses of members to the problems and opportunities the institutional structure and the political environment present to them as they pursue, as individuals or collectively, their goals of reelection, influence in the chamber, and good public policy (Fenno 1973; Sinclair 1995).

The alterations in the legislative process since the 1970s are the latest installment in an ongoing story. Examining them sheds light not only on the contemporary legislative process (what is happening on Capitol Hill today) but also on the broader political process. The study also provides insight into how democratic institutions such as the Congress evolve and adapt.

Chapters 2 through 5 describe the procedures and practices that make up the new legislative process and document their frequency. Chapter 2 begins with the introduction of a bill and proceeds step by step through the process in the House, examining and illustrating frequently used procedures at each stage. Chapter 3 traces the path a bill takes through the Senate. Before 1970 one could speak of a standard legislative process that most major legislation traversed, but as these chapters show, there are now many routes from introduction to enactment. Once the House and Senate have passed legislation, the two different versions must be reconciled, as I explain in Chapter 4. Chapter 5 addresses omnibus legislation, the budget process, and legislative-executive summits.

In Chapter 6 the historical origins of contemporary lawmaking are explored and the change in frequency of particular practices over time is documented. Chapters 7 through 9 use case studies to analyze unorthodox lawmaking. In addition to demonstrating how the contemporary legislative process works, all of the case study chapters are intended to illustrate how the political environment influences that process. Chapter 7 traces the enactment of stimulus legislation in response to economic crisis in the 110th and the 111th Congresses. It illustrates that nominally similar legislation can take quite different paths depending, at least in part, on the political context. In the 110th (2007–2008), Democrats had just regained control of Congress after twelve years in the minority but Republican George W. Bush was still president; in 2009 at the beginning of the 111th Congress, Democrat Barack Obama had just become president and Democrats held big majorities in both chambers. The tortuous saga of the enactment of the Patient Protection and Affordable Care Act in Chapter 8 shows how difficult it is to pass major, nonincremental legislation in a period of high partisan polarization. Multiple unorthodox processes and procedures were required to enact health care reform. Even the Budget Act came into play. Chapter 9 focuses on the budget process as it was employed to pass the Bush tax cuts of 2001 and 2003.

Chapter 10 examines the impact that the new procedures and practices have on legislative outcomes and on how Congress functions. Congress is the least-liked branch of the national government; only a fraction of the American people expresses confidence in the Congress. Americans are not happy with the congressional process or often with the policy produced (Hibbing and Theiss-Morse 1995; Gallup 2011). According to the Gallup Organization, the 111th Congress (2009–2010) averaged only 25 percent approval from the American people (2011). Is unorthodox lawmaking in part responsible, either directly or indirectly? Does it enhance or inhibit the likelihood of a bill becoming law? What other effects does the change in process have on how Congress functions? Does it foster or discourage deliberation, the development and bringing to bear of expertise, the inclusion of a broad range of interests, and informed and timely decision making?

Americans expect a lot from Congress. Congress should represent the people and pass laws that both reflect the will of the people and work; that is, citizens expect members of Congress to bring into the legislative process the views, needs, and interests of the people they are elected to represent, and they expect Congress to pass laws that are responsive to popular majorities and that deal promptly and effectively with pressing national problems. Has unorthodox lawmaking made Congress more or less capable of carrying out the formidable tasks with which it is charged?

A Note on Data

I argue here that the legislative process on major legislation has changed. To show this is so, I need to define major legislation and then document change over time. Major measures are defined by the list of major legislation in the *CQ Weekly* (before 1998, *Congressional Quarterly Weekly Report*), augmented by those measures on which key votes occurred (again according to the *CQ Weekly*). This provides a list of about forty to sixty bills (and some other measures such as budget resolutions and constitutional amendments) for each Congress that close contemporary observers considered major. I then examine the course these major measures traversed in selected Congresses. I supplement my data by drawing where possible on the work of other scholars.

The Congresses selected are the 87th (1961–1962), the 89th (1965–1966), and the 91st (1969–1970), all prereform Congresses;[3] the 94th (1975–1976), the first reformed Congress; the 95th (1977–1978), the first Congress of the Carter presidency; the 97th (1981–1982), the first Congress of the Reagan presidency; the 100th (1987–1988) and the 101st (1989–1990), the last Reagan and first George H. W. Bush Congresses; the 103rd (1993–1994), the first Clinton Congress; the 104th (1995–1996), the first Congress in forty years with Republican control of both houses; the 105th (1997–1998); and the 107th (2001–2002) through the 111th (2009–2010). Democrats enjoyed unified control of the presidency and both houses of the Congress in the 87th, 89th, 95th, 103rd, and 111th Congresses. Republicans controlled the presidency and the Senate in the 97th; they controlled the presidency and both chambers during the first half of 2001—when, with the switch of Vermont's Jim Jeffords to caucusing with the Democrats, control of the Senate switched to the Democrats—and during the 108th and 109th. The other selected Congresses saw divided control, with Democrats the majority party until the 104th and again in the 110th and the Republicans in the 104th through the 106th.

---

3. The 89th was also the "Great Society" Congress, in which an enormous amount of highly significant legislation was passed—for example, the Voting Rights Act and Medicare. See Chapter 6 for a discussion of the reforms of the 1970s.

Multiple Paths: The Legislative Process in the House of Representatives

THE LEGISLATIVE PROCESS IN THE CONTEMPORARY Congress is varied and complex. The old textbook process depicted in Table 1.1 was predictable and linear, with one stage following another in an unvarying sequence. At many stages there is now no single, normal route but rather a number of different paths that legislation may follow. The best way to understand the contemporary legislative process is to begin with the introduction of a bill and proceed step by step through the process in each chamber, examining frequently used options at each stage. That is what this and the following three chapters do.

This is not a book on parliamentary procedure; procedures that are obscure and seldom employed are of no interest here. Rather, my aim is to make understandable the procedures and practices that occur on the major legislation considered during any contemporary Congress.[1]

For convenience, I begin the journey in the House of Representatives. Most legislation and other measures—budget resolutions and constitutional amendments—may begin in either chamber. The Constitution requires that tax legislation originate in the House, the people's chamber, and by custom the House also acts first on appropriations—that is, spending—bills. The Senate, however, is fully coequal as a policy initiator. Even in the tax

---

1. I have relied heavily on Tiefer (1989), Gold et al. (1992), Oleszek (2004), and Gold (2004) for the fine points of procedure. The people at the Congressional Research Service, especially Stanley Bach, Richard Beth, Walter Oleszek, and Elizabeth Rybicki, were invaluable sources of information. Peter Robinson also was extremely helpful.

area, the Senate can initiate policy change by amending a minor House-passed tax bill. Yet because the House tends to act before the Senate (Strom and Rundquist 1977), I start with action in that chamber. Although action on the same *issue* may take place simultaneously in the two chambers, formal action on legislation is a sequential process: the House and the Senate cannot act on the same *bill* at the same time.

Bill Introduction

To introduce a bill, a member of the House simply drops it into the "hopper," a wooden box at the front of the chamber, when the House is in session.[2] Bill introduction has not changed in recent years. Only members of the House may introduce bills or resolutions in the House, and a member may introduce as many measures as he or she wishes. Thus even the president needs to find a member of the House to introduce legislation, although doing so is seldom a problem.

In fact, the legislation that members introduce has many different origins. Some bills are introduced at the behest of interest groups or even individual constituents, some come from federal government agencies and departments, and some represent a member's own personal policy priorities. The legislative process in Congress is open and permeable. Although only members of Congress can perform official acts such as introducing bills and voting, members' behavior is influenced by the president, interest groups, constituents, the media, and public opinion. That makes all of them significant actors in the legislative process.

Bill Referral

Once introduced, the bill is referred to the committee or committees of jurisdiction. Because committees are the primary shapers of legislation and because they differ in membership and perspective, which committee

---

2. The term *bill* is here used for bills, which are designated by the prefixes HR (for House of Representatives) and S (for Senate), and for joint resolutions, designated H.J.Res. and S.J.Res. There is no practical difference between the two in process and in effect; both become law. I try to use the term *measure* to indicate a broader class of legislative entities, including not only bills but also concurrent resolutions (H.Con.Res. or S.Con.Res.), which do not become law, and constitutional amendments. In process terms the difference between bills and joint resolutions, on the one hand, and concurrent resolutions and constitutional amendments, on the other, is that the last two do not require the president's signature. Resolutions, designated H.Res. or S.Res., deal with matters entirely within the purview of one body and do not require action by the other.

receives the bill can make a difference to the legislative outcome. The parliamentarian, a professional, nonpartisan employee of the House, handles referrals under the supervision of the Speaker, whose prerogative it is to make this decision. Referrals are governed by the rules of the House, specifically Rule X, which specifies what subject matters fall within the purview of each committee, and by precedents. Thus, referral decisions are usually fairly routine, but there may be some discretion, especially when new issues arise (King 1994).

Multiple Referral

In 1975 the House changed its rules and permitted the referral of legislation to more than one committee. The prominent issues had changed: many had become more complex, and they no longer fit neatly into the jurisdiction of a single committee. Since that rules change, multiple referral has become increasingly common, especially on major legislation. From the Congresses of the late 1980s (1987–1990) to the present, about 20 percent of all measures have been referred to more than one committee. When only major legislation is considered, the likelihood of multiple referral is even higher. In most Congresses since the late 1980s about three out of ten major measures were multiply referred.[3]

Most multiply referred measures—two-thirds to three-quarters—are sent to two committees. Again, major legislation is different; in the Congresses of the late 1980s and early 1990s (100th, 101st, 103rd), more than half of multiply referred legislation went to three or more committees and, in some cases, to many more. President Bill Clinton's reinventing government legislation (the Government Reform and Savings Act of 1993), for example, went to seventeen House committees; his health care bill was referred to ten. The big trade bill passed by the 100th Congress (1987–1988) was referred to six committees, and five other committees wrote trade-related legislation that was incorporated into the omnibus trade bill. In 1989 a bill to provide aid to Poland and Hungary was sent to seven committees.

After Republicans gained control of the House in the 1994 elections, the percentage of major bills referred to more than two committees declined and has tended toward one in five ever since. In every Congress, however, there continue to be bills sent to many committees. So, in the 104th, the first Republican-controlled House since the 1950's, the bill

---

3. Tables with the complete data series for this and most of the other "unorthodox processes" discussed in this chapter can be found in Chapter 6.

to abolish the Department of Commerce was referred to eleven committees and immigration reform to seven. In the 108th (2003–2004), the bill to overhaul government intelligence operations was sent to thirteen committees. The climate change bill the House passed in 2009 had been referred to eight committees.

It is easy to understand why many committees had jurisdiction over the bill to reinvent government; the bill concerned many federal agencies, each one under the purview of a different committee. Somewhat similarly, the intelligence operations overhaul bill affected agencies and functions under the jurisdiction of a number of committees—the Intelligence Committee but also Armed Services, Homeland Security, Government Reform (which deals with government reorganization), Judiciary (federal criminal law), and Financial Services (in this case, money laundering). But why was legislation to aid two countries in eastern Europe multiply referred? On the Poland-Hungary bill, the Foreign Affairs Committee, which has jurisdiction over foreign aid, played the lead role, but Ways and Means involved because of its jurisdiction over granting special trade benefits to foreign countries; programs for scholarships for Polish students, for technical training for Polish farmers and businesspeople, and for the promotion of U.S. exports to Poland and Hungary involved still other committees.

The original 1975 multiple referral rule instructed the Speaker to refer a bill to all committees with jurisdiction. Before 1995 the Speaker had three types of multiple referral available (Davidson and Oleszek 1992). The most frequent type was a joint referral: a bill was sent to two or more committees simultaneously. Or a bill could be divided up and various sections and titles sent to different committees. Such split referrals have been relatively rare; dividing up complex legislation can be difficult. More common were sequential referrals: a measure was assigned to two or more committees in sequence. Typically, the first committee had the most jurisdiction and consequently the largest legislative role.

The Speaker also could combine types of referrals. Thus legislation might be sent initially to the two or more committees with the most jurisdiction under a joint referral and then sequentially to other committees with lesser jurisdictional interests. As amended in 1977, the multiple referral rule allowed the Speaker to set a reporting deadline for committees under any sort of referral.[4]

---

4. By custom, time limits were set on sequential but not on joint or split referrals. Since the Speaker could decide the type of referral to use, he or she exercised discretion as to time limits.

The 1995 rule, the aim of which was to streamline the process, abolished the old form of joint referral and instructed the Speaker to designate a primary committee (Evans and Oleszek 1995). As interpreted, the rule actually allows for several primary committees under a split referral. During the first one hundred days of the 104th Congress, split referrals were frequently used. The welfare reform bill, for example, was split among the Ways and Means Committee, the Economic and Educational Opportunities Committee, and the Agriculture Committee. Joint referrals and, to an extent, sequential referrals have been replaced by the referral of legislation to a primary committee (based on "the weight of the bill") and *additional initial referral* to one or more other committees.

Committees that receive legislation on additional initial referral may consider it immediately; they need not wait for the primary committee to report before beginning their work. In that sense the new process is similar to the old joint referral procedure. However, when the primary committee reports, the other committees are subject to time limits at the Speaker's discretion; if time limits are imposed, a committee must report within the specified time or be automatically discharged, that is, have the legislation taken away from it. The usual form of such a referral reads, "referred to the [primary] committee, and in addition to the [secondary] committees, for a period to be subsequently determined by the Speaker, in each case for consideration of such provisions as fall within the jurisdiction of the committee concerned." So, HR 1256 the Family Smoking Prevention and Tobacco Control Act, a bill to give the Federal Food and Drug Administration power to regulate tobacco products, was on March 3, 2009, "referred to the Committee on Energy and Commerce, and in addition to the Committee on Oversight and Government Reform, for a period to be subsequently determined by the Speaker, in each case for consideration of such provisions as fall within the jurisdiction of the committee concerned" (Thomas bill summary).

Once the primary committee has reported, Speakers usually impose time limits on the other committees if they have not yet reported. Those time limits may be short, in some cases one day. After Republicans took control of the House in 1995, turf fights between committees seemed to decline in frequency, although they by no means became extinct. The extent to which the new rule was responsible is unclear. Certainly, when the Republicans first took the majority, committee chairs were under intense pressure from the party leadership and the membership to not allow turf fights to interfere with passing bills on the Republican agenda. And the Republican leadership continued to exert significant control over committee decision making. When the Democrats retook control of the House after the 2006 elections and then with the election of a Democratic president in 2008, the pressure to produce legislation was again intense and worked to damp down any inclinations on the part of committee chairs to allow jurisdictional squabbles to get in the way. In any case, House Speakers now seem sufficiently powerful to keep turf wars from seriously impeding the legislative process.

Committees given additional initial referral do not always report legislation. Quite frequently the record will indicate that the committee was discharged. In the 108th Congress, for example, the bankruptcy bill was referred to the Judiciary Committee and in addition to the Financial Services Committee. Judiciary reported, but Financial Services was discharged. The intelligence overhaul bill referred to thirteen committees was reported by five and discharged from the remaining eight.

The fact that a secondary committee was discharged does not necessarily mean it was not substantively involved in the legislation. In some cases, to be sure, the matter under its jurisdiction may have been so minor that the committee did not see any point in bothering to participate. Fetal protection legislation that made it a separate crime to injure or kill a fetus in vitro was referred to the Judiciary Committee and in addition to the Armed Services Committee because of its jurisdiction over military personnel, including crimes committed by members of the armed forces. It is likely that Armed Services let itself be discharged because of its relatively minimal jurisdictional interest. Alternatively, a committee that allows itself to be discharged may have had its concerns met by the lead committee informally. For example, the American Clean Energy and Security Act (ACES), the climate change bill, was referred to the Energy and Commerce Committee and in addition to eight other committees. All the other committees were discharged after Energy and Commerce reported the bill on June 5, 2009, but their concerns were addressed through informal negotiations. Most difficult was resolving the concerns of the Agriculture Committee; committee members worried about the impact of the carbon limits on farmers and other rural residents. An agreement negotiated by Energy Committee chair Henry Waxman, D-CA, and Agriculture Committee chair Colin Peterson, D-MN, and cleared with other rural Democrats specified that the U.S. Department of Agriculture, not the Environmental Protection Agency as in Waxman's bill, would run the program overseeing agricultural activities that could be used to meet the bill's cap-and-trade program (*Roll Call*, June 24, 2010). Thus, although the Agriculture Committee did not mark up the bill and was discharged from its consideration, its members and the interests they represented actually had a significant impact on the bill. In this case, the deals were incorporated in the legislation that went to the floor on June 26 (see discussion of rules below). A discharged committee may have been promised a floor amendment, or, if the bill amended existing legislation (as is often the case), the committee may have been satisfied by the text of the bill on matters under its jurisdiction, so it saw no need to change it. By not reporting, a committee does not give up any claim to jurisdiction. The committee often will receive representation on the conference committee, as Chapter 4 discusses. When the party leadership is ready to take a bill to the floor, it may ask secondary committees to forgo marking up the bill so as to speed up the process.

What does multiple referral mean for how committees work and for how legislation is processed? Clearly, on much of the most important legislation of a Congress, committees must work together if they are to legislate successfully. Some committees—ones that frequently share jurisdiction—have developed standard operating procedures for working together. Multiple referral has probably also accelerated the tendency to make the real decisions through informal processes, often ones in which only the majority party participates. For example, the intelligence overhaul bill was formally marked up by five committees, but the bill was actually drafted by the Republican committee chairs and the Republican party leadership. In 2009, Speaker Nancy Pelosi, D-CA, asked the chairs of the three committees with jurisdiction over health care to draft one bill before committee consideration; she feared that if three very different bills emerged from the three committees, the result would be delay and infighting. The bill the committees marked up had been drafted by the chairs with considerable participation by the leadership (see Chapter 8).

Some observers bemoan this tendency, but intense partisanship rather than the multiple referral rule is primarily responsible. When legislation is actually considered by a number of committees, multiple perspectives are brought to bear on complex problems. More interests have a voice and a more diverse group of members a say at the committee stage, where it counts most. Given the complexity of today's problems, this is certainly a benefit even if some delay is the cost.

Committee Decision Making

According to the textbook story, the legislative process starts in earnest in a congressional committee. That is still usually true—although less than it used to be and, as discussed earlier, more than one committee may be involved. What happens in committee often differs significantly from what was common in the past. Perhaps the greatest change in House committee decision making since the early 1970s is in the extent to which partisanship now drives the process. Most committees used to strive to avoid or at least restrain partisanship; they attempted to reach decisions through a process of bipartisan accommodation, if not consensus (Fenno 1973). They did so because it greatly enhanced the committee's chances for success on the House floor; when a committee reported a bill unanimously, other House members were likely to conclude that the bill was uncontroversial, or at least that all the problems had been worked out, and so they were inclined to follow the committee's lead. Since members' influence in the chamber depended largely on their committee's success, it made sense for them to work hard to build over-sized coalitions at the committee stage. To be sure, there were always committees on which ideological differences among members made consensus decision making impossible. Throughout the 1950s and 1960s, the House Education and Labor Committee was notorious for its knock-down, drag-out battles within committee and also for its dismal record of floor success. Yet, even a committee with as potentially divisive a jurisdiction as the tax-writing Ways and Means Committee tried hard to restrain internal conflicts and go to the floor with a broadly supported package.

Committees are now much more likely to make decisions on a partisan basis. As the political parties have become more like-minded internally and moved further apart from each other in their policy preferences, bipartisan coalitions have been harder to achieve and less necessary for floor success (see Chapter 6). Since the early 1990s, the committee process on about half of major measures has been partisan in the House, approximately double that of the earlier selected Congresses.[5] In the 111th Congress, the committee process was partisan on 60 percent of major measures. Despite this, not all bills are the products of partisan committee processes. Committees that deal with nonideological, constituency-benefit legislation—Transportation, for example—do try for unity and bipartisanship. And most committees consider a fair amount of reasonably important but largely noncontroversial legislation. For example, Ways and Means, now a highly partisan committee, in 2003 approved consensually a bill cracking down on Medicare fraud and another giving tax breaks to members of the armed services. An important defense acquisition overhaul bill was approved 59–0 by the Armed Services Committee in 2009. And perhaps more surprisingly, in 2008, the notoriously fractious Education and Labor Committee produced the first comprehensive overhaul of the Higher Education Act in a decade by a process not dominated by partisanship and voted it out of committee unanimously. On the most salient and consequential bills, however, committees tend to split along partisan lines.

Partisan polarization affects far more than the final vote in committee. With Democrats and Republicans so distant from each other on many policy issues, the majority often effectively excludes the minority from the

---

5. The figure for the early 1990s forward is based on the 103rd to 105th and the 107th to 110th Congresses and is the mean percentage across these Congresses.

decision-making process. Committee markups are often not true decision-making sessions; the real decisions have been made in informal, behind-the-scenes bargaining among majority-party members of the committee, sometimes with party leadership involvement. The public markups with minority-party members present then become simply a formality. The rules allow the minority to offer amendments, but consideration is perfunctory and all are voted down, with the majority voting in lockstep. The new Democratic majority elected in 2006 had promised to allow more real minority participation in committee than the Republicans had during their twelve years in the majority, but they found, as had the Republican majority before them, that the attempt often produced only delay and frustration. When the two parties' ideas of what constitutes good public policy are far apart as they are on many of the most critical contemporary issues and when, as is now often the case, the minority perceives no electoral benefit in compromise, a sincere working relationship even at the committee level becomes difficult to maintain.

Bypassing Committee

Although legislation is now frequently considered by more than one committee, sometimes bills bypass committee consideration altogether. In the late 1980s almost one in five major measures was not considered by a committee in the House. The frequency dropped to an average of about one in ten in the Congresses of the 1990s but then increased again to an average of one in five in the Congresses from 2001 to 2006 and further to one in three in the 110th and 111th Congresses (2007–2010).

The circumstances under which the committee of jurisdiction is bypassed in the House are varied. A majority of the House membership can bypass an unresponsive committee by the discharge procedure: any member may file a discharge petition calling for a measure to be brought out of committee and to the floor; when half the House members—218—have signed the petition, the measure is taken away from the committee and considered on the floor.[6] In the 97th Congress (1981–1982), in the 102nd (1991–1992), and again in the 103rd (1993–1994), a constitutional amendment to require a balanced federal budget was brought to the floor through the discharge procedure. In all three cases the committee of jurisdiction—the House Judiciary Committee—opposed the measure and had refused to consider or report it.

---

6. Actually, for technical reasons, discharge petitions usually seek to discharge the supporters' rule for the bill rather than the bill itself.

A House rules change in 1993 may have increased the incentives for members to file discharge petitions, even though they know the chances of success are slim. Previously, names on a discharge petition—and thus the names of those who had not signed—were kept confidential until 218 signatures were reached. The rules change specified that the list of who had signed would be public from the first signature, making it easier to pressure members to sign on hot-button issues or at least to use their failure against them in the next election. Still, the discharge procedure is seldom successful (Beth 1994; see also Pearson and Schickler 2009).

The threat of a discharge petition can pressure a committee and the majority-party leadership to bring measures to the floor they would rather not consider. During the 106th Congress (1999–2000), supporters of campaign finance reform and of managed heath care regulation used discharge petitions to convince the Republican leadership to bring these issues to the floor. Although neither petition received the required number of signatures, when the number got close, the majority leadership capitulated. If a discharge petition does get 218 signatures, its proponents—and not the majority leadership—control the floor. In 2002, when Speaker Dennis Hastert, R-IL, refused to bring up the campaign finance reform bill, supporters did succeed in discharging it and, in a rare occurrence, passed it over the majority leadership's opposition.

When a committee is successfully bypassed, the decision to do so is usually made by the majority-party leadership.[7] The rationale for doing so varies widely. Extreme time pressure created by an emergency may dictate bypassing a committee so as to enact a bill quickly. Congress responded to the attacks on the United States on September 11, 2001, by passing on September 14 a resolution authorizing the president to use force in response to the attacks (this was the resolution that authorized attacking Afghanistan) and a bill appropriating funds for this action. In neither case was there time for committee consideration. Other legislation enacted to deal with the aftermath of 9/11, specifically a bill to assist the struggling airlines and another to beef up airline security, also was brought to the floor without committee considerations to expedite the process. The financial crisis in fall 2008 required a swift response, which precluded committee consideration. The bill that became law (the bank "bailout" bill that set up the Troubled Asset Relief Program, or TARP) was not considered in committee in either chamber.

---

7. The most frequent means the leadership uses is extraction by the Rules Committee—that is, by the Rules Committee making the bill in order [for floor consideration] even though it has not been reported by committee (Tiefer 1989, 268–269).

Hurricane Katrina's devastating landfall in late August 2005 prompted the leadership to quickly bring to the floor an aid bill for New Orleans and the Gulf Coast region. Not only had the bill not been considered by committee, but also Congress had been in recess and almost all members of Congress were still in their home districts, so the bill was passed by unanimous consent without a recorded vote, which would have revealed the lack of a quorum. Occasionally, the emergency that creates the time pressure is purely political. When a federal court ruled that the Federal Trade Commission (FTC) had gone beyond the scope of existing law in setting up a national do-not-call-list, the Commerce Committee chair, with the full support of the leadership, immediately and without committee consideration brought a bill to the floor that explicitly gave the FTC that power and so reversed the court decision. Speed was deemed necessary to avoid disappointing the fifty million likely voters who had signed on to the list.

Most often, when committees are bypassed, some sort of political strategic consideration plays an important role. In 2002 the Republican leadership, without committee action first, brought to the floor a bill raising the debt limit. Even though it is essential to maintaining the good credit of the United States, House members hate voting for raising the debt limit, because it can easily be misrepresented as a vote for budget busting and to no good cause. Republicans, who for years harassed the majority Democrats about their debt-ceiling votes, especially detest casting such a vote. Figuring that their best chance of passing the bill was to keep its visibility as low as possible, Republican leaders (with almost no warning) offered an amendment to the rule for another bill that would permit the House to consider the Senate debt limit bill and allow only an hour of debate.

In January 2007 the leadership of the new Democratic majority brought a number of bills to the floor without first offering them for committee consideration. During the campaign, Democrats had promised to pass a specific list of bills during the first one hundred hours that they controlled the House, and delivering on this promise required bypassing committee. Similarly, in early 2009, to give President Barack Obama popular legislation to sign soon after his swearing in, the House Democratic leadership engineered quick passage of the State Children's Health Insurance Program (SCHIP) reauthorization and the Lilly Ledbetter Fair Pay Act, bypassing committee in both cases. Both had, after all, passed the House in the previous Congress.

In most cases now, when the leadership decides to bypass committee, the chair of the committee or committees with jurisdiction is an active participant—if not always the primary actor—in the process of bill drafting; the party and committee leaders also work as allies in making the decisions about strategy. When committees are bypassed, however, rank-and-file committee members, majority as well as minority, do have less influence on the substance of the bill at issue.

Postcommittee Adjustments

After a bill has been reported from committee, supporters often make substantive adjustments. The practice has become almost routine, with an average of a third of major legislation subject to such postcommittee adjustments in the post-1980 Congresses for which I have data. Almost half of major legislation in the 104th and in the 110th, both Congresses with new majorities, was subject to some such alteration after committee action. Rarely will legislation be taken back to committee for formal revision. Much more frequently, changes will be negotiated and then incorporated into a substitute bill or an amendment—often called a manager's amendment because it will be offered by the floor manager. The substitute may supersede the committee bill and become the version (called the base bill) taken to the House floor, or it may be incorporated into the committee bill by the rule; alternatively, the substitute or the amendment may be offered by supporters on the floor.

Such postcommittee adjustments are made to enhance the legislation's chances of passage. Almost always both committee and party leaders are involved, with the majority-party leadership often taking the lead. Major legislation that involves difficult political, substantive, or procedural problems is most likely to require such alterations. The committee leaders have, in most cases, done in committee what they were willing and able to do to ensure passage; and the majority-party leaders are ultimately held responsible for passing the legislation their party members and the House as an institution need and want.

Multiply referred legislation may require postcommittee adjustments to get it ready for floor consideration, either because some of the secondary committees depended on informal processes to get their considerations addressed or because the versions of the bills reported from the several committees need to be reconciled. For example, the 2009 climate bill discussed earlier that was reported by the Energy and Commerce Committee was significantly altered in informal negotiations; the concerns of the various other committees with jurisdiction had to be satisfied. The Speaker could and did discharge the secondary committees, but if a significant number of their members had opposed the bill on the floor, it would have failed. In particular, a compromise that satisfied Democratic members of the Agriculture Committee and other rural members was a prerequisite to passage. Sometimes, too, the party leadership will combine bills from a number of committees into one. In 2007, for example, the

Democratic leadership put together energy-related bills from eleven committees into one big energy bill; the size and scope of the bill, as well as the fact that it was sponsored by Speaker Pelosi, were intended to highlight that Democrats were seriously tackling the range of energy issues. Of course, when many bills, some on highly contentious issues, are combined, postcommittee adjustments are likely to be required.

Controversy and saliency often prompt the need for postcommittee adjustments. Supporters may find that their bill as it emerged from committee does not command enough votes to pass. In 2005 the Armed Services Committee included language in the annual defense authorization bill that would have further restricted female soldiers' proximity to combat—and so also their advancement opportunities in the military. Evidently the committee chair who advocated the change simply did not expect the firestorm of criticism that followed. The party leadership persuaded him to agree to remove the offensive language in a manager's amendment he would offer as soon as the bill went to the floor.

With his thin partisan majorities in the late 1990s and early 2000s, Speaker Hastert often found postcommittee adjustments necessary to pass important bills. Thus, in the 108th Congress, a bill rewriting the Head Start program required postcommittee adjustments to get enough votes from moderate Republicans to prevail. A bill entitled the Gasoline for America's Security Act, which Republicans attempted to pass in the wake of Hurricanes Katrina and Rita in fall 2005, was strongly opposed by environmentalists; supporters were forced to delete language that would have made it easier for utilities to expand without installing new antipollution equipment, "a provision that Republican leaders acknowledged would have doomed the bill," as the *New York Times* reported.[8]

Although their majorities were larger in the 110th and especially in the 111th Congress, Democrats took on some highly contentious issues, and the process of putting together a majority for passage sometimes required altering a bill after committee consideration had been completed. In 2007, for example, a provision exempting certain religious organizations was added to a bill barring job discrimination against gays and lesbians. The status of Guantánamo Bay prisoners was a recurring issue during the 111th Congress. As a candidate, Obama had promised to close the prison, and Republicans saw this—and what to do with the al-Qaida suspects held there—as a politically attractive issue. To assuage the fears of their own electorally vulnerable members, Democrats frequently had to include compromise language in committee; nevertheless, this did not

---

8. October 8, 2005.

always suffice. Thus in spring 2009, Appropriations chairman David Obey, D-WI, had worked out language on the issue and it had been incorporated in the war supplemental funding bill in committee. Republican claims that Guantanamo suspects might somehow be released in the United States continued to garner considerable media attention. This was an extremely difficult bill to pass in any case, and Obey and the leadership knew that the Guantanamo issue was a distraction they did not need. So as a postcommittee adjustment, language was added that, among other provisions, explicitly prohibited the use of any funds in the bill to release any Guantanamo detainees in the United States. Major postcommittee surgery was required to make possible passage of the DISCLOSE (Democracy Is Strengthened by Casting Light on Spending in Elections) Act in summer 2010. Earlier in the year the Supreme Court had ruled in *Citizens United v. Federal Election Commission* that corporations, labor unions, and nonprofit groups could spend unlimited funds from their own treasuries to fund political campaign advertising; to counter what they saw as the possible pernicious effects of the ruling, Democrats drafted a bill that greatly strengthened campaign finance disclosure requirements; for example, any group that ran television commercials would have to disclose its top donors in the ad. With the major business groups against the bill, the opposition of the National Rifle Association (NRA) seemed to spell defeat; the Blue Dogs, moderate and conservative Democrats, many from rural areas, would not vote for a bill with such a formidable set of opponents. The NRA especially is feared in rural and southern districts, where it has many, often fervent adherents. Chris Van Hollen (D-MD), the lead sponsor and assistant to the Speaker, negotiated a postcommittee adjustment to the bill the House Administration Committee had reported. It essentially exempted the NRA from the disclosure requirements. Reform groups and liberal Democrats found this an unappetizing deal, but most swallowed hard and accepted it, since the alternative was no bill at all.

Legislation that involves many issues is likely to be both highly consequential and controversial and, as such, not infrequently requires postcommittee fine-tuning. The broad scope of such omnibus measures, which are discussed more in Chapter 5, means that most members have a keen interest in at least some provisions. Putting together a version that is satisfactory to most members of the majority party and to a majority of the House may be difficult for the reporting committee or committees. Budget resolutions that lay out a blueprint for federal spending in the following year—how much will be spent, for what, whether there will be a tax increase, and what the deficit will be—and reconciliation bills that bring law into accord with the budget blueprint (and thus may include changes in a multitude of programs as well as tax increases) are the sort of omnibus measures that frequently require postcommittee adjustments orchestrated by the majority-party leadership.

In 2005, Republicans struggled to pass a reconciliation bill that would cut $50 billion from entitlement spending, as the budget resolution had required. Whip counts showed that the package that emerged from the Budget Committee simply would not pass. Over the course of several weeks, the leadership negotiated with various party factions; the key, according to Speaker Hastert, was finding a balanced package that satisfied the moderates, the conservatives, and those members focused on energy policy, specifically on opening the Arctic National Wildlife Refuge to oil drilling (*Roll Call,* November 18, 2005). After a first compromise proved to be insufficient—planned floor consideration had to be postponed—the leadership put together a package of changes that allowed the bill to squeak through 217–215. The case studies in Chapters 8–10 provide a number of further examples.

When the president is a copartisan, majority-party leaders now usually work closely with him and see passing his programs as important to the success of the party as a whole (see Sinclair 2006). That too may motivate postcommittee adjustments. In the wake of 9/11, the House Judiciary Committee reported a bipartisan version of what would become the USA PATRIOT (Uniting and Strengthening America by Providing Appropriate Tools Required to Intercept and Obstruct Terrorism) Act. The Bush administration believed that bill too weak, so the Republican leadership substituted a tougher administration-backed version for the committee-reported bill and took that to the floor. In 2009, House Democrats made several strengthening changes to the credit card regulation bill at the request of the Obama administration.

Suspension of the Rules

In the House the majority-party leadership schedules legislation for floor debate. When a committee reports a bill, it is placed at the bottom of one of the House calendars, the Union or House Calendars if it is major legislation. Considering legislation in the order it is listed on the calendar would make little sense, since optimal floor scheduling dictates attention to a host of policy and political factors. The House has developed ways of getting legislation to the floor that provide the needed flexibility. The primary ways of bringing legislation to the floor are through suspension of the rules and through special rules from the Rules Committee, both procedures that the majority-party leadership controls.

Noncontroversial legislation is usually considered under suspension of the rules. The motion to suspend the rules is in order on Mondays and Tuesdays and, since 2003, Wednesdays as well. Legislation brought up under this procedure is debated for a maximum of forty minutes. No amendments are allowed, and a two-thirds vote is required for passage.

During the Congresses from 1989 through 1996, on average 55 percent of all bills that passed the House did so by way of the suspension procedure; from 1997 through 2006, that number rose to 76 percent on average; in the 110th, the first Congress after the Democrats regained control, the proportion fell to 52 percent (Wolfensberger 2002, 11 and later updates). Much of the legislation considered under suspension is narrow in impact or minor in importance. The bills adopted under suspension of the rules on July 1, 2010, included:

> H.Res. 1228—Honoring the veterans of Helicopter Attack Light Squadron Three and their families (Rep. Boozman—Veterans' Affairs)
>
> HR 2340—Salmon Lake Land Selection Resolution Act (Rep. Young—Natural Resources)
>
> H.Res. 1460—Recognizing the important role pollinators play in supporting the ecosystem and supporting the goals and ideals of National Pollinator Week (Rep. Hastings—Agriculture)
>
> H.Res. 1321—Expressing the sense of the House of Representatives that the political situation in Thailand be solved peacefully and through democratic means (Rep. Faleomavaega—Foreign Affairs)
>
> H.Res. 1405—Congratulating the people of the 17 African nations that in 2010 are marking the 50th year of their national independence (Rep. Rush—Foreign Affairs)
>
> H.Res. 1412—Congratulating the Government of South Africa upon its first two successful convictions for human trafficking (Rep. Smith—Foreign Affairs)
>
> H.Res. 1462—Expressing support for the people of Guatemala, Honduras, and El Salvador as they persevere through the aftermath of Tropical Storm Agatha which swept across Central America causing deadly floods and mudslides (Rep. Mack—Foreign Affairs)
>
> H.Con.Res. 290—Expressing support for designation of June 30 as "National ESIGN Day" (Rep. McDermott—Energy and Commerce)

Legislation of more far-reaching significance also may be considered under suspension of the rules. This usually happens if the bill is so broadly supported that using much floor time is unwarranted. So on July 1, 2010, the House also approved:

HR 5609—To amend the Federal Election Campaign Act of 1971 to treat as a foreign national under such Act any registered lobbyist whose clients include foreign governments which are found to be sponsors of international terrorism or include other foreign nationals (Rep. Hall (NY)—House Administration)

HR 5503—Securing Protections for the Injured from Limitations on Liability Act (Rep. Conyers—Judiciary) HR 5503 granted the families of the oil workers killed when the BP oil rig exploded greater rights to sue.

Occasionally the majority party leadership for strategic reasons brings up more controversial legislation on suspension. In the weeks before the August 2008 recess, when soaring gas prices had thrust energy policy to the center of the agenda, the leadership brought several Democratic energy bills to the floor under suspension of the rules. The leadership wanted to give their members an opportunity to show voters they cared about gas prices without giving Republicans an opportunity to force votes on lifting the moratorium on offshore drilling, which a majority of Democrats, especially Californians, opposed, but vulnerable junior and "red" district members did not want to vote against. The suspension procedure not only bars amendments but also a motion to recommit, another way of amending a bill usually available to the minority (see below). The Democratic leaders knew they could not muster a two-thirds vote, but they also knew that, were their legislation to survive the Senate, an unlikely prospect, President Bush would veto it; so little was lost. The leaders accomplished their aim: to give their members the opportunity to vote for energy legislation without having to vote on offshore drilling.

The Speaker has complete discretion over what legislation is considered under suspension. When a committee chair has a bill he or she considers appropriate for suspension, the chair makes a request to the leadership. The Speaker is guided by party rules restricting the use of the procedure. Typical of those rules is the Republican Conference rule in the 109th Congress, which reads:

> The Majority Leader shall not schedule any bill or resolution for consideration under suspension of the rules which: 1) fails to include a cost estimate; 2) has not been cleared by the minority; 3) was opposed by more than one-third of the committee members reporting the bill; 4) creates a new program; 5) extends an authorization whose originating statute contained a sunset provision, or, 6) authorizes more than a 10% increase in authorizations, appropriations, or direct spending in any given year.

The Democratic Caucus rule is similar in thrust. These rules can be waived, but the requirement of a two-thirds vote for passage limits what can be successfully passed under suspension of the rules.

The minor measures typically so considered can be very helpful to members as they seek reelection. As the opportunities to offer amendments on the floor have decreased, the chance to get measures passed via suspension has become more valuable for tending the constituency, pleasing interest groups, or pursuing a policy interest, albeit a narrow one that can garner a two-thirds vote. The examples above are listed as they appear on the floor schedule sent out by the leaderships; note that the sponsor of each measure is prominently displayed.

The two-thirds passage requirement also gives the minority party one of its few points of leverage under House rules. Minority Democrats used that leverage to assure themselves of getting a reasonable proportion of Democratic-sponsored measures considered via the suspension procedure. Dissatisfied with the allocation of suspension measures to the minority, Democrats on October 1, 1997, defeated six suspension measures in a row and forced the majority to postpone consideration of ten others. Thereafter Republicans were more generous (Wolfensberger 2002). And the Democrats when in the majority continued to allow the minority its proportional share. The minority can thus inconvenience the majority; approving bills under the suspension procedure is much less time consuming than other routes. The leverage is, however, limited by the majority's ability to bring up a measure defeated under the suspension procedure via a special rule.

Special Rules

Most major legislation is brought to the House floor by a special rule that allows the measure to be taken up out of order. The Rules Committee reports such rules, which take the form of House resolutions—designated H.Res. A majority of the House membership must approve each one.

The rule sets the terms for a measure's floor consideration. A rule always specifies how much time is to be allowed for general debate and who is to control that time. One or two hours of general debate are typical, although major measures occasionally are granted considerably more time. The time is always equally split between the chair and the ranking minority member of the committee that reported the legislation; if several committees worked on the bill, each will control some of the general debate time.

A rule may restrict amendments, waive points of order (against what would otherwise be violations of House rules in the legislation or in how it is brought up), and include other special provisions to govern floor consideration. The extent to which a rule restricts amendments and the manner in which it does so also may vary. An open rule allows all germane amendments, whereas a closed rule prohibits all amendments other than those offered by the reporting committee. Between the two extremes are rules that allow some but not all germane amendments to be offered.[9]

Currently the Rules Committee labels rules as open, structured, or closed. Open rules include what used to be called modified open rules. Such rules allow all germane amendments that are printed in the *Congressional Record* by a specific time (always before floor consideration begins) and are now labeled "Open with a Preprinting Requirement" or set a time limit on the amending process and allow all germane amendments that can be offered during that time period, labeled "Open with a Time Cap." Structured rules "allow for amendments designated in the rule or the Rules Committee report accompanying the rule to be offered on the floor" (Rules Committee Staff). Thus structured rules include all the rules that put some restrictions on amendments but do not bar them completely. As such they include what used to be called "modified closed" rules, a label which in recent years had tended to be applied to rules that allowed only a minority-party substitute. When the Rules Committee expects to report a structured rule, its chair will usually notify members by a Dear Colleague letter and an announcement on the committee Web site. Members then send to the Rules Committee the amendments that they would like to offer and Rules decides which will be allowed.

In the contemporary House most rules are somewhat restrictive; from 1989 through 2008, on average 68 percent of rules have been something other than simple open rules (modified open, structured/modified closed, or closed.) During the 111th Congress, no legislation was brought to the floor under a simple open rule. Restrictive rules are even more likely to be used on major legislation. In the period 1993–2008, on average 78 percent of major bills were considered under a *substantially* restrictive rule, that is, a structured or a closed rule; in the most recent Congresses, almost all rules have been substantially restrictive—96 percent in both the 109th Republican-controlled Congress and in the 110th, the Democratic-controlled Congress, and 99 percent in the 111th Congress.

---

9. The Rules Committee can and sometimes does allow nongermane amendments to be offered.

Structured rules do vary greatly in how many amendments they allow. For example, the rule for the Tobacco Control Act (HR 1256) allowed only one, a Republican substitute; HR 1664, a bill to prohibit "unreasonable and excessive" executive compensation under TARP, was considered under a rule that allowed seven amendments; the rule for the Department of Defense Authorization Act of 2010 made in order 82 amendments. All were "structured" rules employed during the 111th Congress.

When major legislation is ready for floor consideration, a decision on what type of rule to use must be made. Given the variety in contemporary rules, the choices are many. The Rules Committee is officially charged with making the decision, and the leaders of the reporting committee make their preferences known. But since the majority-party members of Rules are selected by the Speaker, the party leadership strongly influences what is decided. On major legislation the decision on the character of the rule is considered crucial to the bill's success; not surprisingly, the leadership decides.

Because there are many options in the design of a rule, special rules can be tailored to the problem at hand, as even fairly straightforward structured rules illustrate. The Rules Committee's summary of its rule for HR 5019 - Home Star Energy Retrofit Act of 2010 reads as follows:[10]

1. Structured rule.
2. Provides one hour of general debate equally divided and controlled by the Chair and ranking minority Member of the Committee on Energy and Commerce.
3. Waives all points of order against consideration of the bill except those arising under clause 9 or 10 of rule XXI.
4. Provides that the amendment in the nature of a substitute recommended by the Committee on Energy and Commerce shall be considered as an original bill for the purpose of amendment and shall be considered as read.
5. Waives all points of order against the amendment in the nature of a substitute except those arising under clause 10 of rule XXI. This waiver does not affect the point of order available under clause 9 of rule XXI (regarding earmark disclosure).
6. No amendments shall be in order except those amendments printed in the Rules Committee report accompanying the resolution. Provides that the amendments made in order may be offered only in the order printed in the report, may be offered only by a

---

10. The committee's summaries are a bit easier to read and understand than the text of the rule itself and so are used here.

Member designated in the report, shall be considered as read, shall be debatable for the time specified in the report equally divided and controlled by the proponent and an opponent, shall not be subject to amendment, and shall not be subject to a demand for division of the question.

7. Waives all points of order against the amendments printed in the report except those arising under clause 9 or 10 of rule XXI.
8. Provides one motion to recommit with or without instructions.
9. Provides that the Chair may entertain a motion that the Committee rise only if offered by the chair of the Committee on Energy and Commerce or a designee.
10. Provides that the Chair may not entertain a motion to strike out the enacting words of the bill.

This bill was referred to only one committee, Energy and Commerce, so all the general debate time is granted to the chair of the committee, who is a member of the majority party, and his minority-party counterpart (#2). The provisions approved by that committee—an amendment in the nature of a substitute for the bill as originally introduced—are made to the bill that will be amended on the floor (#4) to simplify the parliamentary process. Only specific, listed amendments may be offered and only by the member who made the request to the Rules Committee (#6); eight amendments were made in order, and debate time was specified for each, twenty minutes for one to be offered by the committee chair, ten minutes for each of the others. (The summary lists the amendments, their sponsors, the time allowed, and a short substantive précis, but to save space, that is not reproduced here.) With certain exceptions, points of order that the original bill (#3), the committee's substitute (#5), or the amendments (#7) violate House rules are waived. (Clauses 9 and 10 of rule XXI deal with requiring the disclosure of earmarks and the requirement that new expenditures be paid for.) Certain time-wasting motions are prohibited (#9 and #10).

When a bill is referred to several committees, setting the ground rules for floor consideration can present a host of complicated and delicate problems (Bach and Smith 1988, 18–23). Debate time must be divided. The rule for HR 3221, New Direction for Energy Independence, National Security, and Consumer Protection Act, discussed earlier, provided "two hours of general debate, with 15 minutes equally divided and controlled by the chairman and ranking minority member, of each of the Committees on Energy and Commerce, Natural Resources, Science and Technology, Transportation and Infrastructure, Education and Labor, Foreign Affairs, Small Business, and Oversight and Government Reform." When two or more committees have reported different provisions on a given matter, a decision also must be made about which committee's language will constitute the base text and how the other committees' versions will be considered. In this case, various agreements reached were incorporated into "the amendment printed in part A of the report of the Committee on Rules accompanying this resolution [which] shall be considered as adopted in the House and in the Committee of the Whole. The bill, as amended, shall be considered as the original bill for the purpose of further amendment and shall be considered as read."[11] The rule also provided for the consideration of HR 2776, Renewable Energy and Energy Conservation Tax Act of 2007, which had been reported by the Ways and Means Committee and contained the tax provisions of the energy package. No amendments were allowed. The rule further specified that "in the engrossment of HR 3221, the text of HR 2776, as passed by the House, shall be added at the end of HR 3221"; the point was to bundle the parts of the energy package into one bill to send to the Senate.

The Uses of Special Rules

Special rules can be used to save time and prevent obstruction and delay, to focus attention and debate on the critical choices, and sometimes to structure the choices members confront on the floor in a way that promotes a particular outcome.

Clearly closed rules can both save time and hold together compromises reached at the prefloor stage. During the 2006 campaign, House Democrats had committed to passing a series of measures—the "Six for Six"—in the first one hundred "legislative" hours; even though the bills included were carefully chosen to be easily passable, many with considerable support from Republicans, following the regular process of committee consideration and allowing open debate on the floor would make it impossible to meet the leadership's self-imposed deadline. The deadline, in fact, gave minority Republicans a strong incentive to delay and thereby make the new majority look incompetent. So the leadership bypassed committee on these measures, as discussed earlier, and brought them to the floor under closed rules. For similar reasons, in early 2009, closed rules were employed on the SCHIP bill and the Lilly Ledbetter Fair Pay Act.

Rules that restrict amendments and waive points of order also save time and prevent obstructionism. Before Republicans gained a House majority in the 1994 elections, they had promised that if they took control of the chamber, they would use less restrictive rules than had the Democrats when in power. Yet House Republicans also promised to pass the

---

11. Self-executing rules, of which this is an example, are discussed below.

Contract with America during the first one hundred days of the 104th Congress. When they brought one of the early Contract items to the floor under an open rule, Democrats naturally enough offered multitudes of amendments. Thereafter, the Republican-controlled Rules Committee usually included (in otherwise unrestrictive rules) a time limit on total amending activity.

Any restrictions on amendments, even simply the requirement that amendments be printed in the *Congressional Record* several days before being offered on the floor, help the bill's proponents by reducing uncertainty. Proponents can focus their efforts and plan strategy more efficiently. Opponents lose the element of surprise.

When the rule gives members a choice among comprehensive substitutes but bars votes on narrow amendments, it is focusing the debate on alternative approaches, on the big choices rather than the picky details. Since the late 1980s, rules allowing a choice among comprehensive substitutes have been used to bring to the floor tax bills, budget resolutions, civil rights bills, and social welfare legislation on such issues as parental leave, the minimum wage, and child care. The rule for the consideration of the 2004 budget resolution, which sets an overall spending plan for the next year, made in order votes on four substitute versions: one sponsored by the Congressional Black Caucus; another by the Blue Dogs, a group of conservative Democrats; a third by the Republican Study Committee, a group of very conservative Republicans; and a Democratic Leadership substitute. Debate time for the first three was set at forty minutes; the Democratic substitute was given sixty minutes. In the 111th Congress, Democrats controlled the House but the rule for the budget resolution for fiscal year 2010 was similar in structure; four "amendments in the nature of a substitute" were made in order: a Progressive Caucus substitute, a Republican Study Group substitute, a Black Caucus substitute, and one sponsored by Paul Ryan, the Republican ranking member of the Budget Committee. Each was granted forty minutes of debate time. In this case, the House GOP leadership did not ask to offer its own party substitute.

In addition to reducing uncertainty and focusing debate, carefully crafted rules can structure choices to advantage a particular outcome. The use of rules as strategic tools began to be developed by the Democratic majority-party leadership in the 1980s. The rule for welfare reform legislation in 1988 illustrates how rules can structure choices. Most Democrats—enough to constitute a clear majority of the House—favored passing a welfare reform bill; they believed it constituted good public policy. Many, however, believed that for reelection reasons, they had to go on record as favoring a reduction in the costs of the program. By allowing a vote on an amendment to cut the program moderately but barring one on an amendment that made draconian cuts, the rule gave those members who needed it the opportunity to demonstrate fiscal responsibility and also ensured that legislation most Democrats favored would be enacted.

When the Republicans were in the majority, their leadership frequently used highly restrictive rules to protect legislation and to shield its members from having to cast tough votes. In 2001–2002, the first two years of the George W. Bush presidency, 44 percent of all rules allowed only one Democratic substitute (Wolfensberger n.d.). Amendments that the leadership opposed but that might pass often were disallowed. In 2004, for example, the Workforce Investment Act, the country's main job-training legislation, included a provision that would allow religious groups that run federally funded job-training and literacy programs to hire and fire employees based on their religious beliefs. Republicans had failed to enact Bush's faith-based initiative as a separate bill and were attempting to enact it piecemeal. This provision was politically tricky for some Republicans. So the rule for the bill simply barred the Democratic amendment that would have knocked out that provision. The resolution to establish a congressional committee to investigate the governmental response to Hurricane Katrina was brought up under a closed rule, thereby preventing Democrats from offering an amendment making the investigative body an independent commission rather than a congressional committee with a Republican majority. In 2009, the rule for the climate change bill allowed only one substitute, that sponsored by Republican Randy Forbes, not that requested by Republican leader John Boehner. Rules Committee Democrats argued that the Boehner substitute did not comply with pay-as-you-go rules; Republicans charged that Democrats feared the Boehner substitute might actually pass.

The Federal Housing Finance Reform Act of 2005 (HR 1461) was reported out of the Financial Services Committee on May 25 by a vote of 65–5. Democrats backed the bill and made the strong bipartisan vote possible because the bill included an affordable-housing fund. Many conservative Republicans opposed this fund—one called it an "experiment in socialism"—but failed in their attempt to remove it in committee (*CQW,* June 6, 2005, 1453). To overcome the objections of these individuals, the leadership negotiated and the Rules Committee made in order a manager's amendment making major changes in the bill and prohibited Democrats from amending the amendment. Among the provisions included was one that basically barred nonprofit groups that applied for or received housing grants from using their own funds to engage in nonpartisan voter registration or get-out-the-vote activities. These provisions placated conservative Republicans but infuriated Democrats.

Majority-party members vote for such rules not only because the expectation of supporting your party on procedural votes is now very strong, but also because the amendments at issue often are ones the member believes to be bad public policy but politically difficult to vote against. (For Democrats, amendments on such hot-button issues as homosexual rights or flag burning are often problematic; for Republicans, amendments that increase spending on or benefits under popular domestic programs are.)

If barring a vote altogether is politically infeasible, a rule can force an amendment's proponents to offer it in a parliamentary guise that makes the vote highly obscure. So, for example, rather than allowing the minority party to offer a substitute for the majority's bill, a rule can force the minority party to offer its alternative through a motion to recommit with instructions. When House Republicans brought their prescription drug bill to the floor in summer 2002, for example, they forced Democrats to offer their alternative, which provided more generous drug benefits, through such a motion. In April 2006, although nine amendments were made in order, the Rules Committee did not provide an opportunity for the Democrats' much tougher substitute to the Republicans' lobbying reform bill to be offered as an amendment, thus making the motion to recommit the only way Democrats could get a vote on their substitute. Closed rules, of course, force the minority to offer its alternative through the motion to recommit, which by House standing rules cannot be denied to the minority; and under both Republican and Democratic control, the frequency of closed rules has increased substantially. In the Republican-controlled 109th, 32 percent of special rules were closed; in the Democratic-controlled 110th and 111th, 35 percent on average were.

For the Democratic leadership, passing supplemental appropriations bills to fund the Iraq and Afghanistan wars has presented difficult problems in recent years, ones that cleverly constructed rules played an important role in handling. The first such instance started with a funding request by George W. Bush in spring 2007. The new Democratic majority leaders knew that the bill had to include a meaningful provision on withdrawal to satisfy the many Democratic members who were Iraq War opponents and the voters who expected Democrats to do something about the increasingly unpopular war; at the same time, the language could not be so harsh as to alienate Democrats from more conservative districts or subject marginal members to politically perilous votes. And in the end the troops had to be funded; protecting the party's reputation made that essential. Pelosi and her leadership team were deeply involved in crafting the bill's language and persuading their members to support it. The rule for the supplemental spending bill with the leadership-crafted moderate withdrawal language also made in order a bill requiring the withdrawal of U.S. troops from Iraq within 180 days. Fervently antiwar Democrats were thus given a vote on the stronger provision that they favored and were, in fact, delighted when their measure garner 171 votes altogether. Bush vetoed the bill and the leadership knew getting a two-thirds vote to override was not possible; the funds would have to be provided without the withdrawal language. Yet the leadership could use its control over special rules to structure approval in a way that provided policy and reelection-related benefits to its members. The rule specified separate votes on the two parts of the bill—the domestic and security-related spending that Democratic negotiators had induced Bush to accept and the Iraq War appropriations. The former included a number of widely popular provisions, such as money for veterans' health care and farm disaster relief and also the minimum wage increase; it was approved 348–73, with only one Democrat opposed. A separate vote was held on the war-funding bill without the withdrawal language; that was approved 280–142 with Democrats splitting 86–140. This procedure made it possible for Democrats bitterly opposed to the war to vote for the popular domestic spending without having to vote for war funding.

Once Obama became president, the imperative for the Democratic House to meet his requests for war funding was even more intense, but more and more Democrats were becoming leery of the continuing Afghanistan War. The Democratic leadership used similar rules to split the parts of the supplemental funding bills.

New Parliamentary Devices

New parliamentary devices developed in recent years have made special rules even more flexible and potent tools for structuring choices. A self-executing rule provides that when a rule is adopted by the House, the accompanying bill is automatically amended to incorporate the text of an amendment either set forth or referenced in the rule. The new language is "considered as adopted," and no separate vote on it is held. Rules with self-executing provisions are increasingly frequent. In the three Democratic Congresses of the 1990s (1989–1994), 19 percent of rules on average had self-executing provisions; in the six Republican-controlled Congresses from 1995 through 2006, 27 percent of rules had them; and in the Democratic-controlled 110th, the figure was 28 percent. Some self-executing rules simply substitute the committee's bill for the original bill; thus a rule that states "the amendment in the nature of a substitute recommended by the Committee on ___ now printed in the bill shall be considered as adopted" is essentially "a time saver and vote saver," in the words of former Rules counsel Don Wolfensberger. "By self-executing adoption of the committee amendment in the House, you avoid two votes on the exact same matter (assuming the minority substitute fails) and instead go to the motion to recommit" (Wolfensberger, personal communication, March 2006).

If rules that self-execute only committee amendments are excluded, an increase in the frequency of self-executing rules is still evident—from 16.7 percent of rules during the three Congresses of the early 1990s (1989–1994) to 21 percent in the eight Congresses of 1995–2010. The procedure provides a simple way of inserting last-minute corrections into a bill, and some of the self-executing provisions make only technical changes.

But postcommittee compromises of considerable substantive significance and even totally new provisions also can be inserted into a bill without a floor vote through a self-executing provision. Major postcommittee adjustments that the Republican leadership crafted to the 2005 reconciliation bill were bundled into an amendment sponsored by the Budget Committee chair; the rule stipulated that the amendment "shall be considered as adopted" and barred all other amendments. As discussed earlier, Energy Committee chairman Waxman and the Democratic leadership negotiated a complicated set of agreements with other committees that also had jurisdiction over climate change legislation; those negotiated after the Energy Committee had reported its bill—notably the key deal with the Agriculture Committee—were incorporated into the bill by a self–executing rule. Actually this was a particularly complex version of a self–executing rule; the Energy Committee bill was replaced in its entirety by a version negotiated and then introduced by Waxman and that was then further amended by a 309-page Waxman amendment. Many of the other postcommittee adjustments described earlier were also incorporated into the bill that was considered on the floor through self-executing rules; this was the case for the credit card regulation bill and for the Guantánamo compromise language on the war-funding supplemental appropriations bill in 2009. Self-executing rules were strategically important in the legislative process of the 2009 stimulus bill and the health care bill, as the case studies in Chapters 7 and 8 show. In the case of the stimulus bill several provisions that had become embarrassing for Democrats, such as funding for resodding the National Mall in Washington, D.C., were deleted by a self-executing provision in the rule. Similarly, the omnibus appropriations bill for FY2009 was considered under a closed rule that included a self-executing provision eliminating a cost-of-living increase for members of Congress.

Because a self-executing provision in the rule allows language to be incorporated into legislation without a vote, it can be used to pass matters that members would be leery of voting for openly. Without a recorded vote, the visibility of the issue is decreased and responsibility for it is obscured. In 2004, $12.8 billion in new tax breaks for business were quietly incorporated into the transportation bill through a self-executing rule (*RC*, April 7, 2004). In 2006, in the rule for a bill to rein in 527 groups' participation in elections, Republicans self-executed an amendment to abolish the limits on party-coordinated expenditures, meaning that a party could spend an unlimited amount of hard money in coordination with its candidates (H.Res. 755). In early 2010, Congress confronted the necessity of increasing the debt limit by a record amount. The House leadership used a self-executing rule to make it easier for their reluctant members to vote for such a distasteful measure. The first vote was on the rule, and by adopting the rule, the House adopted the debt limit increase. The second vote was on the much more popular PAYGO budget enforcement rules; that vote cleared the bill (*CQW* Online, February 8, 2010, 334).

Self-executing provisions also serve as tools in even more complex strategic situations. Compelled by political pressure to bring to the floor a Democratic proposal to expand the child tax credit to low-income families, Republicans bundled it with tax breaks for higher-income families. They then brought the bill to the floor under a rule specifying that approval of the rule would automatically and without a separate vote trigger approval of the bill. This forced a conference committee on the bill where House Republicans could kill it.

The rule for the lobby/ethics reform bill the House considered in spring 2006 was, in the words of Wolfensberger, "the mother of all self-executing rules," with three separate self-executing provisions (*RC*, June 19, 2006). A Rules Committee version was substituted for the bills reported by the committees of jurisdiction; this version deleted several major provisions in the Judiciary Committee bill that the leadership had been unable to sell to its members. The Rules Committee version was further altered by deleting another Judiciary Committee provision. Finally, the House-passed regulation of 527 political committees was added to the bill that would go to the Senate. All of this was done automatically, without a vote.

Rules that give the chairman of the committee "en bloc authority" are another variant. In the Survey of Activities that the Rules Committee publishes after every Congress, it states, "This category of rule authorizes the chairman of a committee (usually the floor manager of the bill under consideration) or his designee to offer amendment en bloc consisting of amendments made in order by the special rule that have not earlier been disposed of, as well as germane modifications to any such amendments" (110th Congress, 23). That is, the floor manager can roll a number of amendments into one big amendment and, in the process, with the sponsors' agreement, make changes to the amendments included. Rules for the annual DOD authorization bill, which typically make large numbers of amendments in order, usually grant the chair en bloc authority. As the Rules Committee states, "Such a rule enables the floor manager to maximize efficiency and consensus while minimizing duplicative floor time and consideration" (23). Since en bloc amendments always pass, it also gives the floor manager bargaining leverage to extract changes in amendments in return for inclusion.

"King-of-the-hill" and "queen-of-the-hill" rules, devices that were new and employed with some frequency on major legislation from the late 1980s through the late 1990s, have currently fallen into disuse but are nevertheless still available to leaders should strategic considerations demand it. A king-of-the-hill provision in a rule stipulates that a series of amendments or entire substitutes are to be voted on in a specified order and the last one that receives a majority prevails; the queen-of-the-hill variant also allows a vote on all the versions but specifies that whichever version gets the most votes, so long as it receives a majority, wins. These devices make possible a direct vote on each of several alternatives; in ordinary parliamentary procedure, if an amendment or substitute receives a majority, no further alternative amendments to that part of the bill already amended may be offered. Clearly, when the king-of-the-hill procedure is employed, the amendment or substitute voted on last is advantaged. The last is also advantaged under the queen-of-the-hill procedure because supporters of the last option, unlike those of earlier ones, know how many votes they need in order to win. The leadership, of course, always puts its favored option in the last position. These sorts of rules were often used for budget resolutions.

The procedure also made it possible for members to vote for more than one version, which is sometimes politically advantageous. The rule for the 1991 civil rights bill illustrates how the procedure can be used strategically. That rule stipulated that the three substitutes made in order were to be offered in a specific order under the king-of-the-hill procedure. The rule gave liberals a vote on their much stronger version but put that substitute first in line. Having cast a vote in favor of the tough bill favored by civil rights activists, these members then could support the leadership's more moderate compromise. The rule next gave House Republicans and the George H.W. Bush administration a vote on their preferred version. It put the Democratic compromise last—that is, in the advantaged position.

On the Floor

Floor consideration of a bill begins with debate on the rule. One hour is allotted, half controlled by a majority member of Rules and half by a minority member. The majority member explains and justifies the rule, the minority member gives his or her party's position, and then both yield time to other members who wish to speak. If neither the rule nor the legislation is controversial, much less than the full hour may be used. If the legislation is controversial but the rule is not, members frequently will use the time to discuss the legislation substantively. Since so many of today's rules are restrictive and complex, they are often highly controversial, so debate may well revolve around the character of the rule itself and consume the entire hour. During this period no amendments to the rule are in order.

The House must approve the rule before consideration of the legislation can begin. The Rules Committee member managing the debate on the rule for the majority party will move the previous question. If successful, the motion cuts off debate, and the House then proceeds to vote on the rule itself. The only way to amend the rule is to defeat the previous question motion. If opponents defeat the previous question motion, they control the floor and may propose the special rule they would like to see. Losing on the motion to order the previous question is devastating for the majority party and seldom happens; a member who votes against his or her party on this crucial procedural motion is not quickly forgiven.

One memorable vote on the previous question occurred in 1981 on the reconciliation bill that implemented President Ronald Reagan's economic program. The key battle on that legislation was over the rule. Reagan and House Republicans wanted a single vote on Reagan's package of spending cuts; they could then make the vote a test of whether members supported or opposed the popular president's program to rescue the economy. Democrats, who controlled the House, proposed a rule that forced a series of votes on cutting specific popular programs. Knowing they were likely to lose at least some of those votes and thereby major chunks of Reagan's economic plan, Republicans decided to try to defeat the previous question on the rule. With the help of some conservative Democrats, they were successful and so were able to substitute their own rule that called for a single vote on the package as a whole.

Votes on the previous question are usually far less visible, and disgruntled majority-party members can be persuaded by their leadership to vote yes on that motion and show their displeasure, if they must, by voting against the rule. Fearing they lacked the votes to pass their rule for the consideration of the Department of Interior appropriations bill in summer 1995, Republicans nevertheless made an attempt to do so—but only after forcefully explaining to their freshman members that they had better not join the minority in voting against the previous question. The rule was, in fact, defeated. The leadership then worked out a compromise among House Republicans, got the Rules Committee to incorporate it in a new rule, brought that to the floor, and passed it. When the majority party lost the rule, it did not lose control of the floor as it would have had it lost the previous question vote.

Once the previous question has been approved, the House votes on the rule itself. When the rule is not controversial, the vote may be by voice; on controversial rules the votes will be recorded. These recorded votes are still often called roll call votes, although the House seldom calls the roll as it did in the days before electronic voting. Because rules are frequently contentious, recorded votes on either the previous question or the rule itself, or both, are likely. In 2003–2004, for example, 132 measures were brought to the floor under special rules, and on 81 (61 percent) of them, there was a recorded vote on either the previous question or passage of the rule, or both. In 2007–2008, 89 percent of 194 rules were subject to a recorded vote on either the previous question or the rule itself, or both.

The majority party sometimes loses votes on rules, but not often. The vote on the Interior appropriations rule was the only one that Republicans lost during the 104th; from 1981 to 1992, Democrats lost on average just over one rule per year. During the highly charged 103rd Congress (1993–1994), Democrats lost five rules, and during the 105th, with its narrow partisan majority, Republicans lost five. In the 106th, Republicans lost one rule; in the 107th, two; and in the 108th and 109th, none. The Democratic majority lost none in the 110th or 111th.

Majority-party members are expected to support their party on such procedural votes. Republicans in recent years seldom even systematically checked their members' voting intentions on rules. "Basically we ask all our members to signal if they have any problem with the rule. The general presumption is that otherwise you are expected to vote 'Yes,'" a leadership aide explained. "If you have a problem, you need to let us know. . . . More often than a Whip Count, we'll ask the Whip to do a spot-check of trouble spots—those members who on similar issues have been a problem, just to make sure that they are okay."

Over the period 1987 to 1996 the mean vote by majority-party members in favor on rule passage votes was 97 percent. Especially when the rule is restrictive, most minority-party members now vote against the rule. In 2003–2004, every recorded rule vote for a major measure was a party vote, pitting a majority of Republicans against a majority of Democrats. Every Republican opposed every Democrat on 41 percent of these votes, and no more than two members defected from the party position on another 27 percent; the largest number of Republican defections on any one vote was six. In the 110th all but two of the recorded votes on rules for all measures were party votes; on average 3.4 Democrats voted "nay" and 3.9 Republicans voted "yea" on approving rules.

If the House approves the rule, it usually then resolves itself into the Committee of the Whole, where the legislation is debated and amended.[12] A sort of parliamentary fiction, the Committee of the Whole has the same membership as the House but somewhat more streamlined rules. The quorum for doing business in the Committee of the Whole is 100 members, rather than the House quorum of 218 members (half the full membership). In the Committee of the Whole when a member is recognized to offer or speak on an amendment, it is for only five minutes. The Speaker does not preside over the Committee of the Whole, but since he or she chooses the presiding officer and always picks a majority-party member, the majority party remains in control of the chair.

General debate begins the consideration of the bill in the Committee of the Whole. The rule has specified who controls the time. The chair of the committee or subcommittee that reported the bill serves as floor manager for the majority and actually controls the time allotted to the committee majority; his or her minority counterpart controls the minority's time. If the legislation is the product of several committees, each will have floor managers. The majority floor manager begins with a prepared statement explaining what the legislation does and why it deserves to pass.

The minority floor manager then makes a statement, which may range from wholehearted agreement with his or her opposite number to an all-out attack on the bill. When the committee has come to a broad bipartisan agreement, general debate may be a veritable lovefest, with committee members congratulating each other on the wonderful job they did and on the admirably cooperative way in which they did it. When the committee reporting the legislation is split, especially if it is split along party lines, the tone of floor debate will be contentious and sometimes bitter. Because of the intense partisan and ideological polarization that has developed in recent years, highly charged partisan battles are more likely than lovefests on major legislation. (See Figure 6.1 for the trend in partisanship.)

After opening statements the floor managers yield time—usually in small amounts—to other members who wish to speak. By and large, the

---

12. Rules usually have a provision that reads as follows: "Resolved, That at any time after the adoption of this resolution the Speaker may, pursuant to clause 2(b) of rule XVIII, declare the House resolved into the Committee of the Whole House on the state of the Union for consideration of the bill___." That is, the rule specifies that the bill will be considered in the Committee of the Whole at a time of the Speaker's choosing. Occasionally, the rule will specify consideration in the House; this is effectively a closed rule because in the House the previous question motion, which cuts off debate, is always in order.

majority floor manager (or managers) yields time to supporters of the legislation and to majority-party members, while the minority floor manager yields time to minority-party members and, assuming the bill is controversial, to opponents of the bill.

When general debate time has expired, the amending process begins. What happens next depends on the rule. If all germane amendments are allowed, now a rare occurrence, members are recognized to offer amendments. House rules give the chair of the Committee of the Whole discretion to determine the order of recognition, but by custom members of the reporting committee are given preference in gaining recognition, and they are recognized in order of seniority (Tiefer 1989, 231). Once a member is recognized to offer his or her amendment, the member has five minutes to explain it. The floor manager has five minutes to reply; then other members may speak. They gain time by offering pro forma amendments "to strike the last word" or "to strike the requisite number of words." The member who offers a pro forma amendment does not actually want it to pass, but by offering it he or she gets five minutes to speak on the amendment that is really at issue.

A House member may offer an amendment to the amendment being considered. Such a second-degree amendment may be intended sincerely to improve the amendment to which it is offered. Alternatively, the purpose behind a second-degree amendment may be to lessen the impact or even negate altogether the effect of the original amendment. If a bill's supporters believe they cannot defeat a popular but, in their view, harmful amendment, they may try to come up with a second-degree amendment to at least weaken its effect.

Debate on an amendment under the five-minute rule may go on for a considerable period of time, but eventually, when everyone who wants to has spoken, a vote on the amendment occurs. Sometimes a floor manager has no objections to an amendment or actually supports it and will simply "accept" the amendment without asking for a recorded vote. In that case the amendment is usually approved by voice vote. If the floor manager— or another member—opposes the amendment, a vote will be demanded. The first vote may be by voice, but if the amendment is at all controversial, the losing side in a voice vote will demand a recorded vote. Only twenty-five members are needed to force a recorded vote.

The House uses an electronic voting system. Members have individualized cards that look rather like a credit card; they insert their cards into one of the ten voting stations attached to the backs of seats on the House floor and punch the "yea," "nay," or "present" button. The vote is recorded by a computer, and it also shows up as a green, red, or amber light next to the member's name on a huge lighted display behind the Speaker's dais.

After the amendment has been disposed of, another member is recognized to offer another amendment. Under an open rule the amending process continues as long as there are members who want to offer amendments and who are on the floor prepared to do so. The House can by majority vote to cut off debate, although amendments that have been "preprinted" in the *Congressional Record* at least one day before floor consideration are guaranteed ten minutes of debate (Tiefer 1989, 401–403). Unlike senators, House members have limited patience for protracted floor debate. In January 1995, Republicans brought the unfunded mandates bill to the floor under an open rule; after six days of debate and votes on numerous politically dicey amendments and with 170 amendments still pending, they voted to cut off debate.

A more frequently used way of controlling the length of the amending process is through the rule. Under some rules the amending process proceeds pretty much as described above except that the amendments allowed are limited, perhaps to those preprinted in the *Congressional Record*. Often now the rule specifies which amendments are in order and which member may offer each. In these cases the rule usually specifies a time limit on debate on a specific amendment—usually ten or twenty minutes, or an hour for a major amendment. Structured rules also prohibit second-degree amendments (that is, amendments to amendments).

What happens in the Committee of the Whole thus varies depending on the number of committees involved and the character of the rule. Since most rules for major legislation are restrictive, the amending process is seldom prolonged. Even when the Rules Committee allows a number of amendments to be offered, the debate time it allots is usually short—most often ten minutes for amendments other than a minority-party substitute, which may be given an hour. The Department of Defense authorization bill for 2011, for example, was considered under a rule that allowed eighty-two amendments; the rule specified one hour of general debate, and each of the amendments were allotted only ten minutes of debate time. The chairman was given en bloc authority. The bill was taken up on the afternoon of Thursday, May 27, 2010, and finished on Friday, May 28. Much more typical are rules that allow less than a dozen amendments. Such rules assure the expeditious processing of most legislation on the floor; they make floor proceedings more orderly and predictable. But the sort of freewheeling, unscripted amending process that was still common in the late 1980s is largely a thing of the past.

After general debate and whatever amending is allowed have been completed, the Committee of the Whole rises and reports back to the House. The Speaker again presides, and the rules of the House again are in effect. Amendments adopted in the Committee of the Whole must be approved by the House, which gives opponents of an amendment a second chance to defeat it. Usually, however, the House votes on all the amendments adopted as a package and approval is certain. Occasionally, if a vote was very close and the amendment makes major and unacceptable changes in the legislation, an effort to change the outcome will be made, and now and then it works. Generally, however, amendments that win in the Committee of the Whole win again in the House. After all, the membership of the two bodies is identical.

The minority may then offer a motion to recommit the legislation to committee with or without instructions. A motion to recommit without instructions is essentially a motion to kill the bill and seldom prevails. By this point too many members have a stake in the legislation's enactment; if it lacked majority support, it would probably not have gotten so far. A motion to recommit with instructions—that is, instructions to report the bill back with specified changes—is, in effect, a motion to amend the bill. It is the minority's last chance to change the legislation. The motion may propose substituting the minority's version of the bill for the majority's, or it may propose much more modest changes.

When Republicans were in the majority, their leaders defined that vote as a procedural vote that all party members were expected to oppose; Democrats averaged fewer than two wins per year during the twelve years of Republican control. When Republicans began to use the motion to recommit (MTR) as a weapon against the new majority in 2007, the Democratic leadership decided that asking all their members to vote against every MTR no matter its content would endanger some of the members they most needed to protect. Of the 123 MTRs that Republicans offered during the 110th Congress, 24 won. Although few of the MTRs that won had much substantive significance, the leadership's unwillingness to declare the votes a procedural and thus party vote was controversial among its own members; senior members who managed bills on the floor were especially critical. However, Republicans won much more frequently in 2007 (21 of 88) than in 2008 (3 of 35), suggesting that even vulnerable Democrats became more willing to vote with their party on these "gotcha" votes.

Nevertheless, Democrats considered the MTR problem sufficiently serious to trigger a rules change at the beginning of the 111th Congress: such motions could no longer stipulate that the bill as amended be reported back "promptly;" they had to specify "forthwith," or immediately. If "promptly" is used, the bill is sent back to committee, which may or may not choose to report it again, and the bill loses its floor status; it is thus likely to kill the bill. When Republicans used "promptly" in a motion to recommit with instruction, which they frequently did in 2007–2008, they in essence confronted vulnerable Democrats with either killing the bill or voting against an amendment, designed to cause maximum political embarrassment. No motions to recommit "promptly" prevailed in the 110th Congress, but Democrats were forced to take a number of very tough votes.

In the 111th Congress, Republicans offered sixty-five motions to recommit, of which fifteen passed. Most of those that passed were relatively minor; a number of them did contain annoying "gotcha" provisions. So, the motion to recommit the bill establishing the Home Star Energy Retrofit program, providing consumer rebates for energy-efficient home improvements, included a provision prohibiting participating home repair contractors from hiring anyone convicted of sexual assault or child molestation.

The only major instance was the motion to recommit the America COMPETES (Science and Technology) Reauthorization Act, which prevailed on May 13, 2010. This case illustrates both how the minority party can use the motion to recommit to cause the majority significant grief and how the majority leadership can employ its procedural tools to prevail in the end. Major legislation, the five-year, $86 billion authorization doubled current spending for a variety of existing and new programs under the National Science Foundation, National Institute of Standards and Technology, and the Energy Department and for training in science, technology, engineering, and mathematics. The motion to recommit, including provisions to strike five new programs, cut the bill back from a five- to a three-year authorization and reduced funding to fiscal 2010 levels. Democrats would never have voted for this major surgery on a broadly supported bill had that been all the motion to recommit contained. However it also included a provision barring the use of funds to pay the salaries of government employees disciplined for "viewing, downloading or exchanging pornography on a federal government computer or while performing their duties" (CQ Vote description Vote 270). According to a story much in the news at that time, employees of the Security and Exchange Commission had been caught doing exactly that while Bernie Madoff perpetrated a giant Ponzi scheme and the credit markets crashed. Already facing tough reelection battles, many Democrats were not going to give their opponents the gift of a vote against that provision; the motion to recommit prevailed 292–126, with Democrats splitting 121–125.

The motion to recommit is actually a two-step process. As Don Wolfensberger, former council of the Rules Committee, explains: "First, the House votes on whether to instruct the committee chairman to immediately report back the amendments specified in the motion; and second, if that passes, the chairman reports back the amendments 'forthwith' to the House for votes on adopting them" (*RC*, June 15, 2010). Ordinarily this all takes place within a few minutes and the second vote is by voice.

For example, when the motion to recommit the Home Star Energy Retrofit bill passed, Chairman Waxman immediately said, "Mr. Speaker, pursuant to the instructions of the House in the motion to recommit, I report the bill, HR 5019, back to the House with an amendment." The Speaker pro tempore then stated, "The question is on the amendment." And the amendment passed by voice vote (*CR*, H3248).

However, when the motion to recommit the America COMPETES Act passed, the Democratic leadership, using its control over the floor, immediately pulled the bill from the floor so the second part of the process did not occur. The aim was to find a way to save the bill. The chair of the committee, Bart Gordon, D-TN, attempted a compromise; he introduced a new bill that incorporated the amendments that had passed on the floor and cut the bill down from five to three years, thus reducing its cost; he also included the antipornography provision. This new version was brought to the floor the next week under the suspension procedure; the vote was 261–148, short of the two-thirds required under the procedure.

If Republicans were unwilling to vote for a more modest bill, Democrats saw no reason to cater to their preferences for a cheaper version and returned to their original bill. The leadership brought the bill back to the floor on May 28, and the legislative process picked up where it had been interrupted—before the second part of the two step process, the vote to accept the amendment the motion to recommit contained. But, because the Republicans' motion to recommit with instructions contained nine disparate amendments, Science Committee chairman Gordon was able to demand "a division of the question" and so separate votes on all nine. "The reason such a 'demand for a division of the question' was so unexpected is that it has never been tried before," Wolfensberger explains. The antiporn provision and another barring funds from going to colleges or universities that deny or restrict Reserve Officers' Training Corps (ROTC) or other military recruiting on campus won (*CD*, May 18, 2010). The provisions that cut the bill severely all failed, and then the bill itself passed 262–150.

Assuming the legislation survives, a vote on final passage is taken, usually by recorded vote. Legislation that gets this far will almost certainly pass. The majority-party leadership seldom brings a bill to the floor if it does not have the votes to pass it. In the early 2000s, however, Republican leaders found themselves in a situation that induced them to ignore that maxim on a number of occasions. They were charged with passing President George W. Bush's often ambitious and contentious program, and yet their majority was narrow. The Republican leadership brought to the floor several key elements of Bush's agenda, even though they were not sure of sufficient votes for passage, and then held open the recorded vote until they could pressure or persuade enough party members to support the bill to pass it. A normal recorded vote lasts fifteen minutes and is often extended to seventeen so as to give stragglers time to get to the floor to vote. After all, most members are not on the floor continuously during bill consideration but instead are in committee rooms or in their offices conducting other business. The House rule simply stipulates that a recorded vote must be held open for fifteen minutes and does not specify a maximum time.

The Republican House leadership took advantage of that lacuna. The most blatant example was the vote on the conference report for the Medicare prescription drug bill that lasted about three hours. The vote on passage of that bill also had been extended, to about an hour. Legislation giving the president trade promotion authority in 2001 and approval of the Central American Fair Trade Agreement and the Gasoline for America's Security Act, both in 2005, all got the same treatment. Republican leaders figured correctly that the imminent prospect of a very public defeat for their president and their party would soften up enough Republican members to allow the party to squeak out a victory.

Constitutional amendments requiring a two-thirds vote often are defeated on a floor vote in the House. And bills considered under the suspension procedure, which also require a two-thirds vote to pass, sometimes fail. As discussed earlier, most but not all legislation considered under suspension is uncontroversial. Occasionally the majority leadership uses suspension simply to give their members a chance to vote for a measure even though it is not likely to prevail; the several energy bills that Democratic leaders brought up under suspension in 2008 are examples. With gasoline prices rocketing up, Democrats wanted to be able to tell their constituents they were trying to help, but the leadership wanted to avoid a vote on allowing big increases in offshore drilling. Sometimes the leadership just misjudges, perhaps because of late-breaking developments. In 2005 a bill to impose new trade restrictions on countries that allowed the sale of arms and defense-related technology to China had overwhelming support until last-minute but intense lobbying from the defense industry. It was defeated 215–203. Sometimes too the leadership seems to put measures on suspension "on spec." If the bill gets the two-thirds vote, considerable floor time has been saved; if not, it can be brought up again under a special rule. So in early 2009, Democrats tried to pass under suspension a several months' delay of the requirement that television broadcasters switch to digital; enough Republicans opposed that, so it failed 258–168; a week later it passed under a rule 264–158. In late June 2010, a bill extending unemployment benefits failed to get the two-thirds vote it needed to pass on suspension; in that case, Democratic leaders brought the bill back up the next day under a rule and passed it.

Bills that require only a majority seldom fail on the House floor. In the 100th, 101st, 103rd, and 104th Congresses, the only major bills to be defeated at this stage were two competing proposals to aid the Nicaraguan contras, one President Reagan's and the other sponsored by the Democratic leadership in 1988; the first 1990 budget summit agreement (although that technically was the defeat of a conference report); and the campaign finance bill in the 104th, legislation the Republican leadership opposed. The narrow partisan majority in the 105th resulted in a higher number of defeats; four bills lost at this stage, including two that were leadership priorities (school vouchers and the waiving of environmental regulations on emergency flood control projects).

In the 107th Congress, the bankruptcy reform bill died on a House floor vote when the rule for consideration of the conference report failed, a case discussed more in Chapter 4. A bill to set severe limitations on federal spending was badly defeated—146–268—on the House floor in 2004. To get enough votes to pass the budget resolution that year, the Republican leadership had promised conservatives a vote on their budget process reform proposals. To fulfill their pledge, the leaders brought the bill to the floor even though it badly split Republicans and, given unanimous Democratic opposition, was doomed to defeat. In the 109th and 111th Congresses not a single major measure brought up under a procedure requiring only a simple majority failed. In the 110th the first incarnation of the extraordinarily unpopular measure to bail out the banks went down on the floor; but a second TARP bill passed (see Chapter 4). Thus when a bill is defeated on the House floor, extraordinary circumstances are almost always involved; bills that get to the House floor almost always pass.

If the legislation does pass, a motion to reconsider is made and laid upon the table. This ensures that the issue cannot be reopened. The legislation is then sent to the Senate.

Unorthodox Lawmaking in the House

If the textbook legislative process can be likened to climbing a ladder, the contemporary process is more like climbing a big old tree with many branches. The route to enactment used to be linear and predictable; now it is flexible and varied. To be sure, the textbook model was never a complete description of how bills became laws. There have always been alternative routes. In the past, however, the alternatives were infrequently used on major legislation. Now variation is the norm. As the case studies in Chapters 7 through 9 show, no two major bills are likely to follow exactly the same process.

Although the practices and procedures of unorthodox lawmaking arose in response to different problems and opportunities (see Chapter 6), their consequences are similar. The practices and procedures in the House facilitate lawmaking. Most make it easier for the majority-party's leadership to advance its members' legislative goals. The leadership now has more flexibility to shape the legislative process to suit the particular legislation at issue. As is becoming increasingly clear, however, unorthodox lawmaking also entails costs. The way in which the majority-party leadership has used the tools and techniques of unorthodox lawmaking in recent years has tended to have the result of excluding the minority from meaningful participation in the legislative process.

Routes and Obstacles:
The Legislative Process
in the Senate

IN THE SENATE LEGISLATION MUST TRAVERSE the same basic path as in the House, and the alternatives at the various stages are, in many cases, similar—at least on the surface. Yet the Senate is a quite different body from the House (Matthews 1960; Sinclair 1989, 2006; Smith 1989; Koger 2002). Smaller in membership, the Senate is less hierarchical and less formal. Senate rules give senators as individuals great power: A senator may hold the floor indefinitely unless the Senate invokes cloture, which requires an extraordinary majority; further, any senator may offer an unlimited number of amendments to almost any piece of legislation, and those amendments need not even be germane. Current norms allow senators to use extended debate and floor amendments expansively (Sinclair 1989). Like the House, the Senate is now polarized along coinciding partisan and ideological lines, and it is often the minority party that makes use of these Senate prerogatives.

The differences in the two bodies are reflected in their legislative processes. The Senate does much of its business by unanimous consent—both an acknowledgment and an augmentation of the power of senators as individuals. Any one senator can block a unanimous consent request. The Senate is not a majority-rule chamber like the House. In the House the majority can always prevail; in the Senate minorities can often block majorities.

Bill Introduction

In the Senate, as in the House, only members—that is, senators—may introduce legislation, and each may introduce as many measures as he or she pleases. Senators may introduce their bills from the floor or just submit them to the clerks while the chamber is in session. The sources of ideas for legislation—constituents, the executive branch, interest groups, the legislator's own issue interests—are similar in the two chambers. Because senators represent whole states and serve on more committees than the typical House member, they tend to offer legislation concerning a broader range of issues.

Bill Referral

When a bill is introduced or arrives from the House of Representatives, it is normally referred by the presiding officer, on the advice of the parliamentarian, to the committee of predominant jurisdiction. Senate rules do not encourage multiple referral, as House rules do.

Multiple Referral and Multiple Committees

Multiple referral is possible in the Senate. A 1977 rule provides that the joint party leadership (that is, the majority and the minority leaders acting together) can by motion propose that legislation be multiply referred, but this route is never used (Davidson 1989, 379–380). A few types of bills are multiply referred by standing order (standing orders are adopted by Senate resolution, have the same authority as Senate rules, and remain in effect until they are repealed). Thus under a standing order, the intelligence authorization bill is multiply referred to the Intelligence Committee and the Armed Services Committee. Otherwise, when legislation is multiply referred, it is done by unanimous consent; the consent request may specify time limits for each committee's consideration of the legislation, as the 1977 rule allows.

Multiple referral is much less frequent in the Senate than in the House; less than one in twenty bills is multiply referred, and the proportion has been dropping in recent Congresses (see Table 6.2). Even major measures are only a little more likely to be multiply referred, with less than one in twenty sent to more than one committee in recent Congresses.

Much of the legislation sent to multiple committees in the House is referred to only one committee in the Senate; the reverse is seldom the case. In the 109th Congress, for example, the welfare reauthorization bill in the House was sent to the Ways and Means Committee and in addition to Energy and Commerce, Education, Agriculture, and Financial Services; in the Senate it went to Finance only; the bill to overhaul port security went to the Homeland Security Committee in the Senate but, in the House, to Financial Services and in addition to

Energy and Commerce, International Relations, and Homeland Security. In the 110th, a bill requiring health insurance policies to provide mental health coverage equivalent to that provided for physical health was referred in the House to the Energy and Commerce Committee and in addition to Education and Labor and Ways and Means; in the Senate it went to HELP (the Committee on Health, Education, Labor, and Pensions).

Multiple referral may be infrequent in the Senate, but the involvement of multiple committees in what at some point becomes a single bill is not. The bulk of a big transportation bill the Senate passed in 2004 was considered and reported by the Environment and Public Works Committee, but tax provisions drafted by the Finance Committee and a section authorizing mass transit programs drafted by the Banking Committee were incorporated into the bill after floor consideration began. The port security bill passed by the Senate in 2006 was reported by the Homeland Security Committee; however, the Commerce Committee had reported a bill that touched on port security in 2005 and the chairman of the Commerce Committee claimed jurisdiction. Under pressure from the majority leader, who refused to bring the bill to the floor until the dispute was settled, the two chairs worked out an agreement on language. Based on its jurisdiction over the customs service, the Finance Committee also involved itself in the negotiations. The bill that went to the floor was an amended version that incorporated the deal among the three committees (*CQ Weekly*, September 4, 2006, 3215; December 18, 2006, 3356). As this example shows, legislation that overlaps committee jurisdictional lines can entail complications whether or not they are multiply referred or not. Energy bills typically involve the Energy and Natural Resources Committee, the Environment and Public Works Committee, the Commerce Committee, and the Finance Committee.

In the Senate when legislation impinges on the jurisdiction of more than one committee, the committee chairs often informally work out any problems among themselves. Thus in 2005, legislation overhauling federal pension laws was multiply referred in the House to the Education and the Workforce Committee and in addition to Ways and Means; in the Senate, the HELP Committee and the Finance Committee each approved its own draft bill, and then the leaders of the two committees agreed to combine their bills before taking the legislation to the floor (HR 2830; *CQ Weekly*, October 3, 2005, 2625). Sometimes, as the port security example illustrates, pressure from the leadership is required. And more often than in the past, when top priority legislation is at issue, the majority leader closely oversees the negotiations or takes the central role in putting together agreements himself. Thus, after the HELP Committee and the Finance Committee reported separate and quite different health care reform bills in 2009, Majority Leader Harry Reid, D-NV, put together the bill that went to the floor (see Chapter 8).

Senate Committee Decision Making

Judged by floor voting patterns, the Senate is about as highly polarized along partisan lines as the House is (see Figure 6.1). Polarization affects committee decision making in the Senate but to a lesser extent than it does in the House. In the Congresses of the 1960s and 1970s, the Senate committee process was partisan on fewer than one in ten major measures; that increased to about one in seven in the 1980s. In the Congresses of the 1990s and 2000s (103rd–110th), the Senate committee process was partisan on about a quarter of the major measures considered. In the 111th Congress, that figure rose to almost 40 percent. So, certainly, Senate committee decision making is now more likely to be partisan than it used to be; yet, compared with the House, where about half of the major measures reported by committee are the product of partisan committee processes, partisanship in Senate committees is still moderate.

Senate rules largely account for this difference between the two chambers. In the Senate, unlike in the House, partisan ratios on even the most powerful committees closely reflect chamber ratios, and in recent years the Senate has often been narrowly split. Most Senate committees are relatively small, so when the chamber margin is narrow, the majority party may have only one more member on each committee than the minority, as was the case during most of the early 2000s. Under those circumstances, excluding the minority party from committee decision making and relying on a purely partisan coalition in committee is problematic.

Furthermore and more important, because Senate rules give individual senators so much power, any senator, whether a committee member or not, can cause problems for legislation later in the legislative process. Consequently, a bill's supporters have a strong incentive to put together a broad support coalition at the committee stage, one that accommodates interested senators who are not committee members as well as those who are, and that means a bipartisan coalition.

Senators hold multiple committee assignments and usually at least one and often more subcommittee leadership positions. In the 108th Congress, for example, senators averaged 3.9 committee assignments and 8.1 subcommittee assignments each; majority-party members averaged 1.7 chairmanships.[1] Thus senators are stretched very thin. The time pressure this creates, combined with the openness of Senate floor proceedings,

---

1. *CQ Weekly,* April 12, 2003, C2–C17.

contributes to Senate committees' tendency to explicitly put off conflict, including partisan conflict, until the floor stage; that is, major divisive amendments are held to be decided on the floor. Committee chairs may "figure that if they get into these controversial subjects in committee, they'll never get the bill out," as a leadership staffer explained. Committee members are willing to go along because they know they will get their chance on the floor. And, further, why have a time-consuming fight in committee when the battle will have to be refought on the floor, the reasoning goes.

Still, Senate committee decision making has been considerably more partisan since the mid-1990s than it was before. The figures for partisanship in committee decision making are not higher, in part, because frequently now committees are bypassed on the most partisan issues. Despite incentives in Senate procedures to avoid narrow supportive majorities, partisan polarization has made finding compromises acceptable to both political parties much more difficult.

Bypassing Committee

In the Senate, as in the House, committees are sometimes bypassed altogether. In the Congresses of the 1990s and 2000s, the proportion of major measures that were considered on the Senate floor without first going through committee varied considerably but on average was much higher than before; in the Congresses of the 1960s through the 1980s for which data are available, the committee was bypassed in the Senate on 7 percent of major measures; for the 103rd through 110th Congresses, the average increased to 26 percent; in the 111th Congress it was 45 percent. In the Senate bypassing a committee is technically simple; under Rule 14, if any senator objects to committee referral (more precisely, objects on the floor to further proceedings on the measure after the second reading, which occurs right before the bill would be referred to committee), the bill goes directly to the calendar (Tiefer 1989, 594). When legislation reported by a Senate committee awaits floor action and a companion House-passed bill arrives in the Senate, this procedure is frequently used to put the bill directly on the calendar rather than sending it to a committee that has already dealt with the issue. In a similar vein, when a Senate committee is still working on a bill and the House sends over its version, the House-passed bill is commonly held at the desk by unanimous consent. The use of these procedures does not, of course, constitute bypassing the committee in any real sense.

Any senator's power to put legislation directly on the calendar simply by objecting to the bill's being referred to committee would seem to make bypassing committee easy; however, the majority leader, through the position's scheduling powers, effectively has a veto over other senators bringing bills to the floor directly by this route. Although procedurally simple, the direct route really requires the majority leader's assent to work.

The majority leader or a Senate committee chair, with the majority leader's agreement, sometimes uses this rule to speed up the legislative process, particularly on relatively uncontroversial legislation. Republicans, newly in the majority in 1995, were determined to pass quickly legislation requiring that Congress abide by various regulatory laws; the House had passed its bill on the first day of the session. A similar bill had passed before and had bipartisan support, so the Senate by unanimous consent placed the legislation directly on the calendar. Despite this maneuver, the Senate still took a week to pass the bill. The bill to postpone the transition date to digital television was uncontroversial in the Senate, and getting it done quickly was important, so it bypassed committee and was passed by unanimous consent in January 2009.

In recent years, debt limit increase bills frequently bypass committee. There is usually some time pressure, and they are sufficiently straightforward that committee consideration seems to be seen as a waste of time. To ensure immediate action, Senate leaders took the resolution authorizing the use of force to respond to the September 11 attacks directly to the floor.

Political considerations may dictate bypassing committee. In 2001 the evenly split Senate Budget Committee was unable to agree on a budget resolution, so Majority Leader Trent Lott, R-MS, bypassed the committee and brought a Republican resolution directly to the floor. Tom Daschle, D-SD, the majority leader in late 2001, got committee chair Jeff Bingaman, D-NM, to cancel further energy legislation markups in the Energy and Natural Resources Committee when it appeared that the committee might approve drilling in the Arctic National Wildlife Refuge, a position opposed by most Senate Democrats. Daschle and Bingaman put together a Democratic bill, and Daschle used Rule 14 to get it directly to the floor. In the Terri Schiavo matter, politics and time pressure were involved. Schiavo had been in a persistent vegetative state since she suffered severe brain damage in 1990. Her husband had received court permission to remove life support, but her parents were opposed. The case became a cause célèbre for social conservatives, and Congress involved itself. During the Easter recess, Congress rushed through a bill allowing her parents to appeal the state court decision to the federal courts. The bill not only bypassed committee in both chambers, but also the Senate passed it by voice vote, a necessity, since most senators were not even in Washington. At the beginning of the 110th Congress, the new Democratic House and Senate leaderships needed to pass appropriations bills that should have been finished by the previous Congress but were not; they also wanted to begin to shift spending priorities. So they charged the chairs of the House and Senate Appropriations Committees with drafting a continuing (appropriations) resolution, often called a CR, that accomplished both purposes. (On CRs, see Chapter 5.)

The party leadership itself negotiates some major legislation, and that may well entail bypassing committee. In 2007, for example, Majority Leader Harry Reid and Minority Leader Mitch McConnell, R-KY, negotiated a bipartisan deal on lobbying reform legislation; on an issue that impacts members so directly, intensive leadership involvement is likely to be necessary. The Emergency Economic Stabilization Act (the bill that set up TARP, or the Troubled Asset Relief Program), passed in the wake of the financial crisis in fall 2008, was the product of negotiations among Democratic and Republican party and committee leaders and the George W. Bush White House; speed was essential, and delicate issues of congressional–executive branch powers were involved.

Senators have available another—and, in some ways, even easier—way to bypass committee, one that does not require leadership acquiescence; they can offer their legislation as an amendment to another bill on the floor. In most cases the "amendment" need not even be germane. The original Gramm-Rudman budget-balancing legislation was never considered by committee; Texas Republican Phil Gramm, its lead sponsor, simply offered it on the floor as an amendment to legislation raising the debt ceiling. During the 108th Congress, Democrats repeatedly attempted to attach an increase in the minimum wage and a rejection of President Bush's administrative changes in overtime pay rules to unrelated legislation. They succeeded several times with the overtime pay rules amendment, though it never became law. Arizona Republican John McCain's amendment barring the "use of cruel, inhuman, and degrading treatment against detainees," which President Bush vigorously opposed, was added to the Department of Defense (DOD) appropriations bill on the floor in late 2005; despite a veto threat, it did become law (*CQW,* October 10, 2005, 2725). Ted Kennedy, D-MA, added a provision expanding federal hate crime law to include attacks based on gender, gender identity, and sexual orientation as an amendment to the DOD authorization bill in 2007; it was, however, removed in conference. In 2009 it was again added to the DOD authorization bill and subsequently did become law.

As these examples suggest, the legislative process is often less formal in the Senate than in the House. Individual members are more important and committees less important than in the House. Given the power that senators as individuals wield and each senator's enormous workload, informal negotiations and agreements sometimes supplant more formal procedures.

Postcommittee Adjustments

To enhance its chances of passage, legislation in the Senate, as in the House, may be altered after it has been reported from committee. In the Congresses of the 1990s and 2000s, on average about a third of major measures were subject to such postcommittee adjustment.

Often in the Senate committee leaders or even individual senators take the lead. In 1999, Senator McCain, as chair of the Commerce Committee, had to make a number of postcommittee compromises to pass legislation setting liability limits for potential Y2K problems, thus protecting high-tech companies. As he explained on the Senate floor:

> Mr. President,[2] we are about to culminate the work of many months: investigation, drafting, negotiation, and compromise. . . .
>
> I want to remind my colleagues that many compromises have been made in this bill since it passed out of the Commerce Committee. It is certainly not as strong a bill as that passed by the House. These compromises have been made in order to get a bill that can have bipartisan approval and can be signed into law. (*Congressional Record,* June 15, 1999, S6976)

In 2009 the Senate Banking Committee reported out a credit card regulation bill by a 12 to 11 vote, with no Republican support. Chairman Chris Dodd, D-CT, fearing the bill could not pass against united GOP opposition, negotiated a deal with Richard Shelby, R-AL, the ranking Republican on the committee. Agriculture Committee chair Tom Harkin, D-IA, took the lead in negotiating postcommittee compromises to the farm bill in 2002, and Finance Committee chair Charles Grassley, R-IA, worked out a package of sweeteners that made possible Senate passage of a big corporate tax bill in 2004. In both of these cases party leaders also were involved.

The effort to craft a postcommittee compromise may be led by the party leadership. On the clean air bill in 1990, Majority Leader George Mitchell, a Democrat from Maine, orchestrated the complex negotiations that finally produced a bill that could pass the Senate (Cohen 1992, 81–98). He was similarly active on child care legislation in 1989; when it became clear the liberal Labor Committee's bill could not pass on its own, he put together a substitute based on elements of the Finance and Labor Committees' versions. In 1995, when Republican supporters of two line-item-veto bills could not work out their differences, Majority Leader Bob Dole of Kansas helped craft a version quite different from either one.

---

2. The Constitution designates the vice president of the United States as the president of the Senate; the presiding officer of the Senate is always addressed as "Mr. President," even though the vice president seldom presides.

With margins of control often narrow and partisan polarization escalating, party leaders have become increasingly involved in the legislative process on major legislation. On "flagship" legislation, "it's kind of cradle-to-grave," a leadership aide explained. The aide went on to say:

> On the really big bills, he [the majority leader] starts meetings right away, as soon as the issue comes up, well before committee markup. On ___, he had [the chairman] in right away and he talked to [a committee member active on the issue] and to others. On this sort of flagship effort, he reaches out to dissenting parts of the committee and tries to help the chair.

Frequently the working out of postcommittee compromises is a significant part of the majority leader's effort to pass major legislation. Thus, Tom Daschle as minority and majority leader took a highly active role on issues ranging from farm legislation to energy to trade promotion authority. Bill Frist, R-TN, also was frequently engaged in attempts to work out compromises on priority legislation. In the 108th Congress, he brokered a postcommittee deal on a measure limiting class action lawsuits that picked up a number of Democratic votes; a partisan fight over nongermane amendments stalled the bill, but the deal allowed it to pass in early 2005. The central role of Majority Leader Harry Reid in negotiating postcommittee adjustments to health care legislation in the 111th Congress is recounted in Chapter 8.

Of course, the strategy of altering the bill substantively to increase support is not always successful; it may not be possible to make sufficient changes to pick up needed new votes without altering the measure in a way that alienates its supporters. And often doing so successfully requires threading a tiny needle. In putting together a health care reform bill that could pass the Senate, the prospect of losing the liberals when making changes to pick up needed moderates confronted Reid numerous times.

The difficulty of crafting legislation that can pass the Senate is enormously increased by Senate rules and how they are used. Senators now use their right of extended debate—their right to talk and thus block action indefinitely—much more frequently than in the past. Since cutting off debate requires sixty votes, supporters of legislation must build a coalition that is bigger than a simple majority. Doing so will likely require considerable compromise and may require the sort of postcommittee adjustments discussed here. Republicans could have passed strong Y2K legislation and the class action lawsuit bill in their preferred form if only a majority had been required. Similarly, what made passing the big stimulus bill in early 2009 and the health care reform bill in 2009 and 2010 so hard was the willingness of the minority Republicans to use the filibuster and consequently the Democrats' necessity to build an oversized supportive coalition. (See Chapters 7 and 8.)

Scheduling Legislation for the Floor

The Senate does not use special rules to bring legislation to the floor. The majority leader, by motion or unanimous consent, just takes the bill to be considered off the calendar. Senate precedent provides the majority leader with the right of first recognition; when several senators seek recognition, the majority leader is recognized first and the minority leader second. Otherwise, Senate rules require the presiding officer to recognize the first senator to seek recognition, giving the presiding officer much less discretion than his or her House counterpart has. (When the Senate is debating legislation, the bill's managers have the right to be recognized after the leaders but before other senators.)

Although the procedure seems simpler than that used by the House, the Senate majority-party leadership actually has much less control over the scheduling of legislation and over the terms for its consideration. On any debatable motion any senator can hold the floor indefinitely unless or until sixty senators vote to shut off debate. The motion to proceed to consideration of a bill is debatable, so senators can filibuster against bringing legislation they oppose to the floor.

This fact shapes the process by which legislation is actually scheduled for floor debate in the Senate. The majority leader has usually moved bills off the calendar for floor consideration by unanimous consent; a study of 247 matters considered by the Senate in the 98th Congress (1983–1984) found that 98 percent came up by unanimous consent (Tiefer 1989, 563). Another study shows that between 1981 and 2002, only 11 motions to proceed per year were made on average (Beth 2003, 3). In the last several Congresses, however, achieving unanimous consent to bring up major, controversial legislation has gotten harder and majority leaders have had to resort to using the motion to proceed, a motion that can be filibustered (see below).

The Consultation Process

Since any senator can block a unanimous consent request, the majority leader, if he or she wishes floor business to proceed smoothly, must check with all interested senators before bringing legislation to the floor. Leaders of the reporting committee and the minority leader are always consulted; in the Senate effective scheduling requires bipartisan cooperation, and that requires intensive consultation between the majority and minority leaders. Unlike the House, where floor scheduling is a task of the majority-party leadership alone, the Senate cannot function if the two leaders do not work together.

The more contentious and partisan the issue, the more consultation is required. During the impeachment trial of President Bill Clinton, Majority Leader Trent Lott and Minority Leader Tom Daschle checked with each other multiple times a day. Partisan battles strained their relationship, yet Majority Leader Bill Frist and Minority Leader Harry Reid worked together on a daily basis during the 109th Congress (2005–2006). In the 110th and 111th Congresses, majority Democrats believed the minority leadership was "slow walking" the process and attempting to block them from accomplishing anything, yet Majority Leader Reid had no choice but to consult with Minority Leader McConnell, often multiple times a day when the Senate was in session.

Since any senator can object to considering the legislation and since time constraints make it impossible for the leaders to check with every senator on every piece of legislation, senators without an obvious interest in the bill are expected to inform their party leadership if they do have an interest. For every bill, the party secretaries, who are employees of the majority and minority leaders, keep a record of senators who have asked to be informed before the bill is brought to the floor, and these senators must be consulted. In addition, once the majority and minority leaders have tentatively agreed on a unanimous consent agreement (UCA), that information is put on the "hot line," an automated telephone line to all senators' offices; the recorded message specifies the terms of the agreement and asks senators who have objections to let their leader know in a given period of time. Today, e-mail also is being used for hot-lining.

Senate party leaders contend that their only responsibility to senators who have asked to be informed is to tell them when the leaders are ready to bring a bill to the floor, and that may well be all a particular senator expects. The senator may simply want to be sure he or she is prepared to offer an amendment when the legislation comes up. In other cases, however, a senator may object to the legislation's floor consideration at any time or until the bill's supporters have altered it to his or her liking. The notification by a senator to his or her party leader is called a hold; a typical hold letter, addressed to Republican leader Mitch McConnell, reads:

> Dear Mitch:
>
> I am hereby requesting that I be consulted prior to the entering into of any Unanimous Consent Agreements with regard to the Senate's possible consideration of [bill name], or any other similar legislation.
>
> Respectfully
>
> [signature]

A more explicit hold letter, addressed to then majority leader Lott and copied to the majority secretary, reads:

Dear Trent:

   I will object to any time agreement or unanimous consent request with respect to consideration of any legislation or amendment that involves [the matter in question], as I wish to be accorded my full rights as a Member of the Senate to offer amendments, debate and consider such legislation or amendment.
   Many thanks and kindest personal regards.

   [signature]

The party secretaries confer every morning and inform each other about new holds on legislation or nominations. They do not, however, reveal the names of their members who have placed the holds, so a hold may remain anonymous. The intelligence reauthorization bill "has now been held up for months as a result of a secret hold," Sen. Ron Wyden, D-WA, charged in March 2006 (*CR*, March 8, 2006, S1872). Rules to require that senators disclose their holds after a certain number of days have passed the Senate several times, but they have proved largely ineffective. A "revolving hold" is one easy way around the rules; just before the requisite number of days for reporting are over, a senator lifts his hold and another places a hold on the matter. Legislation mandating that senators post their campaign finance forms electronically, as House members do, was subject to that tactic for much of 2007.

Of course, if the purpose of a hold is to invite negotiations, senators make their identity known. And that is most often the case.

Holds are frequent, and placing them has become standard operating procedure in the Senate. This little story appeared deep in *CongressDaily*'s roundup of Capitol Hill news on July 2, 2003; it was reported with almost a yawn, even though there was little news competition, since Congress was home for the Fourth of July recess:

   Senate Majority Leader Frist and Finance Chairman Grassley are continuing to negotiate with Alabama Republican Sens. Richard Shelby and Jeff Sessions over a hold they have placed on a bill that benefits hundreds of U.S. businesses by cutting tariffs on products they import, according to a Senate leadership aide. Sixty-six senators wrote Frist late last week urging him to bring the bill to the floor "without further amendments" to force a cloture vote to beat the holds. While the letter gives Frist more leverage in negotiating with the Alabamians, he "wouldn't bring it up until he has exhausted his ability to work things out amicably," the aide said. Shelby and Sessions want provisions added to the bill that would require country-of-origin labeling on packages of socks, among other demands. (*CongressDaily*, Wednesday, July 2, 2003)

Holds are not granted by Senate rules; they are an informal custom. What gives holds their bite is the implicit or explicit threat to filibuster the motion to proceed. Of course, a hold cannot block consideration of such must-pass legislation as appropriations bills. The majority leader will also sometimes go ahead with less essential legislation despite a hold, and may find that the threat implicit in the hold was a bluff.

On the other hand, the majority leader may face a filibuster on the motion to proceed and, if that is overcome, a filibuster on the bill itself. Even if both filibusters can be overcome, the time consumed is substantial. Especially when floor time is short—before a recess or near the end of the session—most legislation is not likely to be considered worthy of so much time. After all, if scarce time is used trying to end a filibuster, other legislation will be sacrificed. Supporters of legislation are under increasing pressure to make concessions that will remove the threat of a filibuster. In July 2006, Senator Wyden put a hold on a major telecommunications bill because he objected to its weak language on "Net neutrality." *Congressional Quarterly* reported matter-of-factly, "Senate leaders have said they will not bring the bill to the floor until sponsors line up enough votes to overcome a potential Democratic filibuster" (*CQW*, September 4, 2006, 2321). As time becomes scarcer, a hold increasingly becomes a veto.

Senators' willingness to hold up one matter in order to extract concessions on another, sometimes known as hostage taking, has further complicated Senate floor scheduling. A particularly Byzantine instance occurred in 1995, when Jesse Helms, R-NC, chair of the Senate Foreign Relations Committee, sponsored a State Department reorganization bill that the Clinton administration and many Democrats opposed. Helms brought the legislation to the floor, but after two attempts at imposing cloture failed, Majority Leader Dole stopped floor consideration. Frustrated, Helms began bottling up ambassador nominations, the START II treaty, and the Chemical Weapons Convention. Democrats responded by blocking action on a flag desecration constitutional amendment and a Cuba sanctions bill, both priorities for Helms. Negotiations and concessions eventually unstuck the impasse, although only the Cuba sanctions bill actually became law.

The majority leader thus schedules legislation under severe constraints. When the majority leader rises to make a unanimous consent request that the Senate proceed to consider a particular bill, this action has almost always already been cleared with the leader's party colleagues and has received agreement from the minority leader, who has cleared it with minority-party members.

Nominations

The Constitution gives the Senate the power to advise and consent on high-level presidential appointments. This has come to mean that the Senate must approve by majority vote the president's nominations of cabinet secretaries and other high-level executives, ambassadors, and judges, including Supreme Court justices. A motion to proceed to consider a nomination is not debatable, but the motion to approve the nomination is, and, consequently, it can be filibustered.

Party polarization has made the confirmation process an increasingly confrontational one. Senators use holds to block nominations they oppose, even if a Senate majority clearly supports the nomination. In 2003, Democrats blocked the nomination of Miguel Estrada to an appellate court judgeship; after seven failed attempts to impose cloture, Estrada withdrew his name from consideration; on each of those cloture votes, a majority voted in favor. In 2009, Republicans held up the nomination of Robert Groves, the highly respected head of the Survey Research Center at University of Michigan, to head the Census Bureau, because they feared he would favor statistical sampling in the 2010 Census. Republicans placed holds on former Yale Law School dean Harold Hongju Koh's nomination as the State Department's legal adviser to protest his support for a more international approach to resolving disputes. In both cases, the nominee was eventually confirmed after cloture was invoked by wide margins. President Barack Obama's nomination of Craig Becker to the National Labor Relations Board failed despite a majority, but not sixty, voting for cloture. (Using his power to make recess appointments, Obama appointed Becker to the post "temporarily" while Congress was out of session.)

During the Reagan and George H.W. Bush administrations, Democrats blocked judicial nominees whom they considered too conservative; in the second half of the 1990s, Republicans blocked many of Clinton's nominees because they believed them too liberal. (See Epstein and Segal 2005 on the judicial confirmation process.) When the opposition party controls the Senate, it often can block presidential nominees it finds offensive in committee so that the nomination never makes it to a floor vote. Democrats considered many of George W. Bush's appellate court nominees right-wing extremists. In the 108th Congress, Republicans were in the majority, so they could vote Bush nominees out of the Judiciary Committee, but they could not overcome Democratic filibusters.

Frustrated, Senate Republicans threatened to change Senate rules to disallow filibusters on presidential nominations. The Republicans did not have the two-thirds vote that changing Senate rules in the ordinary way requires; however, their plan entailed having the Senate's presiding officer (presumably, Vice President Dick Cheney) rule that cutting off debate on nominations requires only a simple majority. Democrats would, of course, appeal the ruling, but only a simple majority is required to uphold a ruling of the chair. The plan was dubbed the "nuclear option" because of its likely explosive consequences (see Chapter 10).

Since implementing the plan would require the presiding officer to make a ruling that contravenes Senate precedent, one can consider the plan a highly unorthodox response to what Republicans considered the Democrats' unorthodox use of Senate rules (see Beth 2005). The showdown was averted at the last moment by a bipartisan group of fourteen senators. The Democrats in the group agreed to not support filibusters of judicial nominations except under extraordinary circumstances; the Republicans, in return, promised not to support the nuclear option. This agreement held throughout the 109th Congress. In 2005 the Senate approved two Bush Supreme Court nominees, even though both were seen as quite conservative; the agreement played a part, but most Democrats also feared that public opinion would not support filibusters against the nominees, since both were perceived as highly qualified. In the 111th Congress, the Democrats' majority was wide enough that they could usually impose cloture if they were willing to take the time to do so, but because of time constraints, the backlog of unconfirmed nominees reached unprecedented levels.

Increasingly often in recent years, senators have taken to holding nominations hostage in order to extract concessions on other matters from the administration; that is, senators block nominees they do not oppose in order to gain a bargaining chip vis-à-vis the administration. Thus Senators Bob Bennett (R-UT) and Lisa Murkowski (R-AK) put holds on the nomination of David Hayes to be deputy secretary of the Interior Department because, they claimed, the agency had not adequately explained its decision to cancel oil and gas leases in western states (*RC,* May 13, 2009). Reid attempted to invoke cloture but failed on a 57–39 vote. "It has nothing to do with him, it has to do with what's going on in the department," Orrin Hatch (R-UT) explained. After Secretary of the Interior Ken Salazar promised Hayes would promptly review all the disputed leases, the holds were lifted and Hayes was confirmed. In February 2010, Richard Shelby (R-AL) placed a hold on more than seventy Obama nominees; Shelby demanded funding for the KC-135 Air Force tanker fleet, a project that could generate thousands of jobs in Alabama, and the restoration of funding cut from the budget for the FBI's Terrorist Explosive Device Analytical Center, also located in Alabama. After intense media attention and widespread criticism, Shelby lifted his holds on most of the nominees, claiming he had accomplished his purpose: "to get the White House's attention" (*WP,* February 8, 2010).

Even members of the president's own party sometimes use the strategy. Russ Feingold (D-WI) along with John McCain (R-AR) placed a hold on Obama's nomination of John Sullivan to the Federal Election Commission. They would release their hold only if Obama made nominations to all the expired seats. "The FEC is currently mired in anti-enforcement gridlock," read the senators' joint statement. "The president must nominate new commissioners with a demonstrated commitment to the existence and enforcement of the campaign finance laws" (*Politico,* June 30, 2009). And Democratic senator Robert Menendez, NJ, put a hold on the confirmation of Obama science adviser John P. Holdren, a former Harvard professor; he lifted it after several weeks, but it was seen as a shot across the bow warning the administration that he would strenuously oppose any overtures to Cuba (*CQW,* July 13, 2009).

Processing Noncontroversial Business

Congress considers and passes many bills and nominations that are not at all controversial. To expedite such business, the House uses suspension of the rules; the Senate uses unanimous consent.

To determine if a measure is sufficiently noncontroversial that it can be passed by unanimous consent, it needs to be "cleared," a process handled by staff in the party secretaries' offices. "The first I hear about a bill will usually come either from the sponsor or from a committee," a majority aide explained. "And they will say, 'We want to pass such-and-such a bill. Can you hot-line it?'" The aide will check the calendar to see if a senator has sent a hold letter on the matter. If so, the aide went on to explain:

> I'll call that person or those people and see what's going on. Either they'll say, "I just hate that bill," or they'll say, "[it has] this sort of problem or that sort of problem." Or maybe it was just that they wanted to be apprised of the fact that it was going to come up. I will allay their concerns or maybe find that there are other problems, and that might mean that I have to kick it up to someone else.

If the problems can be taken care of at the staff level, the aide will ask the majority leader and the appropriate committee, "Is this okay to hot-line?" At that point, the staffer's minority counterpart will be informed, and much the same process then takes place on the minority side. "Then I'll hot-line the item. After the hot-line, then any office with problems will have to call us. I'll call those offices and then, if it's cleared by both sides, it will go on wrap-up," the staffer concluded.

The "wrap-up" occurs at the end of the day. One measure after another is brought up by the majority leader or his designee, no debate occurs, and the measure is passed by unanimous consent; the minority leader or designee is always present to protect minority members' rights, but, in fact, everything brought up has already been cleared (Oleszek 2004, 198; Gold 2003, 79–80). On September 29, 2010, for example, Senate majority whip Dick Durbin, D-IL, called up and the Senate passed in quick succession twelve bills and twelve Senate resolutions or Senate concurrent resolutions. The bills ranged from a measure providing for a one-year extension of the authorizations for the Work Incentives Planning and Assistance program and the Protection and Advocacy for Beneficiaries of Social Security program and the Oil Spill Prevention Act requiring new vessels for carrying oil fuel to have double hulls, to the CALM Act to regulate the volume of audio on commercials, to four bills naming post offices. The resolutions mostly honored or recognized some person or entity, the Hudson River School painters, in one case, but also included a resolution urging the development of a comprehensive strategy to ensure stability in Somalia (*CR* S 7770-71).

Senators' aggressiveness in scrutinizing matters that the leadership is attempting to clear and their views of what is acceptable affect how this procedure works. In the 1980s liberal Democrat Howard Metzenbaum (OH) had his staff examined every such bill looking for corporate give-aways. He so regularly objected to otherwise noncontroversial bills that Majority Leader Howard Baker's, R-TN, staff took to consulting him on a routine basis before bringing legislation to the floor (see Gold 2003). The conservative Republican Steering Committee and Sen. Tom Coburn's office do that now, though what they consider objectionable is, of course, quite different. They scrutinize every hot-lined bill and place a hold if they believe it is bad legislation from a conservative perspective or even just warrants a closer examination. "A lot of things will go through otherwise if nobody is paying attention and nobody is kind of watching out for the tax-payer," a staffer involved in the process explained. Because the amount of time specified in the hot-lined message may be short, the staffer continued, "our theory is to put a hold on it at first. A senator can lift a hold. He cannot un-pass a bill."

Ordinarily the process—even when there are objections—goes on "below the radar," but in late 2008 and early 2009 the struggle over passing a group of public lands bills broke out into a public battle. The Senate Energy and Natural Resources Committee had reported ninety public lands bills, doing such things as designating wilderness areas, wild and scenic rivers, hiking trails, heritage areas, water projects, and historic preservation initiatives. These are the sort of bills that are traditionally passed by unanimous consent on wrap-up, but when the leadership attempted to clear them, Coburn put holds on them all; he was concerned about the total cost and about a variety of issues affecting private property rights (Wolfensberger, April 13, 2009, in *RC*). The bills did eventually become law—in an Omnibus Public Lands bill, though, not until the next Congress and only after Senate and House leaders had had to expend a considerable amount of time and effort (see Chapter 5).

Unanimous Consent Agreements

The Senate often considers legislation under formal unanimous consent agreements. The majority leader and senior staff, especially the party secretary, negotiate an agreement setting terms for the consideration of the legislation. A UCA may specify time for general debate and time limits for the debate of specific amendments; it may completely bar nongermane (or, more frequently, nonrelevant) amendments or those not explicitly listed;[3] and it may specify the time for votes on specific amendments and on final passage (Tiefer 1989, 573–584; Smith and Flathman 1989). Here is an example of a comprehensive, complex unanimous consent agreement. It was offered and agreed to on June 26, 2008:

> Mr. REID. Mr. President, I ask unanimous consent that on Tuesday, July 8, at a time to be determined by the majority leader, following consultation with Senator *McConnell*, all postcloture time be yielded back and the motion to proceed to Calendar No. 827, H.R. 6304, be agreed to, the motion to reconsider be laid upon the table, and the Senate then proceed to the consideration of the bill; that once the bill is reported, the only amendments in order be the following: Dodd-Feingold-Leahy amendment to strike immunity; a Specter amendment which is relevant; a Bingaman amendment re: staying court cases against telecom companies; that no other amendments be in order; that debate time on the Bingaman amendment be limited to 60 minutes, equally divided and controlled in the usual form, and 2 hours each with respect to the Dodd and Specter amendments, equally divided and controlled, with 10 minutes of the Dodd time under the control of Senator *Leahy*; that upon the use or yielding back of all time, the Senate proceed to vote on the pending amendments; there be 2 minutes of debate equally divided and controlled in the usual form prior to each vote; that after the first vote in the sequence, succeeding votes be limited to 10 minutes each; that upon the disposition of all amendments, the bill, as amended, if amended, be read a third time and the Senate then proceed to vote on a motion to invoke cloture on the bill, with the mandatory quorum waived; that prior to the cloture vote, there be 60 minutes plus the time specified below for debate time, equally divided and controlled between the two leaders or their designees, with 10 minutes under the control of Senator *Leahy*, with an additional 30 minutes under the control of Senator *Feingold*, with an additional 15 minutes under the control of Senator *Dodd*; further, that if cloture is invoked on H.R. 6304, then all postcloture time be yielded back, and without further intervening action or debate, the Senate proceed to vote on passage of the bill, as amended, if amended; further, that it be in order to file the cloture motion on the bill at any time prior to the cloture vote, with the mandatory quorum waived, notwithstanding rule

---

3. Relevance is, in most cases, a less strict standard than is germaneness.

XXII, if applicable, and that if applicable, postcloture time be charged during this agreement.

The PRESIDING OFFICER. Without objection, it is so ordered. (*CR*, June 26, 2008, S6224; see also Wallner 2010)

This UCA provided for the consideration of the Foreign Intelligence Surveillance Act (FISA) Amendments Act. As the first sentence of the UCA indicates, it was offered after cloture had been voted on the motion to proceed; note that, as a time-saving measure, it does away by UC with postcloture debate time and with the actual vote on the motion to proceed. It then lists the amendments that will be in order, specifies debate time for each—for example, sixty minutes for the Bingaman amendment—and who controls the time—"equally divided and controlled" means half controlled by the sponsor and half by an opponent. The UCA goes on to specify that the amendments are to be voted on in order after they have all been debated. After the amendments have been disposed of, debate on the bill itself occurs, with the UCA specifying how much time and who controls it—sixty minutes for the party leaders, ten minutes for Senator Leahy, thirty minutes for Senator Feingold, and fifteen minutes for Senator Dodd. "The Senate then [will] proceed to vote on a motion to invoke cloture on the bill," according to the UCA, and if that vote is successful, no more debate occurs before a final vote on the bill itself.

As this UCA suggests, unanimous consent agreements in the Senate may lend order to floor consideration and do often include time-saving provisions, but they nevertheless allow for considerably more debate time than is typical in the House.

Comprehensive UCAs that are worked out before the bill comes to the floor and that govern the entire process of consideration are fairly rare (Smith and Flathman 1989, 366; Evans and Oleszek 1995). In the 108th Congress, for example, only two major measures were brought to the floor under what could be considered comprehensive UCAs. These days, the leader more often will be able to work out only a partial agreement before debate begins. The agreement may just stipulate that the bill will be brought up, in effect, that no one will object to the motion to proceed to consider the bill.

As consideration progresses, senators are likely to become clearer about what amendments they want to offer and how much time they will need, and further agreements may become possible. These may be worked out on the floor during the debate, sometimes by the bill managers and sometimes by the party leaders. Thus, several partial UCAs may govern a bill's consideration. The major measures that came to the floor in the 108th Congress averaged about six UCAs each. As an expert participant explained:

Usually you have a UCA only to bring something to the floor, and then maybe you have another one that will deal with a couple of important amendments, and then perhaps a little later, one that will start limiting amendments to some extent, and then perhaps one that specifies when a vote will take place. So it's done through a series of steps, each of which sort of leaves less and less leeway.

This is the series of UCAs for consideration of HR 1105, an omnibus appropriations bill:

2/27, 2009
Omnibus Appropriations Act—Agreement : A unanimous-consent agreement was reached providing that at 2 p.m., on Monday, March 2, 2009, Senate begin consideration of H.R. 1105, making omnibus appropriations for the fiscal year ending September 30, 2009.

3/2
A unanimous-consent-time agreement was reached providing for further consideration of the bill at 10 a.m., on Tuesday, March 3, 2009, and that the time until 11:45 a.m. be for debate relative to McCain Amendment No. 592 [this is a substitute] (listed above), with the time equally divided and controlled between Senators Inouye [chairman of the Appropriations Committee] and McCain, or their designees; and that no amendment be in order to the amendment prior to a vote on or in relation to the amendment; provided further, that at 11:45 a.m. Senate vote on or in relation to McCain Amendment No. 592.

3/3
A unanimous-consent agreement was reached providing for further consideration of the bill at 9:30 a.m., on Wednesday, March 4, 2009.

3/4
A unanimous-consent agreement was reached providing for further consideration of the bill at approximately 10:30 a.m. on Thursday, March 5, 2009.

3/5
Cloture Motion—Agreement : A unanimous-consent agreement was reached providing that the previously scheduled vote on the motion to invoke cloture on the bill, be vitiated.
  Subsequently, the motion to invoke cloture on the bill was withdrawn.
  A unanimous-consent agreement was reached providing for further consideration of the bill at 10 a.m., on Friday, March 6, 2009.

3/6
A unanimous-consent agreement was reached providing that Senate resume consideration of the bill at 2 p.m., on Monday, March 9, 2009, and that the following amendments in this agreement be the only first-degree amendments

remaining in order to HR 1105; that no amendment be in order to any of the listed amendments prior to a vote in relation thereto; that the amendments must be offered and debated Friday, March 6, 2009; Monday, March 9, 2009; or Tuesday, March 10, 2009; provided further, that upon disposition of the amendments, and Senate has voted on the motion to invoke cloture on the bill, and cloture having been invoked, all post-cloture time be considered yielded back, the bill be read a third time, and Senate vote on passage of the bill: Ensign Amendment No. 615, Vitter Amendment No. 621, Sessions Amendment No. 604, McCain Amendment No. 593, Thune Amendment No. 662, Barrasso Amendment No. 637, Enzi Amendment No. 668, Kyl Amendment No. 631, Kyl Amendment No. 629, Kyl Amendment No. 630, Kyl or designee amendment relative to dues notification, Cornyn Amendment No. 673, and Bunning Amendment No. 665. (excerpts from *CR Daily Digest* of the date referenced)

The bill passed the Senate on March 10, 2009.

A unanimous consent agreement provides some of the predictability that a special rule provides in the House. The difference is that a simple majority can approve a special rule, whereas a UCA requires unanimous consent—one senator can veto it. This difference, of course, has an enormous impact on the legislative process in the two chambers.

Clearly, unanimous consent agreements make the majority leader's job easier; a comprehensive UCA gives the leader a much better idea of how long the legislation will take on the floor. Even a partial one provides some predictability. The bill's supporters value the reduction in uncertainty that UCAs accomplish. But why do other senators agree to unanimous consent agreements? For other senators, with their extremely busy schedules and their own legislative priorities, the more predictable schedule and the more efficient use of time that UCAs make possible are important benefits and may dictate acquiescing to a UCA even for a bill the senator does not support. But if the senator strongly opposes the legislation, he or she can always object.

In recent years, the minority party sometimes objects to the consideration—not just the passage—of major legislation it strongly opposes. The majority leader in some instances has brought such legislation to the floor without an agreement and so, instead of asking unanimous consent that the bill be considered, has moved to proceed to consider the bill. The leader may know that he lacks the votes to break a filibuster against the motion to proceed but wants to make a political point by at least having a debate on the issue (though the debate is technically on the motion to proceed). During the 108th Congress, three major measures were killed when Democrats filibustered and so blocked an up-or-down vote on the motion to proceed to consider the bill in question. In the 110th Congress, the bill allowing Medicare to negotiate prescription drug prices, a bill making labor organizing easier, one giving the District of Columbia voting representation in the House, another overturning a Supreme Court decision severely narrowing plaintiffs' ability to sue in job discrimination cases, the bill rescuing the U.S. auto industry, and the Dream Act essentially legalizing the children of undocumented workers who had graduated from high school in the United States and had never been in legal trouble all died when Republicans filibustered the motion to proceed. Yet even under these highly contentious and partisan circumstances, the party leaders reached UCAs specifying when the debate would take place, how much time for debate would be allowed, and when the cloture vote would occur.

The minority party now is seldom willing to agree to UCAs that limit amendments or debate initially. In the 108th Congress, for example, only five initial UCAs for major measures restricted amendments in some way. Special circumstances did make comprehensive UCAs a bit more frequent in the 110th and 111th Congresses. Although Democrats gained control of the Senate in the 2006 elections, Bush was still president, so Republicans had a stake in enacting at least some legislation and in a timely fashion. A particularly dramatic example was the Emergency Economic Stabilization Act (setting up TARP). The bill was negotiated by the Senate Democrats and Republicans and the White House, and it was considered on the floor under a comprehensive UCA that allowed a vote on only one amendment (other than the compromise that was itself offered as an amendment to a House bill on other subjects entirely). In the 111th Congress, the Democratic majority sometimes persuaded Republicans to agree to comprehensive UCAs in return for guaranteed votes on their amendments. The UCA for the bill raising the debt limit in January 2010 is a good example. The comprehensive UCA gave Republicans votes on a series of amendments, and this was a must-pass bill in any case. More frequently, though, it is only after a period of debate and amending activity that the minority will entertain the possibility of limiting amendments. As a consequence, both in the abstract and in practice, the majority party's floor agenda control is limited.

The Senate Floor

Assume the Senate has agreed to consider the legislation. Floor debate begins in the same way it does in the House: with opening statements by the majority and minority floor managers. As in the House, the chair and the ranking minority member of the committee or subcommittee usually manage the legislation on the floor, but in the Senate a bill sponsor who holds no such official position may act as floor manager.

Debate is unlimited unless constrained by a unanimous consent agreement, and even then it will not be as restricted as in the House. Senators' statements are likely to be considerably longer than those of representatives. When the Senate is engaged in a great debate, such as on the resolution in 1991 to authorize the Persian Gulf War, the lack of tight time limits makes for better and certainly more dramatic debate. On less momentous occasions Senate debate can drag on interminably.

Especially if the Senate is operating without a complex UCA, debate on amendments is quite unstructured. Even when the House is operating under an open rule, it often amends bills by section or title so that, at any given time, only amendments to a particular section or title are in order. In the Senate measures are open to amendment at any point. Although it is not required, senators often do submit their amendments to be printed in the *Congressional Record* before offering them on the floor. The floor manager may know when a senator intends to offer an amendment, and if that senator is not on the floor at the planned time, the floor manager is likely to wait! The House, in contrast, waits for no member and certainly not for a rank-and-file member who wants to offer an amendment.

Quorum calls are used to kill time. A senator can make a point of order that a quorum is not present, and the presiding officer will ask the clerk to call the roll.[4] The Senate does not use electronic voting. The clerk will very slowly call the names of the senators while everyone waits for the senator who is supposed to be offering the amendment to show up. When the senator comes in, the quorum call is vacated (that is, called off), usually without a quorum ever having shown up. Similarly, when senators need some time in the midst of floor consideration to negotiate in private, quorum calls make possible a kind of time-out. For example, the floor manager and a senator offering an amendment may want to see if they can work out a compromise version of the amendment that both find acceptable.

Amendment Rules and Their Consequences

Senate rules, under most circumstances, allow any senator to offer as many amendments as he or she wishes to legislation on the floor. For most bills the amendments need not even be germane to the legislation; that is, if a senator wants to offer a civil rights provision to an agriculture bill or vice

---

4. In fact, a quorum is seldom present, since senators are in their offices or in committee working. Even if a quorum is present, the presiding officer must have the roll called; only under cloture may the presiding officer determine the presence of a quorum by counting.

versa, Senate rules do not prohibit it. Senate committees, therefore, have considerably less power than their House counterparts to kill legislation by refusing to report it. The language can be offered as an amendment to some other bill on the floor. Amendments to general appropriations bills (that is, spending bills) must be germane according to Senate rules, but senators often prefer not to enforce the rule. Some unanimous consent agreements require that amendments be relevant (a less stringent standard than germaneness) unless they are explicitly listed, and after cloture is invoked amendments must be germane. The Congressional Budget and Impoundment Control Act of 1974 (hereafter the Budget Act) requires that amendments to budget resolutions and reconciliation bills be germane.

In fact, senators frequently offer nongermane amendments. Throughout his long Senate career Jesse Helms used nongermane amendments on such hot-button topics as busing, homosexuality, pornography, and abortion to get his issues to the floor and force senators to vote on them. In the late 1980s he successfully attached to an education bill an amendment outlawing dial-a-porn services (900-number telephone services that provide explicit sexual messages for a fee).

But Helms was by no means an anomaly; most senators use the tactic at least occasionally. In 2004, senators offered amendments to the annual defense authorization bill that set higher monetary penalties for broadcast indecency (Sam Brownback, R-KS), increased the top income tax rate to 36 percent (Joseph Biden, D-DE), broadened the categories covered by federal hate crime laws (Gordon Smith, R-OR), and declared it the sense of the Senate that legislation should be enacted imposing an excise tax on plaintiffs' attorneys in tobacco litigation (Jon Kyl, R-AR). Senator Tom Coburn (R-OK) and other conservative Republicans regularly offer gun amendments to unrelated legislation; in the 111th Congress, for example, they successfully offered such amendments to the bill granting the District of Columbia a voting seat in the House of Representatives and to the legislation regulating credit cards.

Senators' ability and willingness to offer nongermane amendments have major implications for the majority leadership's control of the schedule and of the agenda more broadly. The leadership cannot keep issues off the floor by refusing to schedule legislation. A senator can simply offer the legislation as a nongermane amendment. In the 104th Congress, Majority Leader Dole and most Republicans would have dearly loved to keep off the floor the issue of open hearings on the ethics case involving Sen. Bob Packwood, R-OR. But Sen. Barbara Boxer, D-CA, offered it as a floor amendment to the defense authorization bill and forced a recorded vote. Democrats would much rather avoid gun rights issues, but Coburn forces them onto the Senate agenda.

As the Senate became more partisan in the 1990s, the Senate minority party became increasingly adept at using the Senate's permissive amending rules to force its issues onto the floor. In 1996, Senate majority leader Dole and most Senate Republicans did not want to vote on a minimum wage increase that most opposed but that was popular with the public. Senate Democrats were prepared to offer the minimum wage increase as an amendment to every important piece of legislation brought to the floor, and to avoid a vote, Dole was forced to put off votes, bringing the legislative process in the Senate to a standstill. Eventually, Dole's successor as majority leader, Senator Lott, capitulated, the bill came to a vote, and it passed handily.

Using similar tactics, the minority Democrats, sometimes with the help of dissident Republicans, forced debates on campaign finance reform, tobacco taxes, HMO regulation, Bush administration rules limiting overtime pay, and further minimum wage increases, all issues the majority party would rather have avoided. In 2004, Democrats used the debate on the defense authorization bill discussed earlier to highlight their concerns about the war in Iraq by offering amendments that required President Bush to submit a report on U.S. strategy for stabilizing Iraq and specifying the number of troops that would be needed (Kennedy, D-MA) and that ordered the Department of Defense to prepare and give Congress a number of reports related to the treatment of detainees in U.S. military prisons around the world (Leahy, D-VT). In the 111th Congress, Republican used the Senate's loose amendment rules to force debate on issues ranging from what do about the Guantánamo Bay military prison and the people detained there to the federal budget deficit.

Amending rules make it much more difficult for the majority party and the leadership to control the agenda in the Senate than in the House. Senate leaders sometimes bring bills that they oppose to the floor because attempts to keep them off would be highly disruptive to their schedule and likely not successful. In 2001, for example, Majority Leader Lott did not attempt to keep campaign finance reform legislation off the floor, even though most Republicans (including President Bush) strongly opposed the bill. Republican John McCain and his Democratic allies had threatened to add the bill as a nongermane amendment to every bill Lott did bring to the floor. The result of trying to block it would have been gridlock on the new president's program. The UCA on the debt limit increase in 2010 provided for votes on an amendment eliminating the extremely unpopular TARP and on amendments rescinding already appropriated spending on the legislative branch and other not-so-popular programs; Reid agreed and, in fact, negotiated that UCA because he needed to pass the bill and because he knew he could not keep those issues off the floor indefinitely, in any case. With his big majority—and a sixty-vote require-ment (see below)—Reid did defeat the amendments.

That limited agenda control can also create problems for legislation the majority wants and has the votes to pass. The minority can sometimes come up with "killer" amendments that result in the defeat of a bill that otherwise would command a majority. Thus in March 2004, Republicans brought to the Senate floor legislation to shield the firearms industry from lawsuits; the bill had more than sixty supporters and seemed assured of passing. And had the House's restrictive rules been available, it surely would have. Democratic opponents of the bill failed to stop floor consider-ation when cloture on the vote to proceed to consider the bill was invoked 75–22.

Then, however, an amendment sponsored by Dianne Feinstein, D-CA, John W. Warner, R-VA; and Chuck Schumer, D-NY, passed on a 52–47 vote. The amendment extended for ten years the ban on nineteen types of military-style, semiautomatic assault weapons, which was set to expire in September. Minutes later, the Senate approved, 53 to 46, a proposal by John McCain and Jack Reed, D-RI, to require criminal background checks for purchases from unlicensed as well as licensed dealers at gun shows, closing a loophole in existing law blamed by gun control advocates for sales of weapons to criminals and terrorists. After the National Rifle Asso-ciation let the bill's chief sponsor, Larry E. Craig, R-ID, know that from its perspective the amended bill was worse than no bill, Craig took the Senate floor to say the bill had been "so dramatically wounded it should not pass" and the bill was defeated on a 90–8 vote (*WP*, March 3, 2004). In a turn-around, in the 111th Congress conservative Republicans offered an amendment to the District of Columbia Voting Rights Act that would repeal the District's strict gun control provisions; although the amend-ment's passage did not prevent the bill, which Republicans strongly opposed, from passing the Senate, it killed the bill in the House.

Senators today consider it their right to offer as many amendments as they wish on the floor and to be accommodated in doing so. For example, under Senate rules, once an amendment has been offered, it is pending and no other first-degree amendment is in order until it has been disposed of. But this rule can be waived by unanimous consent; the amendment being considered is "set aside" by unanimous consent but remains pend-ing, and another amendment can then be offered. The Senate frequently does this so as to accommodate senators. The result is that a number of amendments are pending simultaneously, which can lead to confusion. Yet if the majority leader refused unanimous consent to offer more amend-ments under such circumstances, minority-party senators complain bit-terly. The Senate sometimes considers "side-by-side" amendments; that is,

it considers simultaneously two first-degree amendments on the same subject—often alternatives. The regular Senate rules do not allow this, so it is
possible only by unanimous consent. A unanimous consent agreement
may provide for the offering of side-by-side amendments. Both amendments will be voted on, and even if they are conflicting alternatives, if both
pass, both stay in the bill; the problem this creates is taken care of in the
postpassage process.

Although overall the number of amendments offered on the Senate
floor and pushed to a roll call vote has declined since its peak in the 1970s
(Lee 2010), amending activity on major legislation is often high, and
amending marathons[5] (when ten or more amendments are offered and
pushed to a recorded vote) are far from rare. In the Congresses of the
1990s and 2000s, on average about 30 percent of the major measures considered on the Senate floor were subject to ten or more amendments
decided by recorded vote.

What sort of legislation is likely to provoke a high rate of amending
activity, and does such activity usually represent an attempt to legislate or
to stop legislation? Legislation that must pass, as well as legislation that
seems highly likely to pass, more often than other legislation evokes high
amending activity, suggesting that senators are using such bills as vehicles
for legislating. Appropriations bills, which must be enacted to keep the
government functioning, make up a regular part of legislation on which
amending marathons take place, as do defense authorization bills. Legislation that is very broad in scope often provokes extensive amending activity;
budget resolutions, major tax bills, and omnibus appropriations bills are
examples. On the six budget resolutions from 2003 through 2008, on average thirty-six amendments were offered and pushed to a recorded vote;
there were fifty amendment votes on the 2003 budget resolution.

And, of course, controversial legislation stimulates amending activity
as opponents attempt to alter or even kill it, or at least to place supporters
on the record on controversial provisions. The Medicare prescription drug
bill that passed the Senate in 2003 occasioned thirty-four amendments
pushed to a roll call vote. The immigration bills in the 109th and 110th
Congresses were subject thirty-six and thirty-four amendment votes,
respectively, and the health care reform reconciliation bill was subject to
forty-one roll calls on amendments (see Chapter 8). Defense authorization
bills have stimulated high amending activity in recent years because they
are quite broad in scope and parts are highly controversial (missile

---

5. This is my term, not an official designation. "Indirect" votes on amendments
such as votes to table an amendment and to waive the Budget Act to allow the
offering of an amendment are counted.

defense, for example); and since they are considered nearly must-past legislation, the minority party has seen them as a convenient vehicle for getting votes on issues it wants to highlight. There were thirty amendments pushed to a roll call vote on the 2004 DOD authorization bill, including a number, such as the Kennedy and Leahy amendments mentioned earlier, that were intended to draw media attention to Democratic critiques of Bush administration policies regarding Iraq and to put Republicans on the spot. Republicans offered an amendment to the 2009 defense authorization bill that would allow individuals with a valid permit in their home state to carry concealed firearms in any state that has permits for firearms or does not prohibit residents from carrying them.

One must remember that amendments that are pushed to a roll call are only the tip of the iceberg. For example, the 2004 intelligence reform bill was subject to only 7 amendments that were decided on a roll call vote, but a total of 262 amendments were proposed and the bill was on the Senate floor for nine days. There were roll calls on 18 amendments on the very controversial energy bill in 2003, but hundreds more had been introduced before Majority Leader Frist gave up on passing the Republican version of the bill.

To expedite the legislative process on the Senate floor, a floor manager will often agree to accept many amendments, either as is or with some negotiated changes, and roll them into a big "manager's amendment" that the floor manager then offers. After a number of grueling days on the floor, the manager may be willing to accept "just about anything," staff report (only half jokingly). Some of these amendments, everyone knows, will be dropped in conference. Even so, senators are able to claim credit for an amendment passing the Senate.

If a senator wants a recorded vote on his or her amendment, the senator can almost always get one. Senate party leaders cannot protect their members from tough votes in the way that House leaders sometimes can. To be sure, bill proponents often move to table an amendment. This is a nondebatable motion, and if an amendment is successfully tabled—which requires only a majority vote—debate on it is cut off and it is killed without a vote ever being taken on the amendment itself. However, the tactic makes an ineffective fig leaf for senators who oppose the amendment but fear the political consequences of voting against it.

The consideration of reconciliation bills is governed by Budget Act rules that are highly complex and require sixty votes to waive. Many of the amendments offered to reconciliation bills can be killed by making a point of order against them for violating the Budget Act, and this is routinely done. The amendment's sponsor can, however, demand a recorded vote on waiving the act. While the requirement of sixty votes to waive makes it relatively easy to defeat the motion, senators are forced to go on the record. The parliamentary language does not provide much of a screen to hide the opposition of senators to the substance of the amendment. (In fact, a senator who believes that waiving budget rules is a mistake, and thus votes against such motions on principle regardless of the substance of the amendment at issue, may have a hard time convincing constituents of his or her motives.)

Each senator's prerogative under the rules to offer as many amendments as she or he desires on almost any piece of legislation has many uses and, in fact, is employed to a variety of ends. Committee and party leaders know that the Senate's permissive amending rules give disgruntled senators a potent weapon. Therefore, before the bill reaches the floor, leaders have a considerable incentive to bargain and compromise with any senator who expresses dissatisfaction. Senators not on the committee of jurisdiction can influence the shape of legislation at the prefloor stage in a way not possible for similarly situated House members. If senators alert a bill's sponsor, informally or through a hold, that they have a problem with certain of a bill's provisions, the sponsor must seriously consider trying to placate them. A single dissatisfied senator, even a junior senator who is a minority-party member, can cause a great deal of trouble.

Extended Debate and Cloture

A bill's supporters must concern themselves not just with the barrage of amendments opponents may offer on the floor but also with the possibility that opponents will use extended debate to block action altogether. In the Senate, debate ends on a matter when every senator has said all he or she wants to say or after cloture is invoked. The cloture process is the only way in which debate can be shut off in the Senate over any senator's objection.

Any senator may circulate a cloture petition. When the senator has gathered sixteen signatures, the petition is filed; after a one-day layover, the Senate votes. On most matters three-fifths of the entire Senate membership (usually sixty) must vote for cloture for the motion to pass. If the measure at issue changes Senate rules, two-thirds of those present and voting are required to shut off debate.

Even after a successful cloture vote, debate does not necessarily end immediately. Senate Rule 22, the cloture rule, places a cap of thirty hours on consideration after the cloture vote. The thirty hours does include time spent on quorum calls and voting as well as on debate. The rule also requires that amendments considered after cloture must be germane.

If cloture fails, the bill's supporters may try again. There is no limit on the number of cloture petitions that may be filed on one measure, and sometimes supporters file a new petition even before a vote has been taken on a previous one so as to minimize the delay caused by the requirement that there be a day in session between the filing of the petition and the vote. In 1987 and 1988, Majority Leader Robert C. Byrd, D-WV, made eight attempts to impose cloture on campaign finance reform legislation before he gave up. In 1999, Republicans tried and failed to impose cloture three times on Y2K legislation before John McCain, the bill's sponsor, decided he had to compromise; on the Social Security "lockbox," Republicans tried unsuccessfully five times. In the 108th Congress, Majority Leader Frist attempted seven times to impose cloture on the nomination of Miguel Estrada to an appellate judgeship; he was never successful.

The cloture process is time consuming and cumbersome. Furthermore, if the opponents are determined, supporters may need to impose cloture at more than one stage in a bill's progress through the chamber. Thus extended debate can occur on the motion to proceed to consider the measure, on specific amendments, on the measure itself, on various motions related to going to conference, and on the conference report. No single measure has ever been subject to filibusters at all these stages, but it is not uncommon for cloture to be sought at several stages. On the "motor voter" bill in 1993, for example, cloture votes took place on the motion to proceed, on the measure itself, and on the conference report. To pass the tobacco regulation bill in 2009, supporters had to win cloture votes on the motion to proceed; on the Dodd amendment in the nature of a substitute, which was the committee bill; and on passage. The process took two weeks of Senate floor time. As Chapter 8 describes, passing the health care reform bill required winning five cloture votes.

The purpose of the cloture rule is to give the Senate some way to end a filibuster—the use of extended debate to block or delay legislation. Yet filibusters are not as easy to identify as one might think, especially since modern filibusters seldom resemble the famous ones of the past (Beth 1995). The word *filibuster* conjures up images of Sen. Huey Long, D-LA, in the 1930s reading from the Constitution, quoting the Bible, and offering "pot liquor" recipes; of Sen. Strom Thurmond, D-SC, in the 1950s holding the floor for twenty-four hours at a stretch; or of round-the-clock sessions with senators sleeping on cots in the Capitol as occurred during the great civil rights battle of 1964. Modern filibusters are seldom so dramatic, and threats to filibuster now frequently take the place of actual filibusters. A hold may keep legislation off the floor altogether.

Because filibuster threats are frequent and may also be nebulous, a bill's supporters may file for cloture before opponents have clearly indicated they intend to engage in extended debate, and undoubtedly sometimes when opponents actually had no such intention. The requirement that all amendments must be germane after cloture is invoked sometimes encourages supporters to try for cloture. Finally, when senators spend a long time debating and amending a measure, they may simply be performing their deliberative function rather than trying to kill the measure. Many filibusters have as their purpose forcing a compromise on the legislation rather than killing it outright. Therefore, distinguishing between deliberating and filibustering becomes even harder.

Filibusters, defined as those instances where an attempt to invoke cloture on a given measure or nomination has been made, are now very frequent in the Senate. The Congresses of the early 1990s through 2006 (103rd through 109th) averaged 30 each, and the number rose to 54 in the two recent Democratic-controlled Congresses, 2007–2010 (Beth 1995; DSG 1994; *Congressional Quarterly Almanac; CQWeekly* online, various years). The number of cloture votes averaged 53 per Congress for the period 1993–2006, indicating that on many measures more than one cloture vote was taken. In the 110th Congress, the Senate voted on cloture 112 times and in the 111th Congress, 91 times.

Filibusters occur on a broad variety of matters. Not just legislation but also presidential nominations may be subject to extended debate. In 1995, Republicans killed by a filibuster the nomination of Henry Foster to be surgeon general of the United States. A majority of senators was ready to confirm Foster, but since only fifty-seven voted to cut off debate, no vote on confirmation ever took place. Democrats blocked ten of Bush's appellate court nominees in 2003–2004, including Estrada. The twenty-one cloture votes all failed, although in every case more than half of the senators voting voted in favor of invoking cloture. In the 111th Congress, there were twelve cloture votes on Obama nominees, but with their bigger majority, Democrats won all but two. In every case, a majority voted in favor of confirmation.

Extended debate is not confined to the great issues of the day; senators sometimes hold up minor and parochial legislation or more major bills for parochial reasons. A bill adjusting Hoover Dam rates was filibustered; senators concerned that Cuba would interfere with radio broadcasting in their states filibustered a bill setting up Radio Marti to broadcast to Cuba; and a Maryland senator filibustered the Metropolitan Washington Airports Transfer Act. As the 102nd Congress was rushing to adjourn in October 1992, Sen. Alfonse D'Amato, R-NY, held the floor for fifteen hours and fifteen minutes to protest the removal from an urban aid tax bill of a provision he said could have restored jobs at a New York typewriter plant (*CQW*, October 10, 1992, 3128). The bill containing the agreement on appropriations bills between President Clinton and Congress in November 1999, a bill that had to pass before the Congress could adjourn for the year, was filibustered by the senators from Minnesota and Wisconsin because it included the Northeast Dairy Compact, which they claimed hurt their dairy farmers, and by Sen. Max Baucus, D-MT, because the bill excluded provisions making satellite television more accessible to rural areas.

Major legislation is especially likely to encounter an extended debate-related problem—a hold, a filibuster threat, or a filibuster. Since the early 1990s, about half of all major measures have. In the 110th the figure soared to 70 percent and then to 72 percent in the 111th. In 1999, Y2K legislation passed the Senate only after Republicans agreed to compromises, and the Social Security lockbox bill failed because Republicans were unwilling to satisfy Democrats. In 2002, Republicans, then in the minority in the Senate, refused to allow a vote before the elections on the Democrats' version of the bill setting up the new Department of Homeland Security; Democrats had the votes to pass the bill in a form President Bush disliked, and Republicans wanted to use the fact that a bill had not passed as a campaign issue. In the 108th, Democrats used the Senate supermajority requirement to kill energy legislation, welfare act reauthorization, legislation tightening class action lawsuits, and malpractice law changes. At the beginning of the 110th Congress, Republicans held up the new Democratic majority's signature ethics reform legislation until they extracted a promise from Majority Leader Harry Reid for a future vote on their line-item veto legislation. Throughout the Congress, they prevented Democrats from getting a clean vote on President Bush's Iraq policy and killed large parts of the Democrats' domestic agenda. Even though Democrats had a large majority in the 111th Congress, Republicans managed to kill some major Democratic and President Obama priorities including the DREAM Act.

The filibuster is not a tool of the minority party alone, however. Majority Republicans repeatedly filibustered campaign finance legislation in the late 1990s. In June 1999, Phil Gramm, a senior member of the majority party, blocked passage of a broadly supported bill allowing the disabled to keep their Medicaid and Medicare benefits when they take paid jobs, until supporters agreed to drop the funding mechanism he disliked (*WP*, June 17, 1999). In the 108th Congress, the Internet tax moratorium bill was initially held up by Lamar Alexander, R-TN, a former governor concerned about the bill's impact on state and local taxing powers. He was joined by three other former governors, two Democrats and one Republican, in leading the charge for the states. After months of stalemate, they forced proponents to accept a major compromise. Even more than the Senate's permissive amending rules, the right of extended debate provides the individual senator with a powerful weapon few can refrain from using.

Since the early 1990s, extended debate has become a routinely employed partisan tool, and that has magnified its impact. Except for a few months in 2009, the Senate minority party has been big enough that if its members stick together, they can block any nomination and most bills (budget resolutions and reconciliation bills are the exception; see Chapter 5). As a consequence, controversial measures almost always need sixty votes to pass the Senate, and amassing the necessary support often requires significant concessions.

Majority leaders are not completely without weapons to counter senators' use of Senate rules for partisan and individual advantage and, to the extent Senate rules allow, they have adapted to the routine use of extended debate by the minority party. The Senate's permissive rules combined with the chamber's large workload make Senate floor time a scarce and valuable commodity, so for the majority leader, imposing cloture is problematical quite apart from needing to get a supermajority. The process takes time. As Majority Leader Reid declared in response to Senator Shelby's holds on seventy nominations, "There isn't enough time in the world—the Senate world, at least—to move cloture on every one of these" (*CR*, quoted in *WP*, March 6, 2010). With the minority party now frequently refusing to grant unanimous consent on motions to proceed to consideration of legislation, the majority leader often moves to proceed to consider a measure, then immediately moves for cloture on the motion, and then follows that by immediately withdrawing the motion to proceed. This makes it possible for the Senate to conduct other business during the period that is required to elapse before the cloture vote (that is, while the cloture motion "ripens," in Senate terminology). If cloture fails, the majority leader now frequently moves to reconsider the cloture vote. (To do so, he needs to be recorded as voting on the prevailing side with the result that the official list of how senators voted shows some very peculiar votes—the majority leader who has just spent enormous effort attempting to impose cloture on a key party agenda item voting against cloture on it.) Moving to reconsider the cloture vote—but then postponing action on the motion—allows the majority leader to bring up the reconsideration whenever he thinks he has the votes. It is unnecessary to go through the whole cloture process again. This can save time and give the majority leader greater flexibility on timing (Beth et al. 2009).

Once cloture has been successfully invoked, consideration of the matter can go on for an additional thirty hours. At this point the minority may agree by unanimous consent to shorten or dispense with that time. The minority may have extracted concessions in return for voting to impose cloture, or it may simply capitulate; however, the minority party—or just some of its members—can insist on the thirty hours. Furthermore during that time consideration of any other business is prohibited, except by unanimous consent. On July 20, 2010, Democrats finally managed to impose cloture on legislation extending emergency unemployment insurance, which had lapsed in June because of GOP opposition to doing so without paying for the cost with spending cuts elsewhere. Once Democrats got the sixty votes for cloture—by virtue of Sen. Robert Byrd's replacement being seated and some trimming of the bill to get the two moderate Maine Republicans on board—the bill's passing was no longer in doubt, but Republicans still insisted on using the thirty hours; presumably they believed that their message would get more media attention before the final passage vote than in other circumstances.

Once cloture has been invoked, amendments must be germane—a boon to a bill's supporters. Additionally, the majority leader may be able to block all amendments in conjunction with cloture. The majority leader can "fill the amendment tree," that is, use the majority leader's prerogative of first recognition to offer amendments in all the parliamentarily permissible slots, thus preventing other senators from offering their amendments. If the bill's supporters can then invoke cloture, the majority leader can run out the postcloture time and thereby prevent any other amendments from being offered or voted on. Although no complete list of all the instances when majority leaders have used this parliamentary tactic is available (identifying them is not easy), experts agree that the practice has increased in recent years (Beth et al. 2009, 11). Majority Leader Frist appears to have done so on initial consideration of legislation six times in 2005–2006; Reid did it nine times in 2007–2008 and even more frequently in 2009–2010. Minority Leader McConnell claimed that Reid filled the tree forty-three times in the 2007–2010 period (*CR*, December 18, 2010). Not surprisingly, the minority party complains bitterly when the tactic is used; however, when the majority party is required to get a supermajority to pass almost everything, then once the sixty votes are in hand, the majority leader has every incentive to fill the tree and cut off amendments.

Of course, from the majority leader's perspective, the limitation of the strategy is that unless cloture can be invoked, the bill at issue cannot be brought to a passage vote. In the late 1990s, Majority Leader Lott used the tactic a number of times, but because Democrats maintained high cohesion on cloture votes, it usually just led to gridlock. In eight of the fifteen times it was employed by Frist and Reid in the 109th and 110th Congresses, the majority leader had to either pull the bill off the floor or withdraw his amendments so as to allow other senators to offer theirs. Unless the majority is very large, the strategy requires special circumstances to work. In early 2007, Reid filled the amendment tree on the continuing resolution that was necessary because Republicans had not passed most of the appropriations bills for FY2007; he then filed for cloture, a vote Democrats won. The result was that the CR passed the Senate quickly and in a form identical to the House bill, which was the aim. Reid was able to succeed with such aggressive tactics because the CR was must-pass legislation, the deadline was imminent, and Republicans were leery about calling attention to their own dereliction.

Because filibuster threats in their various forms have become so routine, sixty-vote requirements are now sometimes written into unanimous consent agreements. The majority agrees because it saves time; the minority may extract substantive concessions or may not, for a variety of possible reasons, want to go through the time-consuming cloture process either. CRS experts report that sixty-vote requirements can be found in UCAs going back to the early 1990s, but they have become much more frequent in recent years. Majority Leader Bill Frist agreed that passage would require sixty votes on three bills—all relating to stem cell research—in the 109th Congress (*CQW,* August 14, 2006, 2214; Beth et al. 2009, Table 2). In 2007 a stem cell bill again came to the floor under a UCA specifying a sixty-vote requirement. Altogether eleven bills in the 110th Congress were considered under UCAs that stipulated passage would require sixty votes. In early 2009, the UCA negotiated by Reid on the Lilly Ledbetter Fair Pay Act specified that passage would require fifty-nine votes (three-fifths of the total number of senators sworn, which at that time was ninety-eight). Democrats were eager to chalk up a legislative accomplishment quickly and had a big agenda awaiting action, so they were eager to avoid spending the time to go through the cloture process. To get Republicans' assent, however, Democrats had to agree to a weaker bill than had passed in the House.

UCAs still more frequently specify that certain amendments require sixty votes to pass. In the 109th Congress, six amendments were subject to a sixty-vote requirement in UCAs; this shot up to thirty-three in the 110th. Clearly opponents of the amendment are advantaged by such provisions, and since the majority party has the predominant say in the drafting of the bills that come to the floor, amendment proponents are more likely to be minority-party members. Why then do minority-party members agree to such UCAs? Most often it is because they know their amendment will, in any case, fail to get a simple majority (they are, after all, the minority) and the UCA gives them an up-or-down vote on the amendment. The sponsors' primary motive may be to publicize their own proposals or to force their opponents to cast a difficult-to-explain vote. If the minority forces the majority to go through the cloture process, the majority leader may "fill the amendment tree" and prevent a vote on the amendment.

In the procedural arms race that characterizes the contemporary Senate, minority senators have recently come up with a tactic that gets them an indirect vote on their amendment after cloture even if the tree has been filled. First employed by Sen. Jim DeMint (R-SC), it entails moving to suspend Senate rules to permit consideration of a specific amendment. Because suspending the rules requires a two-thirds vote, the minority does not expect to prevail, but the mover can insist on a recorded vote, thereby forcing opponents on the record.

The majority party's latest version of procedural hardball entails forcing the minority to actually stay all night and use all of its postcloture time or agree to less than thirty hours for when final passage can occur. Knowledgeable staffers expect that to become a regular practice.

The majority leader's weapons are more effective as negative than as positive tools. Any senator can make a motion to proceed to consider, but in more than half a century, only two such motions that the majority leader opposed have won. In negotiating UCAs, he may be able to, in effect, trade allowing clean votes on amendments for sixty-vote thresholds for amendment passage. He can "fill the amendment tree" to block votes on amendments. But in the end, to pass legislation he needs either the cooperation of all senators or sixty votes.

Senators' desire to—in the words of a knowledgeable participant—"have a life" does give the majority leader some leverage. Senators' enthusiasm for offering their less crucial amendments tends to lessen on Friday afternoon, when the airport beckons. Similarly, if the majority leader schedules a bill right before a recess and insists it be finished before the Senate can depart, action tends to speed up. A former high-ranking leadership aide explained:

> Many times now you bring bills to the floor without a [comprehensive] consent agreement. And this is a kind of informal assessment period. You have a couple of days of debate. If you see it's not going anywhere, you go to the Democrats [then the minority party]. You see how many amendments they have. . . . And then . . . say, on Thursday, things are just not seeming to go anywhere. You'll go to the Democrats and say, how much more do you have? The Democrats will say, well, we've got another hundred amendments. You let it go fairly far into the evening. Then essentially they'll want to get out; they'll want to go home. So you kind of grind them Thursday nights. And, soon enough, they'll say, well, we've got one more amendment. And that'll be it.

Yet these tactics work only when no senator feels really intensely on the matter at issue.

Finally, senators have to consider whether their exploitation of Senate prerogatives is likely to entail an electoral cost. If legislation is widely popular, being seen as responsible for its demise is a high-risk strategy, and few elected politicians are risk takers. Thus if a measure is popular and if its supporters can raise the visibility of the process sufficiently to pin public responsibility on the blockers, the costs may become too high. During the 111th Congress, Republicans went all out to oppose health care reform, but they were not willing to filibuster the credit card regulation bill and their opposition to the financial services regulation bill aimed at ultra-unpopular Wall Street was somewhat restrained.

If legislation reaches the point of a passage vote, it almost certainly will pass. After all, passage of a bill requires only a simple majority. In recent Congresses almost all of the major measures that lost on passage votes in the Senate were constitutional amendments, which require a two-thirds vote. Among the few exceptions were a bill barring employment discrimination against homosexuals, which was opposed by most Republican senators who were then in the majority and was only brought to the floor as part of a package deal, and the gun liability bill, after killer amendments won and its sponsor called for its defeat.

Unorthodox Lawmaking in the Senate

Because the Senate's legislative process has always been less formal than the House's and thus more flexible, the distinction between the orthodox and the unorthodox is less clear in the Senate than in the House. Senators have always had the right under the rules to talk as long as they wished, offer multitudes of amendments, and propose nongermane amendments. They have always used those prerogatives. Yet all the evidence indicates that the frequency of such behavior has increased enormously in recent decades. The contemporary legislative process in the Senate is of necessity predicated on the assumption that senators, now most often as party teams, will regularly and fully exploit their prerogatives. The extensive consultation that is a standard part of legislative scheduling and the deference to senators as individuals are all responses to senators' hyperexploitation of their prerogatives under the rules. In addition, in recent years the parties—especially the minority party—are fully exploiting Senate rules to further their partisan objectives. When employed by an organized and sizable group of senators, the Senate's permissive rules become a formidable weapon.

Unlike unorthodox lawmaking in the House of Representatives, the changes in the legislative process in the Senate, on balance, make legislating more difficult. Given senators' willingness to exploit their prerogatives and the lack of much cost to them within the chamber of doing so repeatedly, successful lawmaking requires accommodating individual senators and the minority party, and most controversial legislation requires a supermajority for Senate passage. Yet there is an upside to unorthodox lawmaking in the Senate. The greater necessity of building oversized coalitions has made excluding any sort of minority from meaningfully participating in the legislative process more difficult. Minorities, partisan or otherwise, can make themselves heard. And, for better or worse, they can often influence outcomes.

Getting One Bill: Reconciling House-Senate Differences

S<small>INCE THE HOUSE AND SENATE</small> differ in membership and rules, major legislation is unlikely to emerge in identical form from the two chambers. Even if exactly the same bill were introduced in the House and the Senate, the changes necessary to pass it would likely result in differences by the time it worked its way through the two chambers' quite different legislative processes. Yet before the bill can become law, both chambers must approve the identical wording; after all, a law cannot exist in several different versions. How would people know which they were expected to obey?

A number of alternative ways of reconciling House-Senate differences are used. One chamber can simply accept the other chamber's version of the legislation. A procedure based on amendments between the chambers entails a kind of public bargaining back and forth. A conference committee of members from both chambers can be appointed and charged with coming up with a compromise, which is then taken back to both chambers for approval.

By and large, conferences are restricted to settling differences on major legislation. Studies that examine all bills that passed or all those that became law in a specific Congress have found that only 9 to 13 percent went to conference (Smith 1995, 406; Oleszek 2004, 255). That figure was even lower in the 109th and 110th Congresses; in 2005–2006, 5 percent of the bills that became law had been to conference, and in 2007–2008, only 4 percent were reconciled in conference (*RC,* March 10, 2010).

Traditional Nonconference Reconciliation Procedures

On minor legislation or when the differences between the two chambers' bill versions are small, one chamber may be willing to accept the other's bill. Early in 2009, the House, rather than going to conference, accepted the Senate version of a bill extending and expanding the State Children's Health Insurance Program (SCHIP). The two chambers' bills were very similar, and the Democratic leaders wanted to get the legislation to new president Barack Obama as quickly as possible so as to rack up an early accomplishment.

Sometimes political expediency dictates that one chamber simply pass the other's bill. The judicial threat to the enormously popular National Do Not Call Registry led the House to immediately pass a bill and prompted the Senate to accept that legislation without change only hours later. Right before the August recess in 2009, the Senate passed without change the House bill adding funds to the "Cash for Clunkers" program. The program, which gave cash rebates to consumers who replaced their older, less fuel-efficient cars—their "clunkers"— with new vehicles had run through its initial funding in a week. Unless the Senate passed the House bill without amendments, the popular program that was also providing much-needed economic stimulus would be in hiatus at least until Congress returned in September.

Late in a Congress, when time is tight and the alternative is the probable death of the bill, one chamber may accept the other's version of even major legislation; if the choice is to let the legislation die and start over in the next Congress or to take a less preferred version, supporters may well opt for the latter. In late 2004, for example, the House agreed to the Senate version of a bill extending the moratorium on Internet taxes even though that meant accepting a temporary rather than a permanent ban.

In 1980, in a more striking example, the House in a lame-duck (that is, postelection) session accepted the weaker Senate version of the massive bill on Alaskan lands. Since Republicans had won control of the Senate in the elections, House supporters of a strongly pro-environment bill knew they would fare worse if they waited until the next year. They also knew that if they did anything other than simply accept the Senate bill, Senate opponents of a strong bill could easily use extended debate to kill the legislation in the few remaining days of the session. Similarly, during the lame-duck session in 2006, the House grudgingly accepted a much more restrictive Senate version of a bill allowing expanded drilling off the Gulf Coast. House Republicans had intended to hold out for their more permissive bill, but when the Democrats won control of both chambers, they knew the Senate bill was the best they were going to get. The power of extended debate as an obstructionist tool, especially late in a session, can put the House at a disadvantage, confronting the chamber with the choice of accepting Senate legislation as is or taking a chance that opponents in the Senate will kill it if more action is required.

In general, now when one chamber accepts the other's legislation for strategic reasons it is to avoid the possibility of delay or worse in the Senate. Thus in the 108th Congress (2003–2004), minority Democrats had managed to derail bankruptcy and class action overhaul legislation, both high on the Republican majority's priority list. With a bigger Senate Republican majority, prospects seemed better in the 109th Congress; nevertheless, the Republican leaderships wanted to avoid giving opponents any more opportunities for delay than absolutely necessary. Thus Speaker Dennis Hastert and Majority Leader Bill Frist agreed that the Senate would pass both bills first and the House would then pass the Senate bills without change. The strategy succeeded. Frist got both bills through the Senate without killer amendments, though Republicans did have to invoke cloture on the bankruptcy bill and the House accepted the Senate bills without change.

Sometimes, however, strategic considerations dictate that the Senate accept the House bill. In 2004, when the Republican-controlled House passed the Shays-Meehan campaign finance reform bill over the Republican leadership's objections, Senate minority leader Tom Daschle, D-SD, engineered passage of that bill without change in the Republican-controlled Senate. The bill's supporters knew that were the bill to go to conference with the Senate-passed McCain-Feingold bill, Republican opponents would kill it.

House-Senate differences on most minor and some major legislation are reconciled through a process known as amendments between the chambers—also sometimes referred to as "ping-ponging." Assume the House has passed legislation and sent it to the Senate. The Senate then amends the bill, perhaps by substituting its own version for the House's, and sends it back to the House. At this point the House floor manager of the bill may ask that the House by unanimous consent (or under suspension of the rules or by a special rule) "agree to the Senate amendment with an amendment." The Senate amendment referred to is actually the Senate version of the bill, and the amendment the House is adding is the House's initial offer of a settlement of interchamber differences. Generally, the House will stick to its own position or move least on those issues its members care about most. If the House agrees to the motion, the bill as amended goes back to the Senate and the Senate can either accept the House offer or respond with an offer of its own.

The parliamentary language can become mind-bogglingly complex; for example, on July 26, 2008, the Senate "agreed to the motion to concur in House amendment to Senate amendment to House amendments to Senate amendment to the [housing reform] bill." What is actually going on formally is fairly straightforward bargaining, with each chamber making offers in succession. The legislation may go back and forth between the chambers several times (Tiefer 1989, 778; Oleszek 2004, 257–258). Often differences are resolved through informal, behind-the-scenes negotiations between the House and Senate committees and, if major legislation, party leaders and then incorporated in the amendment one house sends the other.

Nonconference resolution procedures have become both more frequent and more complex since the early 1990s. A late section discusses variations on the procedures described here and why and how they are used.

Conference Committees

Until recently, interchamber differences on major legislation were routinely resolved by conference committees (Longley and Oleszek 1989). From the 1960s through the 1990s, 76 percent of major measures that got to the resolution stage were sent to conference; in some of these cases, amendments between the chambers were also used. In the 2000s (107th through 110th Congresses), however, the figure dropped to 47 percent and then dropped further—to 22 percent—in 2009–2010.

Both chambers must approve sending legislation to conference; the first house requests a conference, and the second agrees. Usually this approval is obtained by unanimous consent, but it can be done by motion and a majority vote, although in the Senate the motion can be filibustered. Occasionally, though, one chamber will refuse to go to conference. In 2006, House Republicans, then in the majority, refused to go to conference with the Senate on immigration legislation. President George W. Bush supported the Senate-passed bill that House Republicans abhorred. By refusing to go to conference, House Republicans killed the bill.

The Appointment of Conferees

In both chambers the presiding officer appoints conferees: House rules give the Speaker sole power to do so; the Senate's presiding officer must receive unanimous consent. In the Senate, with its weak presiding officer, committee leaders, increasingly with the participation of the party leaders, actually make the choice. The chair of the committee of origin, after "consultation" with the ranking minority member, "recommends" a list of conferees to the presiding officer, who accepts it without change. By tradition, conference committees are bipartisan; the ratio of majority to minority members roughly reflects the ratio in the chamber, and the majority allows the minority to choose its own members.

The process is similar in the House, except that the Speaker has more discretion. House rules explicitly require the Speaker to appoint "no less than a majority of members who supported the House position as determined by the Speaker." The rule continues: "The Speaker shall name Members who are primarily responsible for the legislation and shall, to the fullest extent feasible, include the principal proponents of the major provisions of the bill as it passed the House" (Gold et al. 1992, 339). Since the decision about which members meet these criteria is solely the Speaker's, the rule actually gives the Speaker more leeway to choose, if so desired, junior members or members not on the committee of origin.

During the 104th Congress, Speaker Newt Gingrich, R-GA, was unusually assertive in exercising the Speaker's discretion; he appointed freshmen and even, on occasion, Democratic supporters of the legislation that the minority had kept off its conference delegation. In 1999, after managed care legislation that the Republican Party leadership opposed passed the House, Speaker Dennis Hastert, R-IL, employed his discretion to keep Republican supporters of the successful bill off the conference committee. Despite protests from a number of the sixty-eight Republicans who broke ranks to support the Norwood-Dingell bill, neither Charlie Norwood, R-GA, the chief sponsor, nor Greg Ganske, R-IA, another prominent backer, was appointed.

Senate leaders have also, from time to time, attempted to stack conference delegations, as Majority Leader Bob Dole, R-KS, did on the Kennedy-Kassebaum health care reform bill in 1996. However, the fact that so many conference-related motions are debatable and can be filibustered holds Senate leaders in check. Dole's attempt to stack the conference delegation with supporters of medical savings accounts, which he favored but a majority of the Senate had voted against, was stymied by Senator Ted Kennedy, D-MA, who threatened to filibuster the naming of conferees.

In both chambers most of the conferees will be members of the committee (or committees) that reported the bill and, by and large, fairly senior ones. Today, both chambers include leaders of the subcommittee responsible for the bill. The conference delegation will not simply consist of the most senior members of the committee, as was often the case before the mid-1970s.

When several committees have considered the legislation, all expect representation on the conference committee. Even if a committee was discharged, it still regards itself as entitled to conference representation, and, in fact, when committees agree to be discharged, they are not waiving their jurisdictional rights. Frequently, the chair of the discharged committee sends a letter to that effect to the lead committee, and the letter is then printed in the *Congressional Record*. The prevalence of multiple referral in the House led for a time to very large conference delegations. On the conference committee for the 1988 trade bill were 44 senators from nine Senate committees and 155 House members from 14 House committees (Tiefer 1989, 798–799). Although this is an extreme example, multicommittee conference delegations are common. In addition to multiple referral putting pressure on the size of conferences, so does the Senate's penchant for added nongermane amendments to bills. The House committees whose jurisdictions these amendments impinge on expect to be included in the conference.

When Republicans took control of the House in 1995, Gingrich attempted to reduce the size of conference delegations to speed action, with some success. On the line-item-veto bill, the House delegation of eight was actually considerably smaller than the Senate delegation of eighteen. Speaker Hastert also kept conference delegations small when he could. He appointed only three conferees for both the 2001 and the 2003 tax reconciliation bills and for the 2001 and 2003 budget resolutions and only eight, from two committees, on the Medicare prescription drug bill. Nancy Pelosi (D-CA) as Speaker followed the same path when time was of the essence; she appointed only five conferees for the big stimulus bill in early 2009; Democrats believed this bill had to be enacted quickly to prevent the economy from sinking into a depression (see Chapter 7). Yet some bills are so broad in scope and affect the jurisdiction of so many committees that large conference delegations are nearly unavoidable. The reconciliation bill that implemented the spending provisions of the 1997 balanced budget deal was the product of eight committees in each chamber. The conference numbered seventy-three members in total. The conference for the 2010 financial services reform bill consisted of forty-three members—thirty-one from the House and twelve from the Senate.

Speaker Hastert responded to the problem of very large conferences on bills impinging on the jurisdiction of a number of committees by instituting a "2–1" rule. Any committee that made a jurisdictional claim recognized as valid by the nonpartisan parliamentarians got conference representation. Only the lead committee (or, occasionally, committees) received more than three conferees. The other committees all were granted two majority-party conferees and one minority-party conferee. The House conference delegation for the big transportation reauthorization bill in 2005 consisted of Majority Leader Tom DeLay, R-TX, thirty-four members of the Transportation Committee, and three members of each of the following ten committees: Budget, Education, Energy, Government Reform, Homeland Security, Judiciary, Resources, Rules, Science, and Ways and Means. Pelosi followed the same rule; thus she appointed as conferees on the 2010 financial services reform bill sixteen members from the Financial Services Committee and three members of each of the following five committees: Agriculture, Energy and Commerce, Judiciary, Oversight and Government Reform, and Small Business.

Typically, only the conferees from the lead committee have the authority to negotiate on the entire bill. In the case of the 2005 transportation bill, only DeLay had authority over the entire bill, and the Transportation Committee members had authority over all but two tax titles of the bill. In the case of Financial Services Reform, only the conferees from the lead committee, Financial Services, had authority over the entire bill. House conference appointments for large, complex bills now usually specify in great detail the precise titles or sections that particular conferees can negotiate, as they did for each of the other committees' conferees for the financial services reform bill. Thus, for example, the conferees from "the Committee on Agriculture for consideration of subtitles A and B of title I, secs. 1303, 1609, 1702, 1703, title III (except secs. 3301 and 3302), secs. 4205(c), 4804(b)(8)(B), 5008, and 7509 of the House bill, and sec. 102, subtitle A of title I, secs. 406, 604(h), title VII, title VIII, secs. 983, 989E, 1027(j), 1088(a)(8), 1098, and 1099 of the Senate amendment, and modifications committed to conference" (Thomas Bill Status Report for HR 4173). The authority of House conferees has always been jurisdiction specific, but the extent to which that is spelled out in the appointment process seems to have increased considerably.

On the most important and controversial legislation—especially top priority items on the party's and the president's agenda—Hastert regularly appointed a member of the House party leadership to the conference and made that individual a general conferee who had authority over the entire bill. Thus Majority Leader Dick Armey, R-TX, was a conferee on the 2001 reconciliation tax bill. Tom DeLay, as whip and then as majority leader, served on conferences on energy bills, the Medicare prescription drug bill, and transportation bills. None of this is completely unprecedented. Speaker Jim Wright, D-TX, appointed Majority Leader Tom Foley, D-WA, to the conference rewriting the Gramm-Rudman budget-balancing law in 1987. Yet a routine leadership presence on such conference delegations was new. Pelosi did not appoint members of the leadership to conference delegations, but she herself took an informal part in negotiations.

Senate conference delegations are usually—although not always—quite small. The Senate conferees on the 2002 farm bill numbered seven, whereas the House delegation included fourteen members of the Agriculture Committee plus three members from each of nine other committees. The conference on the 2008 farm bill showed a similar imbalance: eleven senators and forty-nine House members—fourteen from Agriculture, three each from eleven other committees and two other members. Furthermore, the Senate seldom spells out the sections or titles over which a conferee has authority. Often the committee the conferee represents is not even specified. Thus the twelve Senate conferees on the financial services reform bill were from the Banking and Agriculture Committees, but their committee position was not mentioned when they were appointed, nor was any limitation on their authority spelled out.

Reaching Agreement

The conferees are charged with coming up with a compromise between the House and Senate positions that can win the assent of a majority in both chambers. Sunshine rules instituted in the mid-1970s require that conference committee meetings be open to the public. However, because a public forum inhibits the hard bargaining that is often necessary, much negotiation takes place informally behind the scenes. To reach a compromise, members may need to retreat from positions they have advocated, often ones they have argued for strongly and ones with ardent interest group and constituency support; that is easier done behind closed doors. Staff typically work to resolve the often myriad minor differences between the bills; members become directly involved in the behind-the-scenes negotiations when major, controversial provisions are at issue. Often formal, open conference meetings simply ratify deals worked out elsewhere.

The difficulty of reaching agreement depends, of course, on how far apart the two chambers' bills are, as well as on how strongly the participants feel about their positions. Certain kinds of differences lend themselves to compromise more easily than others. When an appropriations bill goes to conference, it typically includes hundreds of items in disagreement, but the differences in dollar figures usually are resolved easily by splitting the difference or trading off among items. The tough fights are more likely to be over substantive provisions (for example, the Hyde amendment barring federal funding for abortions with certain, often contested exceptions).

When the two chambers take completely different approaches to a problem, the conference faces the most difficult task; splitting the difference is meaningless in this context. In 1995 the House passed a line-item-veto bill that would allow the president to make a proposal to rescind spending for specific items previously approved by Congress. Unless both chambers of Congress voted to overturn the proposal, it would become law. The Senate's line-item-veto bill was very different. The Senate proposed that, after passage, appropriations bills be broken down and sent to the president as hundreds of separate bills, thus enabling the vetoing of individual items. Clearly, there was no way of splitting the difference between the two approaches; the conferees had to choose one or the other or come up with a different approach altogether.

Differences between the two chambers' bills on volatile political issues also can complicate resolution. The bankruptcy law overhaul bill the Senate passed in the 107th Congress included a provision preventing anti-abortion groups from using the bill to avoid paying court judgments, and many senators were strongly committed to keeping that language in the final bill. The House bill had no such language, and many House members were just as strongly committed to barring it from the final bill.

The "torture" issue split the chambers for most of 2005. The Senate added to several bills a provision sponsored by John McCain, R-AZ, that would prohibit torture or cruel and inhumane treatment of enemy combatants. House Republican committee and party leaders opposed the McCain amendment, and the House defense authorization and appropriations bills did not contain the McCain language. (In late 2005, after the House voted overwhelmingly for a motion to instruct conferees to the Department of Defense [DOD] appropriations bill to accept the antitorture language, the House Republican leaders could no longer maintain their opposition and the conferees included the provision in the conference report.) In 2007 an amendment expanding the definition of hate crimes became a sticking point on the defense authorization bill. Hoping thereby to avoid a Bush veto, Democrats added the nongermane amendment on the Senate floor, but House conferees insisted they could not pass a conference report that included it; House Republicans opposed the amendment and too many anti-Iraq House Democrats opposed the DOD authorization bill.

Conferences with many conferees from a number of different committees can be much more unwieldy than the traditional small, one-committee conference. The House's current standard operating procedure of spelling out the sections or titles of the bill over which the "limited jurisdiction" conferees have authority eases the problem to some extent. Conferences with a number of sets of limited jurisdiction conferees ordinarily work through subconferences, with the House's limited jurisdiction conferees negotiating with their Senate committee counterparts.

Although they have authority over the entire bill, the House general jurisdiction conferees get involved in the provisions under other committees' jurisdiction only if the matter threatens the success of the conference. Since the Senate seldom expressly limits its conferees' authority to specific parts of a bill, senators can, if they wish, dabble in any aspect of the legislation. In fact, staff report that even senators not on the conference may insert themselves into the negotiations if they feel strongly about an issue. Time constraints do tend to keep Senate conferees focused on the parts of the bill that fall within their committees' jurisdiction.

Subconferences do provide some structure, but when conferees from a number of different committees are involved, someone still must coordinate the work, making sure progress is made and that the parts are reassembled into a coherent whole at the end. The committee chairs of the lead committee have the primary responsibility for this, but the party leadership and the leaders' senior staff often are actively involved as well.

As the legislative process has changed, drawing party leaders more deeply into the process, members have come to expect that their leaders will take a hand on major legislation at the conference stage. Speaker Hastert routinely discussed upcoming conferences with the relevant committee chairs, laying out the parameters of an acceptable agreement: "what's got to be in it . . . [and] things that can't be in it." The Senate leaders also keep a careful eye on conference negotiations. In several notable instances, Majority Leader Harry Reid served as a conferee; the Democratic Senate conferees for the big stimulus bill in early 2009 were the chairs of the Appropriations and Finance Committees and Reid.

Stalemate between the two chambers often requires direct leadership intervention. When conferences on four appropriations bills bogged down in late 1995 over the abortion issue, House majority leader Dick Armey and Senate Republican whip Trent Lott stepped in to broker agreements that both adamantly antiabortion House Republicans and more moderate Senate Republicans could accept. In March 1996, Senate majority leader Bob Dole almost single-handedly broke the stalemate on the line-item-veto bill. Having established himself as the almost certain presidential nominee of the Republican Party, Dole made getting a bill out of conference and to the president a top priority and so a test of his ability to get things done. Under these special political circumstances Republican senators, even those with severe substantive doubts about the bill, were unwilling to hold out against Dole's position of basically agreeing to the House version of the bill. Doing otherwise would have crippled their nominee. The line-item-veto bill was approved by the conferees and signed by the president, who in negotiations with Majority Leader Dole and Speaker Gingrich had decided what the effective date of the legislation would be. Majority Leader Frist and House Speaker Hastert made the final big decisions on the bill adding prescription drug coverage to Medicare in 2003 when the conference committee bogged down. Frist had, in fact, appointed himself to the conference committee. This was a signature bill for President Bush and the Republican Party, and it fell to the leadership to get it done. The FY2007 supplemental appropriations bill funding the Iraq War was vitally important to the new Democratic majorities. Speaker Pelosi and Majority Leader Reid were deeply involved throughout its legislative life, crafting withdrawal language, deciding what else to include, and making the key decisions on compromises. That involvement very much included conference proceedings. These examples illustrate that when the choices facing conferees are highly salient and consequential ones that affect the political fate of members and of their party, party leaders are likely to make the final decisions.

In conference, decisions require the assent of both the House and the Senate. Traditionally, the position of a chamber has been determined by the majority of its conferees, and the final agreement also has required a simple majority of the conferees of each chamber. That is still the Senate's interpretation. The House, however, requires that on each part of the bill a majority of the total of the general conferees plus the jurisdiction-specific conferees must sign (Beth and Rybicki 2003). Conferees formally indicate their approval by signing the conference report, which consists of the compromise legislative language agreed on by the conferees. The House form is broken down by sections that coincide with the jurisdiction-specific authority for which conferees were appointed.

Rarely, at least when both chambers are controlled by the same party, are conferees unable to reach an agreement and the legislation dies in conference. In recent Congresses on average fewer than one major measure per Congress died in conference. In the 108th Congress the big transportation reauthorization measure never emerged from conference, but the problem was finding a deal that satisfied the president, who was unwilling to go along with as high a spending figure as both the House and Senate wanted. By the time legislation gets to conference, many people, and especially many of the conferees who may well have worked on the bill for months, have a considerable stake in the legislation's enactment. A compromise, therefore, is usually found even when House and Senate versions are very different.

Conferees' Power and Its Limits

Conferees have considerable power over the substance of legislation. House and Senate rules specify that conferees are limited in the agreement they reach to the differences between the House and Senate versions of the legislation. However, in those cases—the majority—in which the Senate has passed a substitute to the House bill (rather than a series of specific amendments to the House bill), Senate rules interpret this requirement quite broadly. In the House the conferees can get around the rule by taking their conference report to the floor under a special rule from the Rules Committee that waives the requirement. Since many conference committees finish their work late in a Congress, when everyone works under severe time constraints, senators and representatives not on a conference committee often lack the time to study the conference report and thus to be able to challenge it. Furthermore, the "layover" require-ments stipulating that members have the conference report available for a period of time before floor consideration often are waived, further limit-ing access to the report.

Although House members or senators can (by majority vote) instruct their conferees about the substance of the legislation, these instructions are not binding (Tiefer 1989, 780–833; Gold et al. 1992, 337–347). Motions to instruct are frequently offered, more than ninety in the House during the 108th Congress and an average of forty-nine per Congress in the House from 1991 through 2002. In response to the majority's increased use of highly restrictive rules, the minority party in the House often turns to motions to instruct conferees to force floor debate on its issues. A con-siderable number of such motions do pass—thirty-four in the 108th. Occa-sionally they do have an effect, as the 308–122 House vote on the Murtha motion to instruct conferees to accept the Senate's antitorture language did in 2005. Of course, since the motions are not binding, voting for a popular provision can be a cheap vote for a majority-party member.

Not only can conferees ignore instructions, but also they can and sometimes do jettison provisions that both chambers have approved. Party leaders dropped a number of provisions that Bush opposed but both chambers had voted for from the omnibus appropriations bills in 2002, 2003, and 2004. Democrats complained bitterly, but given that appropria-tions bills are must-pass legislation, they had little recourse. In June 2006 a bar on the funding of permanent U.S. military bases in Iraq, a version of which was included in both chambers' bills, was deleted from the emer-gency supplemental Iraq War appropriations bill even before conference. The Bush administration had opposed any such language.

On occasion a provision that neither chamber included in its respec-tive bill gets added in conference. The conference report for the agricul-tural appropriations bill that passed in late 2005 contained totally new language rewriting and weakening the legal definition of *organic food*; the bills that went to conference did not deal with the issue even peripherally (*RC,* November 16, 2005). (The language was inserted by someone, pre-sumably a senior conferee.) Before recent rules changes, earmarks—projects for specific districts or states—were regularly added at the con-ference stage (Lilly 2005, 2006). Sometimes even most majority-party conferees are unaware of what is being inserted into the conference report. In fact, there often were no formal meetings of the conference to approve the report. Rather, the necessary signatures were gathered by staff and members signed without actually seeing the final language. Rules changes instituted by the new Democratic House majority in 2007 reined in these practices to some extent, though given the decline in the number of conferences, the impact of new rules is hard to gauge.

Once a majority of the House conferees and a majority of the Senate conferees have formalized their approval by signing the conference report, it is returned to both chambers, where the full membership must decide whether to accept what their representatives have done. At this point no amendments are in order; the membership votes up or down on the compromise as a package.[1] Although the overwhelming majority of conference reports are approved, occasionally one is recommitted, that is, sent back to conference—a parliamentary move available only to the chamber that acts first—or simply is voted down.

When the conference report for the 2002 bankruptcy bill came back to the House containing language that prohibited abortion protestors from using bankruptcy to escape fines for harassing staff and prospective clients of abortion clinics, committed antiabortion Republicans joined with those Democrats who opposed the bankruptcy provisions to defeat the rule. That killed the bill for the 107th Congress.

In fall 2005 the House voted down the conference report on the Labor, Health and Human Services, and Education appropriations bill, with twenty-two Republicans joining all the Democrats in opposition. Democrats vehemently disliked the cuts in spending for education and health programs, as did some moderate Republicans, and, according to a Republican leader, there were ten different issues motivating the other Republican opponents (*CQW,* November 18, 2005, 3133). The Labor-H bill, as it is called, is huge, funding hundreds of programs, and the 2005 budget resolution had mandated a tight spending ceiling, ensuring that many popular programs would suffer. Reportedly, the conference committee's dropping of all earmarked projects for specific districts also infuriated some members. Of course, everyone knew that defeat of the conference report was not the last word. The programs the bill funded could not be allowed to go without any money for a year. The Speaker reappointed conferees, and the House sent the bill back to conference with the Senate. Increases in funding for rural health care and a few other changes allowed the Republican leadership to narrowly pass the new conference report a month after the first had failed.

---

1. The exceptions are appropriations bills on which the conferees have exceeded the scope of the differences between the two chambers' bills or to which the Senate has added amendments that constitute unauthorized appropriations; or legislation and bills on which the Senate has added nongermane amendments, so long as the Senate has constructed its appropriations bill via a series (often one hundred or more) of amendments to the House bill. House rules allow separate votes on those matters, but this can be waived by a rule from the Rules Committee. Since the mid-1990s, the Senate has instead produced a substitute for the House bill and this precludes demands for separate votes (Tiefer 1989, 833–848; Oleszek 2004, 276).

These cases (and occasional others) notwithstanding, the recommittal or defeat of a conference report is rare. Yet, as infrequent as the rejection of a conference report is, its occasional occurrence serves to remind conferees that they must be sensitive to the policy preferences of their chambers' membership. Conferees have considerable discretion but only within the limits set by the full membership's tolerance.

Partisan Polarization and Unorthodox Postpassage Processes

High partisan polarization has affected the process of resolving interchamber differences. On major measures, conference committees are less frequently employed and other procedures more frequently than they used to be as recently as the 1990s. To be sure, much major legislation still does go to conference. Regular appropriations bills that become law as such are always the product of conference committees; it is when regular appropriations bills are bundled into an omnibus bill that differences may not be resolved through a formal conference. Budget resolutions and reconciliation bills almost always go to conference for the resolution of interchamber differences. These are complex measures on which multiple differences between the two chambers' bills can be expected. Probably most dispositive, however, is the fact that budget resolutions and reconciliation bills are protected by the Budget Act from filibusters in the Senate. Thus, although these measures tend to be highly partisan, the majority party need not worry about having to muster supermajorities multiple times in the Senate if it decides to use conference procedures.

The annual Department of Defense authorization bill, which is seldom strictly partisan, always goes to conference. In the 110th Congress (2007–2008), a number of other reauthorization bills were reconciled in conference: the 2008 intelligence authorization bill, the agricultural authorization bill, a big water projects authorization bill, the Head Start reauthorization, and the higher education reauthorization bill. Although a number of these bills had controversial provisions and in some cases were hard fought, none were purely partisan measures. Despite the fact that a record low proportion of major measures went to conference in the 111th Congress, several highly partisan and contentious bills—including the big stimulus bill and the financial services reform bill— did.

The decision to use alternative procedures to reconcile House-Senate differences has, in recent years, sometimes been motivated by direct minority-party obstruction of going to conference. Three different motions are required in the Senate: to insist on its amendments, to request a conference, and to authorize the chair to appoint conferees. Although the three are ordinarily bundled together and agreed to by unanimous consent, they can be individually filibustered, thereby making going to conference a time-consuming process at best and impossible in many cases. When Senate Republicans used this strategy to prevent a conference on a campaign finance bill late in the 103rd Congress, it was, according to Majority Leader George Mitchell, D-ME, an unprecedented move (Oleszek 2007, 262). That cannot be said today.

The 107th Congress (2001–2002) began with the Senate equally divided. Because the vice president has the constitutional authority to break ties, Republicans organized the chamber—chose the majority leader and the chairs of all the committees—but only after agreeing to equal numbers of Democrats and Republicans on each committee. No agreement was reached on the composition of conference committees, and Democrats blocked conferences on all but those measures protected by the Budget Act. The effect was small because little legislation that Republicans wanted to send to conference was at that stage of the legislative process before Jim Jeffords, VT, switched to caucusing with the Democrats and thereby gave Democrats control of the chamber.

When Republicans took back the majority in the 2002 elections, they began to exclude minority Democrats from meaningful participation in conference deliberations. So, for example, only two Senate Democrats thought to be amenable to the Republicans' approach were actually included in the conference negotiations on the 2003 prescription drug bill; the other Democratic conferees were completely excluded. In response, Senate Democrats sometimes blocked conferences or extracted promises before agreeing to allow them. Thus on the massive 2004 highway bill, Democrats allowed a conference only after Majority Leader Bill Frist, in a colloquy on the floor, guaranteed Democrats that they would be full participants in the negotiations (*CR*, May 19, 2004, S5838).

When the Democrats took a narrow majority in the 110th Congress, Republicans responded by sometimes blocking conferences. On two major bills, lobbying reform and a big energy bill, it was the right wing of the Republican party that objected. On energy, in particular, many Senate Republicans wanted to go to conference. However, with a straight-forward path to conference blocked, the party leaders reached agreement through informal negotiations. On the lobbying bill, the House passed, on a motion to suspend the rules, S 1, the original Senate bill "as amended," that is, with the compromise language. Then the Senate agreed to the House amendment. HR 6, the vehicle for the big energy bill, was initially passed by the House in January 2007 as part of the "six for '06" Democratic agenda; it passed the Senate in considerably different form (i.e., with amendments) in June. After informal negotiations produced a compromise, the House agreed with amendments (the compromise) to the Senate amendments; then the Senate concurred in the House amendment to the Senate amendment to the text of HR 6.

Minority opposition to going to conference can sometimes produce significant concessions from the majority. Thus in 2007, Republicans refused to allow a bill implementing the 9/11 Commission's recommendations to go to conference until Majority Leader Reid promised to drop a provision giving airport screeners collective-bargaining rights. Senate minority opposition can occasionally kill legislation, as the Democrats' did on parental abortion notification in the 109th; however, this is rare, as legislation that passes both chambers seldom fails at the interchamber resolution stage. Most of the time when the minority blocks a conference, the majority leadership finds a way around the problem through alternative procedures. The majority-party leadership decides what procedure will be used for the resolution of differences and, on major legislation important to the party, is generally deeply involved in the negotiations.

Alternative procedures are now frequently used for reasons beyond avoiding minority-party obstruction of the Senate motions necessary to go to conference. Informal negotiations followed by one of the alternative procedures may well speed action. Conference reports are subject to points of order on "airdrops" (earmarks inserted at the postpassage stage) and on scope (that the agreement goes beyond the scope of the differences between the House and Senate bills); amendments between the chambers are not. House amendments to Senate bills are privileged in the Senate; so no filibuster on the motion to proceed is possible; thus the parliamentary situation is no worse than for conference reports. A potential disadvantage to using amendments between the chambers rather than conference committees is that while conference reports are not subject to amendment, House amendments to Senate bills are. However, the Senate majority leader can "fill the tree" and, if he has sixty votes to invoke cloture, prevent amendments. Majority Leader Frist employed this maneuver twice during the 109th Congress, seemingly the first time it had been employed. Majority Leader Reid used it eight times in the 110th, on major bills such as the reauthorization of SCHIP, the ethics reform bill, and the energy bill (Beth et al. 2009, 16).

Another procedure the leadership now sometimes uses entails negotiating a compromise between the House and Senate bills informally and then introducing the product as a "clean bill," which the chambers subsequently pass in identical form. A standoff between the House and Senate on extending and revising the Foreign Intelligence Surveillance Act during the 110th Congress was resolved in this way. President Bush and most Republicans favored an extension that put few new limits on surveillance and that explicitly granted immunity to telecommunications companies for disclosing presumably private information to the government in the past. The majority of Democrats favored substantially greater restrictions and opposed immunity; but some moderate Democrats leaned toward

Bush's position and electorally marginal Democrats and those from red, that is Republican-leaning, districts certainly did not want to open themselves to charges of being soft on terrorists. The Senate, with its sixty-vote requirement, passed a bill Bush favored; the House bill was much tougher, and Bush threatened to veto it. After months of confrontation, with moderate House Democrats becoming more and more nervous and pressuring their leaders to allow a vote, House majority leader Steny Hoyer, D-MD, engaged in negotiations for a compromise. Working with House minority whip Roy Blunt, R-MS, and the chair and ranking member of the Senate Intelligence Committee, Hoyer hammered out a deal that gave Bush much of what he wanted but did impose more restrictions than the Senate bill did. The compromise was introduced as a clean bill (HR 6304) on June 19, 2008, and was passed by the House on June 20. The Senate passed the bill without amendments on July 9. As this case illustrates, the fact that one chamber accepts the other's bill without change does not necessarily mean there was no initial disagreement between them.

In recent times nonconference postpassage procedures have been used in a most unorthodox way to, in effect, achieve the initial passage of major legislation. An extended example—the passage of the legislation establishing the Troubled Assets Relief Program (TARP)—illustrates how this is possible and why it is sometimes used. With a financial crisis looming menacingly, Secretary of the Treasury Henry Paulson on September 19, 2008, called on Congress to pass rescue legislation immediately. The legislation Paulson proposed was so cursory and gave him so much untrammeled authority that leaders and members on both sides of the aisle balked. Still, the pressure to act quickly was intense, and the regular legislative process would take far too long. So a small bicameral and bipartisan group of congressional leaders and White House negotiators hammered out a bill in closed-door meetings over the course of a week.

To get it to the floor quickly and without the possibility of amendment and to then make swift Senate action easier, House leaders used a bill providing tax relief and protection to military personnel that had passed both chambers in 2007. Interchamber difference on HR 3997 had come close to being resolved through amendments between the chambers, but then the leaders had decided to include modified versions of various parts of it in other bills. So, while the substance of HR 3997 had become law, HR 3997 was still available as a vehicle.

On September 29, 2008, Financial Services Committee chair Barney Frank, D-MA, moved that the House "concur in the Senate amendment to the House amendment to the bill, with an additional amendment," that additional amendment being the bailout package. If it had passed, the Senate could have simply accepted the House amendment, and that would have cleared the bill for the president's signature. However, with public opinion running overwhelmingly against bailing out greedy banks seen as responsibly for the financial mess, two-thirds of House Republicans and 40 percent of Democrats voted against the motion and it failed 205–228.

When the vote triggered a massive sell-off on Wall Street, the Senate leaders took over. They agreed on a package that added to the bailout language a number of "sweeteners"—provisions extending various popular tax breaks, expanding incentives for renewable-energy projects, limiting the reach of the alternative minimum tax for a year, and requiring insurance companies to offer mental health coverage on par with what they offered for other health problems (*CQWeekly*, October 6, 2008, 2692–2009).

The Senate used HR 1424, the mental health parity bill, as its vehicle. The House had passed this bill and the Senate had passed its own bill earlier, but no resolution of the two had been formally attempted because by the time the significant differences between the two had been worked out informally, time had become short. The bill extending the popular tax breaks had stalled because the House insisted on paying for the revenue loss (PAYGO) and the Senate, with the need to get sixty votes, could not pass the bill with tax increases included. HR 1424 was brought to the floor under a unanimous consent agreement requiring that any amendments get sixty votes to pass; the first and critical vote was on the Dodd substitute for HR 1424. When that passed 74–25, the negotiated package—including the Senate's language on the tax extenders and the compromise on mental health—was substituted for the original House-passed bill. The Senate then passed the bill by an identical vote.

Although they had not been included in the negotiations and Senate language had replaced House language on several contentious issues, House Democratic leaders reluctantly accepted the deal. Time was of the essence, and the sweeteners were likely to persuade some Republicans to vote for the legislation. On October 3, 2008, the House approved Frank's motion to concur in the Senate amendment to HR 1424 by a vote of 263–171, with Republican splitting 91–108 and Democrats 172–63. That vote cleared the bill for the president's signature.

A final, hybrid example illustrates still more variations on the use of alternative resolution procedures to accomplish strategic aims. On March 24, 2010, the House passed HR 4899, a supplemental appropriations bill funding disaster relief and summer jobs. The Senate did not act until May, by which time President Obama had requested supplemental funds for the wars in Iraq and Afghanistan. On May 13 the Senate Appropriations Committee ordered reported HR 4899 with an amendment in the nature of a substitute—that substitute was a supplemental appropriations bill that included the war funding and a number of other items but not summer jobs money. The Senate passed the bill on May 27. Because House

Democrats were at odds over war funding, the House Appropriations committee was unable to mark up a bill including supplemental war funding. Democrats did agree finally on a package of domestic spending increases to add on to the Senate supplemental. On July 1, Appropriations chair David Obey moved that the House agree to the Senate amendment (the Senate substitute) with amendments (the domestic add-ons and several antiwar amendments). The complex rule for considering this motion specified that the war funding part of the bill be considered as adopted when the rule passed (so antiwar Democrats would not have to vote specifically on war funding they opposed) and that the four House amendments be voted on separately. The first, the domestic add-ons, passed by a largely party-line vote of 239–182. The other three, all antiwar amendments failed; by allowing the votes, the Democratic leadership gave their antiwar members an opportunity to express their views. By passing the war funding through postpassage procedures, Democratic leaders also avoided a Republican motion to recommit, which is always in order on initial passage but not on postpassage motions. Senate majority leader Reid was not able to muster the votes to impose cloture on the motion to agree to the House amendment (the domestic funding) to the Senate amendment to the bill (HR 4899). So the Senate disagreed to the House amendment to the Senate amendment and sent the bill back to the House. The House then suspended the rules and receded and concurred in the Senate amendment (that is, accepted the Senate bill as initially passed).

After Republicans took back the House in the 2010 elections, President Obama negotiated a deal to extend the Bush-era tax cuts, unemployment insurance, and some other expiring tax provisions with Senate minority leader Mitch McConnell. Time was short and the agenda long in the lame-duck session of the 111th Congress; many liberal Democrats and conservative Republicans were unhappy with the deal. So to move legislation quickly and allow as little opportunity for opponents to unravel the deal as possible, the leadership used a bill that had passed both chambers. HR 4853 was the Federal Aviation Administration Act of 2010 when it initially passed the House in March and the Senate in September. Through a process of amendments between the chambers in December, it became the Tax Relief, Unemployment Insurance Reauthorization, and Job Creation Act of 2010 and was enacted into law as such.

Whatever postpassage procedure is used, once legislation has passed both chambers, it seldom dies because the houses cannot come to an agreement. Only 6 percent of the major measures in my selected Congresses from 1960s through the 2000s did so.

The President in the Postpassage Legislative Process

The executive branch is often an important participant at the postpassage stage. During periods when control of the White House and Congress is divided between the parties, especially in times when the parties are highly polarized, the president is often another source of difficulty in reaching agreement. The president has no official role, but if legislators want their legislation to become law, they must satisfy the president sufficiently to avoid a veto or be prepared to muster a two-thirds vote in both chambers. Under divided control presidents often wield their greatest power over legislation at the postpassage stage. The term *veto bargaining* became current during George H.W. Bush's presidency to describe that Bush administration's frequent attempts to extract concessions from the Democratic Congress by threatening a veto.

After Republicans gained control of Congress in the 1994 elections, President Bill Clinton showed himself to be an adept veto bargainer. Most bills and all major legislation showed the effects of administration involvement, usually at the post passage stage. In 1998 the conferees for a bill authorizing funds for agricultural research and making up a shortfall in the federal crop insurance program added a provision restoring food stamp eligibility for 250,000 legal immigrants who had been denied such eligibility by the 1996 welfare reform bill; they did so because Clinton persuaded them that otherwise he would veto the bill, which was of great importance to their constituents. The Clinton administration was especially effective in conferences on appropriations bills, often extracting more money for education and other favored programs from a less-than-amenable Republican Congress.

When the same party controls Congress and the White House, the administration wields influence throughout the legislative process. It may send Congress draft legislation. Administration officials, of course, testify at committee hearings, but less formal consultation is ongoing and probably more influential. Nevertheless, the House-Senate resolution stage gets special administration attention just because it is the final stage. What emerges goes to the president. White House involvement allowed the airline assistance bill passed in the wake of the September 11 attacks to avoid conference altogether. Formally, the Senate passed the House bill without change. In actuality, the bill was drafted by the White House and congressional leaders from both chambers. During the 111th Congress, the Obama administration worked closely with the Democratic Congress on major legislation and played its most active role at the postpassage stage. The health care reform case study (Chapter 8) illustrates the president's influence throughout the legislative process but especially at the House-Senate resolution stage.

Even though Republicans controlled both chambers of Congress in the 108th Congress, President George W. Bush used veto threats quite frequently; he threatened at least eighteen relatively major bills with vetoes.[2] These veto threats were, by and large, directed at specific provisions in bills that he otherwise supported. Attempts to overturn new Federal Communications Commission media ownership rules, to lift the ban on travel to Cuba, to prevent the administration from revising overtime rules in such a way as to deprive some of those currently eligible of overtime pay, to delay military base closings, to allow concurrent receipts for veterans, and to block the administration's efforts to outsource federal jobs to private companies were the target of veto threats—in some cases, of repeated threats.

Bush's veto threats may well have been intended to give the Republican leadership ammunition against majority-supported provisions the president opposed. On some issues, Bush was forced to compromise, but in every instance the veto threat moved the bill toward his position. Party leaders repeatedly removed offending provisions in conference. Speaker Hastert made sure a transportation bill Bush would feel it necessary to veto did not emerge from conference in 2004. In fact, "[Hastert] made it clear that they would not allow bills that would be vetoed to reach the president's desk," according to Nick Calio, former head of White House liaison for Bush (*RC*, December 15, 2003). Bush did not veto a single bill during his first term and only one before Republicans lost control of Congress in the 2006 elections.

In 2009–2010, Obama had big Democratic majorities, but he too made occasional veto threats; thus when Appropriations Committee chair David Obey proposed paying for other domestic spending by cutting funds from the administrations prized "Race to the Top" education program, Obama threatened a veto. The bill that went to Obama did not include the cut. He also threatened to veto defense legislation if authorization for the F22 fighter plane, an expensive program he wanted to terminate, were included; the final bill dropped the authorization. During the 111th, Obama cast two vetoes, neither of major legislation.

The Final Step

After both the House and Senate have approved legislation in identical form, it is sent to the president, who can sign it, do nothing, or veto it. If

---

2. "Relatively major" includes appropriations bills as well as major measures as defined earlier. Veto threats are identified by their being mentioned in *CQW*.

he signs it or holds it for ten weekdays while Congress is in session, the legislation becomes law. However, if Congress has adjourned *sine die* (that is, indefinitely, which happens at the end of a Congress), the president can kill legislation by holding it for ten weekdays without signing it. In those cases the president is said to cast a pocket veto.[3]

When the president casts a formal veto, the legislation is sent back to the Congress with the president's message of disapproval and his reasons for having cast the veto. For the legislation to become law, both houses must override the veto by a two-thirds vote.

No rules require that Congress vote to override a president's veto within a specified period of time. In the past the vote tended to come fairly soon after the veto. For years this was the expectation and the practice. More recently, however, the chamber that originated the bill (which must be the first to vote to override) has sometimes held the bill to gain political advantage. In 1996, for example, Republican leaders did not schedule veto override votes on the "partial-birth" abortion bill until late September, only weeks before the elections. This was a bill that had passed both houses way back in March and had been vetoed in April.

Mustering a two-thirds vote in both chambers on a controversial matter is a formidable task. George H.W. Bush had only one veto overridden during his four years as president even though politically he was quite weak during much of his presidency. In 1995, despite being enormously weakened by the 1994 elections, Clinton suffered only one override; from 1996 through 2000, only one more of his vetoes was overridden. During the 110th Congress, which the Democrats controlled, George W. Bush cast ten vetoes and was overridden four times (twice on essentially the same bill—an agriculture authorization bill). A bill's supporters know that if they want to enact legislation, they must either satisfy the president or be prepared to amass enough support in both houses to override his veto. The former will usually seem the easier task. Thus the veto gives the president considerable influence in the legislative process, as explored earlier in this chapter.

Reconciling Differences: How Much Change?

Change in the legislative process within the two chambers has spilled over and affected the process of reconciling interchamber differences. Multiple

---

3. For the controversy over whether presidents have the right to pocket veto legislation when the Congress has adjourned but not *sine die* (between the two sessions or over recesses, for example), see Gold 2004, 130–131. Congress seems to have successfully countered this strategy by authorizing an agent to receive messages from the president.

referral and members' desire for broad participation have led to bigger conference delegations, especially on the part of the House. Although House leaders have reined in the size of conference delegations, conferences still often have multicommittee representation; such conferences work in subconferences, which on the House side have authority to make decisions only on specifically delineated parts of the legislation. The coordinating problems such an undertaking entails draw the party leadership, the only central leadership in the chambers, into a process that used to be committee dominated. The party leaders' greater involvement in the legislative process within their chamber—in working out postcommittee compromises that facilitate passage, for example—leads to a greater role for them at the resolution stage as well. If it took leadership intervention to put together the compromise necessary to pass the bill, sustaining the compromise in conference and passing the resulting conference report often will require leadership involvement, too.

Furthermore, the party leadership's more central role—as well as increased obstructionism in the Senate—stimulated the use of various nonconference routes to resolving interchamber differences. Leaders have had to become more creative in the employment of alternative procedures and now sometimes use them in highly unorthodox ways for strategic advantage.

c h a p t e r   f i v e

Omnibus Legislation, the Budget Process, and Summits

UNORTHODOX LAWMAKING IS NOT CONFINED to the sorts of innovations and modifications to what were once standard procedures and practices that the previous chapters examined. Forms of legislation and ways of making decisions that either did not exist at all or were rarely used several decades ago are now prominent. Contemporary Congresses often legislate through enormous omnibus bills, something rarely done before the 1980s. The budget process, established in the mid-1970s but peripheral to legislative decision making until the 1980s, has become central. And on big issues that must be resolved, summits—relatively formal negotiations between congressional leaders and high-ranking administration officials representing the president directly—have become a fairly standard mode of decision making when control of the national government's branches is divided between the parties.

When legislative decisions are made through omnibus legislation, the budget process, and summits, decision making is more centralized than it is on other major legislation; central leaders—congressional party leaders and often the president—play a more important role, frequently the decisive role. These modes of legislating make it possible for Congress to enact comprehensive policy change, always a difficult task for what has usually been a decentralized institution; they also may reduce the opportunities for careful scrutiny of the legislation's provisions and for broad participation by rank-and-file members.

Divided government, partisan polarization, and big deficits are the most important of the environmental factors that fostered these developments. As long as intense partisanship and big deficits persist, the major political conflicts of a Congress likely will continue to revolve around omnibus legislation and the budget process. With the return of divided government, summits too may again become prominent.

Omnibus Legislation

The legislation that Congress deals with varies from the short and simple—the one-sentence bill, HR 3989, "To designate the facility of the United States Postal Service located at 37598 Goodhue Avenue in Dennison, Minnesota, as the 'Albert H. Quie Post Office'"—to the extraordinarily long and complex.[1] The 1990 Clean Air Act was about 800 pages long, and the 2005 energy bill was 550 pages; the length of the Patient Protection and Affordable Care Act of 2010—about 2,100 pages—became notorious. In many cases, nonexperts would need a translator to make sense of the legislation.

Legislation that addresses numerous and not necessarily related subjects, issues, and programs, and therefore is usually highly complex and long, is referred to as omnibus legislation. Although there is no consensus technical definition of what constitutes an omnibus bill, every Congress watcher would classify as omnibus the 1988 trade bill, which spanned the jurisdiction of thirteen House and nine Senate committees, and the anti-drug bill, passed the same year. The latter covered drug abuse education and prevention; treatment; punishment of abusers and sellers, big and small; and the interdiction of drugs flowing into the United States from abroad by air, sea, and land.

Although perhaps not quite as disparate in subjects covered, the 2002 bill setting up the Department of Homeland Security and the 2004 bill reorganizing U.S. government intelligence operations also can be considered omnibus legislation, and the process on each illustrates the problems such bills create and the unorthodox fixes the leadership employs to pass them. When President George W. Bush requested that Congress quickly establish a Department of Homeland Security in spring 2002, the House Republican leadership could anticipate some significant problems. What Bush proposed was the largest reorganization of the federal bureaucracy in a half century, a reorganization that combined all or part of twenty-two federal agencies responsible for counterterrorism. A large number of House committees would have to be involved because they had jurisdiction over programs that Bush wanted moved into the new department, and some of them would likely resist giving up any of their jurisdiction.

---

1. Albert H. Quie is a former member of the House; Congress frequently names federal buildings after former members.

Yet if the House did not move expeditiously, the chamber's and the party's reputation would be damaged.

To handle the political problems as well as the major coordination task of melding the work of a dozen or so committees into a coherent whole, Speaker Dennis Hastert, R-IL, proposed and the House approved a select committee of nine members. Hastert chose Majority Leader Dick Armey, R-TX, to chair the committee and appointed members of the leadership to the remaining Republican slots (*CQ Weekly*, June 22, 2002, 1651). On June 24, the legislation was referred to twelve standing committees under a deadline; on July 16 and 17, ten of these committees presented their recommendations to the Select Committee, which made significant changes to some of the recommendations. Floor consideration on the combined bill began on July 25, and the bill passed on July 26.

The bill reorganizing government intelligence operations in response to the recommendations of the 9/11 Commission was also a far-reaching measure and, on the House side, included myriad loosely related proposals—on such matters as law enforcement and immigration, for example. In the House the bill was referred to thirteen committees, five of which reported. These formal processes, however, masked what really happened. The bill was actually drafted by the chairs of the affected committees under leadership auspices. Only then was the bill introduced—by Speaker Hastert—and sent to the committees, all of which reported or were discharged within ten days.

Revealing the differences between the chambers, neither bill was handled through such unorthodox processes in the Senate. Both were reported by a single committee—Government Affairs. The Homeland Security Department bill did run into a typical Senate problem when minority Republicans, using their right of extended debate, refused to allow a passage vote on a version Bush opposed.

Many of the bills generally labeled omnibus are money bills of some sort. The most common omnibus measures in contemporary Congresses are omnibus appropriations bills, budget resolutions, and reconciliation bills. Omnibus measures have made up about 12 percent of major legislation in recent Congresses.[2]

Authorizations, Appropriations, and Earmarks

Understanding the congressional budgetary process requires grasping the difference between authorizations and appropriations. It is the subject matter committees, such as Agriculture or Education, that are empowered

---

2. The 103rd–105th and 107th–111th Congresses.

to report legislation that creates new programs or alters existing ones. Such a bill typically also authorizes Congress to appropriate the money that will be needed to implement the program. Most of these authorization bills, as they often are called, now authorize specific maximum amounts of appropriations for one or more fiscal years. If the program is going to continue being implemented beyond those fiscal years, Congress is supposed to reauthorize appropriations for it for additional fiscal years. Congress moved from mostly permanent authorizations to mostly temporary, but multiyear, authorizations in the 1960s and 1970s in order to encourage more program oversight and to increase the influence of the subject matter, or "authorization," committees.

The Constitution requires that funds for government programs must be appropriated by law. Congressional rules, especially House rules, require that those appropriations first must be authorized. Once a program has been created by law, the provisions governing its organization, purposes, activities, and so on remain in force unless that law is amended or repealed, or unless the law includes a "sunset" provision that causes the provisions to expire on a certain date or after a certain number of years. It is the authorization of appropriations for a program that is limited to one year or a finite number of fiscal years.

The reason people talk as if the program itself would cease to exist if it were not reauthorized when its limited-year authorization of appropriations expires is because a program without money (appropriations) in effect does not exist. However, the internal congressional rules that bar unauthorized appropriations can be waived and now often are. Thus for various political reasons, U.S. foreign aid programs were not reauthorized for many years, even though they were supposed to be reauthorized every year. Nevertheless, those programs continued to function because money for them was appropriated after the rules prohibiting unauthorized appropriations were waived in the House via a special rule reported from the Rules Committee.

Appropriating funds is the task of the House and Senate Appropriations Committees; every year they must report out and see enacted a series of bills that appropriate money for the federal government's multitude of programs and agencies. The two committees are organized into a number of subcommittees, each of which reports a general appropriations bill that funds a number of government programs and agencies. For example, the Subcommittee on Labor, Health and Human Services, and Education reports a bill that appropriates funds for the programs and agencies that fall under these three cabinet departments.

For many years the House and Senate Appropriations Committees each had thirteen subcommittees with identical jurisdiction. After some changes in the subcommittees' jurisdictions and numbers in the mid-2000s, both the House and the Senate Appropriations Committee now have twelve subcommittees with parallel jurisdictions, each of which has been charged with reporting one general appropriations bill. New Speaker John Boehner (R-OH) has advocated breaking these big bills into smaller pieces in the 112th Congress.

Appropriations bills fund their programs for only one year. Were Congress to fail to pass the Labor-HHS-Education appropriations bill, many of those departments' programs as well as the administrative structure would have to shut down. (Programs such as Social Security that are funded through a mechanism other than annual appropriations would not be directly affected.) The prospect of shutting down programs that people want and depend on is sufficiently horrendous that Congress always passes appropriations bills—although in late 1995 it did so only after a hiatus of several weeks. This was the famous government shutdown of Christmas 1995: House Republicans newly in the majority tried to force President Bill Clinton to agree to their plan for balancing the budget by refusing to pass appropriations. Clinton held tough, and the public blamed the Republicans for the pain of the shutdown—national parks and the Washington Monument closed, government employees unpaid and so unable to buy Christmas presents for their children (Sinclair 2007, chap. 11). Prodded by Senate majority leader Bob Dole, R-KS, House Republicans capitulated and passed a continuing resolution (CR) (see below).

Frequently, Congress cannot pass all the general appropriations bills by the annual deadline of October 1, the beginning of the fiscal year (abbreviated as FY); in that case it passes a continuing (appropriations) resolution that temporarily continues funding.[3] CRs may cover the few appropriations bills that have not yet passed and extend for only a few days or weeks. Sometimes, however, Congress passes a bill that encompasses half or more of the regular appropriations bills and extends through the remainder of the fiscal year—such legislation truly qualifies as omnibus. In 2002, for example, Congress failed to pass eleven of the regular appropriations bills; after multiple CRs, all eleven were wrapped into one omnibus bill and passed in February 2003, more than four months after the beginning of the fiscal year. Similarly, seven regular appropriations bills for FY2004 were packaged into one omnibus bill and finally passed in January 2004. The FY2005 Omnibus Appropriations bill included nine of the regular appropriations bills. The next year, however, Congress managed to pass all of its appropriations bills separately, although some were passed well after the beginning of the fiscal year.

---

3. Funding is usually set at the previous year's level or at the lower of the levels proposed by the House and Senate.

At the beginning of the 110th Congress, only two of the general appropriations bills for FY2007 had been enacted. During a lame-duck session, the outgoing Republican majority had passed a CR funding the programs covered by the other bills through February 15. That CR set funding for each program at its previous year's level. The new Democratic majority was confronted with having to pass nine contentious appropriations bills four months into the fiscal year or doing one big bill. Since the new majority had an ambitious agenda, and the Appropriations Committees would soon have to start work on the FY2008 bills, the chairs of the Appropriations Committees negotiated a combination CR/omnibus appropriations bill that mostly funded programs at the previous year's level for the rest of fiscal 2007 but did make some adjustments to take into account Democratic priorities and to avoid hardships in underfunded programs. This bill never went through committee in either chamber and was considered under a closed rule on the House floor. Here again, severe policy and political problems prompted the use of unorthodox processes.

Passing all the general appropriations bills as separate bills has become increasingly difficult for Congress. From FY1996 through FY2010, almost half of regular appropriations bills were bundled into omnibus measures (*Congress Daily,* June 2, 2008, updated by the author). The Senate has had enormous difficulty passing appropriations bills in recent years; from FY2001 through FY2010, an average of five of the general appropriations bills were never considered on the Senate floor (Lilly 2010, 4). The Senate as a whole voted on the bills only as part of a package, often as a conference report on which only an up-or-down vote is allowed. The root of the problem lies in the Senate's rules and how they are used in this era of partisan polarization. With the minority party routinely using extended debate, Senate floor time has become scarce. When the majority brings to the floor appropriations bills that used to be uncontroversial, the transportation appropriations bill, for example, the minority offers large numbers of amendments, with the result that it takes days to pass the bill. Democrats believe that Republicans have been "slow walking" the legislative process ever since they lost their majority. The majority leader has to weigh how much floor time appropriations bills will consume and how much he needs for other high-priority legislation that, given minority tactics, will also consume inordinate amounts of floor time. The end result is now often that the majority leader does not bring many of the appropriations bills to the floor for initial consideration. The appropriations bills that have never been considered on the Senate floor are added in conference. In 2010 the combination of a big agenda and delaying tactics led to the Senate not passing a single appropriations bill; Republicans blocked an omnibus bill in the lame-duck session, and only a CR extending funding to March 2011 was enacted into law.

Partisan polarization has affected the appropriations process in the House as well but, given its different rules, in a different way. Traditionally appropriations bills were considered on the House floor though an open process that allowed all germane amendments, and this continued even after most other legislation was brought to the floor under restrictive rules. In recent years, however, minority Republicans began to, in effect, "filibuster through amendments." When Democrats brought the first regular appropriations bill to the floor in 2009, Republicans filed more than one hundred amendments and refused to reach a unanimous consent agreement setting out a schedule for consideration, as was traditionally done. The Democrats responded with a structured rule for consideration of the bill, a first for a general appropriations bill. All subsequent general appropriations bills in the House were considered under structured rules during the 111th Congress, though those rules were quite generous in the number of amendments allowed. The rule for the FY2010 Commerce-Justice-Science bill, for example, made in order twenty-three specific amendments plus ten chosen by the ranking minority member from a list of amendments the minority had wanted to offer.

In addition to regular appropriations bills, Congress may pass supplemental appropriations bills. These bills are supposed to address unexpected contingencies—emergencies such as Hurricane Katrina relief (Oleszek 2004, 44). The George W. Bush administration used emergency supplementals to fund the wars in Afghanistan and Iraq, arguing that the amounts needed could not be predicted and so could not be included in the regular budget. The amounts appropriated by supplementals do not count against spending ceilings set by the budget resolution and do not figure into predictions about future budget deficits. Furthermore, the president's request usually is much less detailed and less thoroughly justified than are funding requests in his budget. For these reasons, the administration's use of supplementals to fund the wars became increasingly controversial, even among congressional Republicans. After the 2006 elections, the administration promised to include war funding in the regular budget—after one more big supplemental in early 2007. President Barack Obama's first full budget did include war funding, but a supplemental was nevertheless needed, and with many Democrats increasingly doubtful about the Afghanistan war, it too was highly controversial.

The best-known, most notorious, and most misunderstood aspect of the congressional budgetary process is earmarking. An earmark is a legislative provision that directs funds to be spent for a specific project, a bridge or a university research center, for example. Typically the project is sought by a member for a project in his or her district or state. The provision may be in the bill itself, in which case it is legally binding on the executive branch; or it may be in the committee report that accompanies the bill—in that case it is not legally binding but is usually treated as such by the agency or department so directed. After all, those executive branch officials are dependent on Congress for their future budgets and see little to be gained by making members angry at them by ignoring their directives. Authorization legislation may contain earmarks; the periodic transportation reauthorization bill has always included a long list of specific projects that have been requested by members for their districts. Narrowly drawn tax provisions that are specifically targeted to benefit one or a small number of people are another form of earmark. It is, however, earmarks in appropriations bills that have received the most attention.

The media portray all earmarks as pork—outrageously wasteful and possibly corrupt. The examples that make headlines—the "bridge to nowhere"—seem to bear out that storyline, which is also pushed by some members of Congress and outside groups. Reality is, however, considerably more boring. Most earmarks are for worthy purposes; as an example, here are the first four earmark requests by Sen. Barbara Boxer (D-CA) for inclusion in the FY2011 agriculture appropriations bill:

Applied Agriculture and Environmental Research
Requesting Entity: California State University
Location: CSU campuses throughout California
Amount: $3,000,000
Funds will support competitive grants throughout the CSU system for research into climate change, air quality, greenhouse gas emissions and carbon sequestering; food safety and security; water quality, infrastructure and conveyance; and public health and welfare.

Bay Area Aquatic Pest Prevention Plan
Requesting Entity: County of Monterey
Location: Counties of Monterey, Santa Clara, Alameda, Contra Costa, and San Benito
Amount: $2,500,000
The funding would implement a coordinated prevention plan in five California counties to address the economic threat posed by zebra and quagga mussels. These mussels are invasive aquatic pests that can quickly clog filters, pipes, pumps and critical infrastructure of agricultural, municipal, and industrial water delivery systems.

California County Pest Detection Augmentation Program
Requesting Entity: California Agricultural Commissioners and Sealers Association
Location: Counties throughout California
Amount: $1,350,000

Funds will allow county agriculture commissioners to continue a program to inspect incoming plant material at points of entry in California to prevent the establishment of invasive pests and diseases.

Community Farming and Agriculture Education
Requesting Entity: Orange County Great Park
Location: Irvine, CA
Amount: $850,000
Funds would expand agricultural crop land to 120 acres at the Park's Farm and Food Lab, which is sited on the former El Toro military base. Much of the harvest will be donated to local food banks and the site will be a model for agricultural sustainability. Funding would also support free educational programs focusing on agriculture. (link from Appropriations Committee Web site to Boxer Web site appropriations.senate.gov/cdsr/cfm)

One may question whether these and the many other requests by other members are the best use of the limited funds available, but it is hard to argue that these are outrageously wasteful projects.

Furthermore, the debate over earmarks sometimes ignores the fact that someone has to make the decisions about the specific projects and programs on which the funds appropriated are spent. Congress's constitutional authority over spending gives it the power, should it choose to use it, to earmark every cent it authorizes and appropriates. Of course, given the size and scope of national governmental activities, that is neither feasible nor advisable, so many detailed spending decisions are delegated to the executive branch. Yet were Congress to deprive itself of the power to earmark altogether, that would represent a significant shift in power to the executive branch. On a practical basis, members of Congress often argue that they know the needs and priorities of their own constituencies better than executive branch bureaucrats do.

Some serious problems with earmarking did develop in the 1990s and 2000s. In the aftermath of the Republican takeover of Congress in the 1994 elections, the number of earmarks on appropriations bills exploded. According to a Congressional Research Service count, there were 3,023 earmarks worth $19.5 billion in 1996 appropriations bills. By 2006 the number had climbed to 12,852 valued at $64 billion. Before 1995, when Congress was under Democratic control, a number of appropriations bills—the huge bill funding the Departments of Labor, Education, and Health and Human Services, for example—were largely or completely free of earmarks; in subsequent years, they became replete with earmarks. The sums earmarked on appropriations bills also grew enormously. The last Democratic Labor, Health and Human Services, and Education appropriations bill of the 1990s (fiscal year 1995) contained no earmarks; by fiscal year

2002, over $1 billion in the bill was earmarked. The periodic transportation authorization bill has traditionally included numerous earmarked projects, but in both numbers and value, there were large increases under Republican-controlled Congresses. The number of earmarked projects averaged 325 among the three bills passed in 1987, 1991, and 1995. That increased to 1,850 earmarks (worth $9.5 billion) in 1998 and to 6,371 earmarks (worth $23 billion) in 2005.

Earmarking is not responsible for the big budget deficits; the amounts involved are a tiny percent of the entire federal budget, and, furthermore, most of the money is not additional but comes out of the total amount authorized or appropriated. Some of the projects earmarked are wasteful, but many are worthy. In some smaller programs, however, the extent of earmarking left almost no funds for nonearmarked projects; in other cases, such as the NASA budget, earmarks directed scarce funds to projects that have little to do with the agency's core mission. According to Scott Lilly, former staff director of the House Appropriations Committee, the most deleterious effect of the huge increase in earmarking is that it seriously skews how both members and staff use their time. Pursuing earmarks is a highly time-consuming process for the member, his or her staff, and committee staffs, especially the Appropriations Committee staff. Yet constituent groups increasingly expect earmarks, and an entire lobbying establishment has grown up around the pursuit of them. The result is that members and staff are left with less time to devote to legislation of broader import.

The enormous growth in the number of earmarks and several corruption scandals led to some reforms. The lack of transparency in the process was a major problem, and the reforms have attacked that. In 2007 the House adopted rules requiring "detailed lists of every earmark and its sponsor, a public certification from every Member that they have no financial interest in any earmark request, and identification of earmarks 'air dropped' [i.e., inserted] in conference" (Committee on Appropriations, March 2010). In 2009 all members were required to post online their earmark requests and justifications. In 2010 the House Appropriations Committee decided that it would not approve requests for earmarks that are directed at for-profit entities. The Senate requires all members to post information on their earmark requests on their official Web sites at the time the request is made. "Each Senator must explain the purpose of the earmark and why it is a valuable use of tax payer funds" (http:// appropriation.senate.gov/cdsr.cfm). The Appropriations Committee posts a link to each senator's request page. In early 2011 both the House and Senate agreed to forgo earmarks for at least two years.

Not all programs are funded through annual appropriations. Some of the federal government's biggest programs are entitlement programs— programs stipulating that people who meet certain criteria are entitled to a specified benefit. Social Security, Medicare, Medicaid, agricultural commodity programs, and food stamps are all entitlement programs. Funding for many of these programs is not under the control of the Appropriations Committees. Some of the biggest—Social Security and a part of Medicare—are funded by trust funds, and some have permanent appropriations. Even in those cases, such as food stamps, for which annual appropriations are required, the Appropriations Committees' discretion is highly limited. If the money appropriated runs out before the end of the year, Congress must pass a supplemental appropriations bill to fund food stamps for eligible people. Cutting spending for entitlements requires changing the legislation that authorized the program, and that is in the jurisdiction of the authorizing committee, not the Appropriations Committees.[4]

The Budget Process

To provide some coherence to the process of making spending decisions, Congress in 1974 passed the Congressional Budget and Impoundment Control Act. Before the 1974 Budget Act, Congress made spending and taxing decisions in a piecemeal and uncoordinated fashion. The budget process also provides Congress with a tool for making comprehensive decisions, though it was not initially used as such.

The Budget Act created an entirely new process and superimposed it on the old process by which Congress had made spending and taxing decisions. The new budget process made omnibus measures a regular part of the annual congressional workload and influenced the legislative process in other direct and indirect ways. Although a detailed examination of the budget process and its ramifications cannot be undertaken here, a discussion of the contemporary legislative process would not be complete without some discussion of the budget process. (On the budget process, see Schick 1980; Oleszek 2004; and Thurber and Durst 1993.)

The Budget Act requires that before the appropriations bills are drafted, Congress must pass a budget resolution setting guidelines. The budget resolution specifies how much the federal government will spend

---

4. Aid to Families with Dependent Children (AFDC) was an entitlement program; the 1996 welfare bill changed it from an entitlement to a block grant program that requires annual appropriations.

in the next fiscal year, how much it expects to collect in taxes, and how large the deficit or surplus (the difference between the two) is expected to be. It also specifies how much is to be spent in each of twenty broad functional categories—health or agriculture, for example. The Budget Committee report accompanying the resolution may contain detailed suggestions about policy changes that would produce the overall figures. Although it may suggest that spending on particular programs be cut in order to reach the overall spending figure, its suggestions have no binding effect.

Estimating the deficit or surplus is not a routine technical exercise and may well be a source of controversy. The deficit or surplus depends on expected expenditures and revenues, both of which depend in turn on a number of economic assumptions. Tax receipts, for example, depend on the state of the economy; when the economy is growing, more people have jobs, wages are likely to be going up, and more businesses are making money, and thus people and business pay more in taxes. Federal expenditures depend on economic estimates as well; for example, when the economy is bad, more people will qualify for unemployment benefits and food stamps, so spending for such entitlement programs will go up.

In addition to estimates for the upcoming year, the budget resolution projects expenditures, revenues, and deficits or surpluses for either five or ten years into the future, an even trickier enterprise. Congress relies on the Congressional Budget Office, staffed by nonpartisan experts, for its estimates. The Office of Management and Budget (OMB) provides estimates for the president. In 1995 a dispute over which set of figures to use was at the center of the budget battle. Small differences in assumptions about the growth rate of the American economy over the following seven years made a huge difference in the estimate of how much needed to be cut from spending in order to achieve a balanced budget by the year 2002.

Drafting the budget resolution is the task of a Budget Committee in each chamber. The committees take into consideration the president's budget request, which by law must be submitted to Congress by the first Monday in February. As the Senate committee's description of the budget process explains, "One of the first things Congress needs to know when crafting a budget is what the executive branch believes is necessary to fund the operations of the Federal government" (Committee on the Budget, United States Senate 1998, 10). Other committees send their views on spending on programs within their jurisdictions to the Budget Committee, and the Congressional Budget Office provides reports on the budget and economic outlook as well as an analysis of the president's budget request. Since the resolution sets overall budgetary policy, drafting it is too important and often too politically difficult a task for the committee to undertake on its own. A budget is a statement of priorities, and when resources are tight, it involves painful trade-offs. Congressional party leaders always are involved, and the president may be as well.

The legislative process on a budget resolution looks similar in many ways to the process followed on ordinary legislation. After the committees report, each chamber must pass its respective version. In the House the majority-party leadership always brings up the resolution under a special rule that restricts amendments; usually, only a limited number of comprehensive substitutes are allowed. The Budget Act limits Senate debate to fifty hours and requires that amendments be germane. Thus a budget resolution cannot be filibustered. A conference committee is appointed to come up with a compromise between the two chambers' versions, which must then be approved by both houses. The budget resolution, however, is not legislation; it is a concurrent resolution that does not require the president's signature.

In essence, the budget resolution is a set of guidelines that Congress has agreed on to guide its own—specifically, its committees'—spending and taxing decisions for the year. The budget resolution serves as a framework within which the Appropriations Committees make their spending decisions. The conference report on the resolution divides up total spending by committee. Since the Appropriations Committees are responsible for all spending done through appropriations, they receive the largest allocation. The spending that the Appropriations Committees control is referred to as "discretionary" because in law if not in political reality the committees could simply cut that spending at will. According to the OMB's estimate of outlays (spending) for 2010, discretionary spending accounts for only about 38 percent of federal spending (with 60 percent of that going to defense and homeland security and 40 percent going to domestic); entitlements account for 56 percent; and interest on the national debt, 6 percent (Office of Management and Budget 2010, Table 8.3).

The resolution may—and in recent years often does—include binding instructions to other committees to bring law within their jurisdiction into conformance with the dictates of the budget resolution. If the aim is to cut the increase in spending, as is often the case, entitlements are likely to be targeted. The resolution may instruct an authorizing committee to reduce expenditures in the programs under its jurisdiction by a given amount; doing so requires the committee to change legislation under its jurisdiction. For example, the budget resolution for FY2006 stipulated

> The House Committee on Agriculture shall report changes in laws within its jurisdiction sufficient to reduce the level of direct spending for that committee by $173,000,000 in outlays for fiscal year 2006 and $3,000,000,000 in outlays for the period of fiscal years 2006 through 2010. (House Report 109-062—Concurrent Resolution on the Budget for Fiscal Year 2006)

The budget resolution instructions do not prescribe the details of the changes, only the amount of savings. Similarly, if the resolution specifies that tax revenues need to increase over what current law would bring in, the tax-writing committees—House Ways and Means and Senate Finance— will be instructed to draft a tax bill that raises a specific amount, but they will not be told how to do it—whether by raising the gasoline tax or by increasing income tax rates, for example. Conversely, if the budget resolution instructs the tax committees to cut taxes, the instructions consist of an amount taxes are to be reduced; the report may offer suggestions as to which taxes might be cut, but these are not binding. The instructions in a budget resolution are called reconciliation instructions; they instruct the various committees to reconcile legislation under their jurisdictions with the figures in the budget resolution. Reconciliation instructions also specify a deadline for committee compliance.

Budget Act reconciliation bills can be used as a vehicle for making comprehensive policy change. Without that tool, passing an economic program embodying a significant change in direction, such as President Ronald Reagan's in 1981 or President Clinton's in 1993, would have required enacting a dozen or more separate bills. When the budget process is used as a vehicle for making comprehensive change, the number of committees instructed is often large. The budget resolution in 1981, which carried Reagan's economic program, instructed fifteen House and fourteen Senate committees. The 1993 resolution containing Clinton's program instructed thirteen House and twelve Senate committees. The 1995 resolution encompassing the new Republican majority's economic plan instructed twelve House and eleven Senate committees. The budget resolutions of 2001 and 2003, which carried George W. Bush's economic program, specified only tax cuts, although enormous ones, so they instructed only the tax-writing committees. By 2005 the growing deficit pressured Republicans to attempt to control spending growth, and the budget resolution instructed eight committees in each chamber to cut spending, but it also instructed the tax committees to cut taxes.

The instructed committees draft their legislation and then send it to the Budget Committee, which packages it into an omnibus reconciliation bill.[5] The legislation must then win approval by each chamber. In the House, special rules that tightly restrict amending activity always are used to protect these big and usually controversial packages. The Budget Act protects the reconciliation bill against a filibuster in the Senate by limiting

---

5. Occasionally, two reconciliation bills will be used, one that includes the programmatic changes intended to cut spending and the other that deals with taxes. This was the case in 2005.

initial floor debate to twenty hours and debate on the conference report to ten hours; in addition, amendments must be germane and deficit neutral, that is, they can not increase spending. Sixty votes are required to waive these rules.

Conference committees on reconciliation bills have sometimes been huge. All the committees with provisions in the legislation as well as the Budget Committees are represented, and the totals have run into the hundreds. The conference committee on the 1981 reconciliation bill consisted of 208 House conferees from seventeen committees and 72 senators from fourteen committees (Tiefer 1989, 798). In 1993, 164 House members from sixteen committees and 53 senators from thirteen committees served on the reconciliation bill conference committee. Generally, such conferences work in subgroups; the 1981 conference, for instance, met in 58 subgroups (*CQW* 1984, 1298). Most conferees have authority to make decisions only about the provisions their committee or subcommittee drafted. The House conference delegation for the 1997 spending reconciliation bill, for example, consisted of thirteen subgroups from eight committees, each with authority to negotiate on only a specific title or subtitle of the bill. Conferees from the Budget Committees usually have authority over the entire bill and take on the formidable task of coordination.

Because reconciliation bills are so substantively and politically important, the party leadership is always involved. When the Democrats were in the majority before 1995, the House majority leader served as the leadership representative on the Budget Committee and was routinely appointed a conferee. Speaker Newt Gingrich, R-GA, appointed Majority Leader Armey, Majority Whip Tom DeLay, R-TX, and Chief Deputy Whip Hastert to the 1997 spending reconciliation bill conference; they were three of the five Republican general conferees with authority over the entire bill. The conference delegation for the 2005 reconciliation bill illustrates contemporary practices. The Senate appointed twenty conferees without specifying the committees each represented. The House delegation was forty strong, but only fifteen of those were general conferees; three members from each of eight committees were appointed to negotiate on the matters under their committee's jurisdiction, which were spelled out in detail. Of the fifteen conferees with jurisdiction over the entire bill, thirteen were from the Budget Committee; the other two were from the party leadership—Roy Blunt, R-MO, whip and acting majority leader, and Tom DeLay.[6]

------

6. At that point—December 2005—DeLay had stepped down as majority leader temporarily, as the rules dictating that indicted leaders do so required, but he had not been replaced and was still acting as part of the leadership.

Unlike the budget resolution, the reconciliation bill is legislation, so the president can veto it. This possibility gives the president influence in the process of putting the bill together, even if Congress is controlled by the other party. Unless the congressional majority party has huge majorities in both chambers, its chances are exceedingly dim of amassing a two-thirds vote to override the president on legislation that goes to the heart of the differences between the parties. If the president's own party is in the majority, the president and congressional party leaders likely will work together closely on such a major piece of legislation. The 1993 reconciliation bill followed the outlines that President Clinton had laid out, even though he had to compromise on specific provisions. In 2001 and 2003 the Republican congressional majorities gave Bush most of what he had requested. In both cases, majority-party leaders played a crucial role in delivering for the president of their party. (See the case studies in Chapter 9.)

Reconciliation bills make a multitude of policy decisions through an abbreviated legislative process in which many provisions receive limited scrutiny. It is possible that no committee hearings were held on the changes included in the legislation. With the committees operating under time constraints, many provisions may have received only perfunctory attention during committee markup; as part of a much larger package, they may have been altogether ignored during floor debate. In fact, most members may not have been aware of many of them. Yet the provisions in a reconciliation bill are very likely to become law. The sheer size of the package tends to take attention away from any but the most major provisions. In the House the bill will be considered under a special rule that prohibits most amendments. In the Senate the bill is protected from a filibuster. And a reconciliation bill is considered "must pass" legislation by the majority party.

Given these advantages, the temptation to use a reconciliation bill as a vehicle for enacting extraneous provisions that have nothing to do with implementing the reconciliation instructions is enormous. To counter that temptation, the Senate in the mid-1980s adopted the Byrd rule, named after its creator, Sen. Robert C. Byrd, a Democrat from West Virginia. The rule prohibits extraneous matter in a reconciliation bill and requires a three-fifths vote to be waived (Tiefer 1989, 891–894; Gold et al. 1992, 302–303, 326). Since what is extraneous is not self-evident, a set of rules and precedents defining what does and does not fall under the Byrd rule has developed.

Application of the rule can have major policy consequences; in 1995, for example, Senate Democrats managed to knock out big chunks of the Republicans' welfare reform legislation from the reconciliation bill. Democrats used the Byrd rule to delete a provision from the 2005 reconciliation bill that granted hospitals immunity from malpractice liability if they refused to treat poor Medicaid recipients who could not afford a copayment (*CQW,* December 22, 2005, 3378). Because the conference report was altered by the application of the Byrd rule, the revised version had to be approved in the House; however, most House members had already left town for the Christmas break, so in this case, the move postponed final approval of the bill. In 2010 the Byrd rule dictated what could—and could not—be included in the bill completing the health care reform effort (see Chapter 8). As was the case in this instance, the Byrd rule often adds to the strains between the House and the Senate; House members bitterly complain that a Senate rule dictates what can and cannot be included in reconciliation bill conference reports.

The Byrd rule is only one example of the way in which the budget process has superimposed onto the two chambers' rules another set of highly complex rules. The Budget Act has given rise to a number of points of order, many of which require 60 votes to waive in the Senate. As the Senate Committee on the Budget explains, "Budget Act points of order are a parliamentary device by which any member of Congress can object to an amendment or piece of legislation on the grounds that it is not within the limits set out in the budget" (Committee on the Budget, United States Senate 1998, 16). Most often the points of order maintain that the legislation spends more than the budget resolution allows.

In the House the result is that special rules from the Rules Committee, which can waive budget rules, become even more important in managing the business of the chamber. In the Senate the budget process offers a legislative route protected from filibusters, but it also adds another set of decisions that require a supermajority. For example, the key decision in the Senate's approval of legislation implementing the General Agreement on Tariffs and Trade (GATT) in 1994 was not the vote on passage, which required a simple majority. Before the Senate could vote on approval, sixty votes were needed to waive a Senate budget rule requiring that new legislation be "budget neutral." Since the GATT agreement reduced tariffs, a form of taxes, it did not comply with that rule.

The Congressional Budget Office, created by the Budget Act, is required by law to produce a cost estimate for every bill reported by a congressional committee.[7] As the CBO's Web site states, "Used to determine whether the proposals are consistent with the budget resolution, CBO's cost estimates have become an integral part of the legislative process"

---

7. "Each cost estimate of pending legislation assesses (1) the potential impact on spending subject to appropriation (also known as discretionary spending), (2) any impact on mandatory spending (also known as direct spending), and (3) any impact on federal revenues . . ." (CBO Web site).

(www.cbo.gov). This is, if anything, an understatement. CBO estimates can provide the basis for a point of order. In addition, however, in an era of deficit worries, the estimates can become powerful political weapons. In the legislative battle over enacting health care reform, CBO cost estimates were central; at several points, an adverse report might well have permanently derailed the effort (see Chapter 8).

Congress, the President, and Summitry

The veto, presidents' status as head of their political party, and their capacity to command media attention allow presidents to play a major role in the legislative process. Many legislative proposals originate in the executive branch. Executive branch officials testify before congressional committees on most legislation, and they often are present during committee markups and during conference committee deliberations. In addition, executive branch officials let committee and party leaders know through private meetings and frequent informal contacts what the president wants and will accept.

Even if the president is from the other party and has very different policy preferences, the congressional majority party must pay some attention to his wishes if it wants to enact legislation. Presidents under such conditions of divided control have become adept at veto bargaining—at threatening a veto in order to extract the maximum in terms of substantive concessions from an opposition congressional majority. Of course, if the divergence in policy preferences is very wide, the result may be stalemate rather than compromise.

In recent years the president and Congress have resorted to "summits" when normal legislative processes have been incapable of producing a bill and the costs of failing to reach an agreement have been very high. (For a similar argument, see Gilmour 1990.) As relatively formal negotiations between congressional leaders and high-ranking administration officials representing the president directly, summits really have no official status; they occur when the president and the majority-party leadership decide to engage in such talks. During the 1980s and 1990s, normal legislative processes often ended in stalemate because of divided control, sharp differences in policy preferences, and the tough decisions that big deficits made necessary. The deficit and the budget process, especially as revised in the mid-1980s by the Gramm-Rudman automatic spending cut provisions, often provided the sense of emergency and the statutory deadline that made inaction politically costly.

In 1987, for example, the Democratic-controlled Congress and the Reagan administration were headed toward a potentially bloody and protracted showdown. Congressional Democrats believed some tax increases were essential and had included them in their budget resolution and in the reconciliation bill; Reagan was adamantly opposed. Then the stock market crashed and everyone realized a quick agreement was essential to restore confidence in the economy. Reagan called for a summit, congressional Democrats agreed, and a small group of high-level negotiators worked out a deal.

In 1990 the Gramm-Rudman requirement—that the deficit be cut by a specified large amount or a process known as sequestration would take place—meant that the costs if the president and Congress failed to reach an agreement would be very high. Sequestration would involve draconian automatic across-the-board spending cuts. Furthermore, estimates of the deficit were rising, and the economy showed signs of slowing. This situation made decisive action even more necessary.

Most independent experts agreed that a serious budget reduction package would have to include significant revenue increases, yet in decisions about taxes, the parties saw their future electoral prospects at stake. Attempting to shake the high-tax image that Republicans had successfully pinned on them, Democrats were determined to refuse to take the initiative—and the blame—in proposing new taxes. A great many Republicans believed that their "no new taxes" stance accounted for their party's electoral success; George H.W. Bush had pledged himself to that course during his 1988 campaign. As they saw it, Republicans had a great deal to lose by reneging on that promise.

Under these circumstances, normal processes were unlikely to produce results. So President Bush proposed a summit. The congressional party leaders appointed seventeen members as negotiators. The Treasury secretary, the head of OMB, and the White House chief of staff represented the president. The first meeting was held on May 17, 1990, and sessions continued through much of June. Estimates of the likely size of the budget deficit continued to increase, but no progress toward a plan to deal with it was made.

Finally, on September 30, the day before the beginning of the fiscal year, the president and congressional leaders announced that a deal had been reached. Even after Bush had conceded the need for some new revenues, differences over taxes and domestic spending cuts had continued to block progress. Eventually, the congressional negotiating group was pared down to include only the top party leaders, and it was this small group of key leaders and high-ranking administration officials that forged the agreement. Neither Bush nor the Democratic House leadership was able to sell that agreement to their troops, and it was defeated in the House. A revised version, however, was approved soon thereafter and sequestration was avoided (Sinclair 1991).

In 1995 a budget summit between the new majority congressional Republicans and President Clinton failed to produce an agreement; Republicans believed they could force Clinton to accept their priorities, which were very different from his own. Clinton not only refused but also won the public relations battle over who was to blame for the government shutdown that resulted from the impasse. In the end, the Republicans were forced to retreat. In 1997, after another summit, Clinton and the congressional Republicans managed to agree on a budget deal that balanced the budget. By then, Republican expectations about what they could extract from the president were more realistic and a booming economy made it much easier to reach the necessary deals (Sinclair 2007, chap. 11).

During the second half of the 1990s, reaching agreement on appropriations bills increasingly came to require summits. Even after the budget reached balance, President Clinton and the conservative Republicans who controlled both houses of Congress differed enough in policy preferences to prevent the normal process from being sufficient. Appropriations bills must pass every year or the government shuts down. Since the president can veto appropriations bills, Congress must either satisfy him or be able to muster a two-thirds vote to override. In the partisan 1990s, the latter was never a realistic possibility for Republicans; but satisfying Clinton meant spending more for programs they disliked. Often, only some of the appropriations bills could be enacted through the regular process; the rest had to be rolled into a big omnibus spending bill, the contents of which were negotiated between congressional leaders and high-ranking White House officials. In 1998, for example, eight of the thirteen appropriations bills were packaged into one omnibus bill; in 1999, five were, including the huge Labor, Health and Human Services, and Education appropriations bill.

Under difficult circumstances, a summit may offer the only hope of agreement between Congress and the president, but as a decision-making mechanism it is relatively expensive for party leaders and the institution; it not only short-circuits the normal decision-making process but also excludes most members and is therefore likely to lead to discontent. Furthermore, summits are not a magic bullet; as the 1995 example shows so dramatically, if the president and the congressional majority are too far apart in their legislative preferences, and if one or both overestimates its bargaining strength, the result may be stalemate, not agreement.

When the president and the congressional majority share a partisan affiliation, summits are much less likely to be necessary. The White House and the majority-party leaderships in the House and Senate communicate continuously and work together regularly. The president and most members of his party in Congress share policy preferences. Consequently, informal processes are likely to be adequate for reaching agreements. Not surprisingly, there were no summits during George W. Bush's first six years as president or, arguably, during Obama's first two.

The 2008 stimulus bill, the Emergency Economic Stabilization Act of 2008 (which set up the Troubled Asset Relief Program, or TARP), and the tax cut extensions deal in late 2010 were negotiated between the White House and congressional leaders of the other party, but, except for the Stabilization Act, the top party leaders did most of the deal making, so the process was less formal—and even less participatory—than the summits of the 1980s and 1990s. The tax cut extensions deal was, in fact, largely negotiated between Obama and Senate minority leader Mitch McConnell. It may be that summitry of the form described earlier represented a transitory phase; with the greater centralization of power in the hands of the congressional party leadership, the bargaining group may frequently include solely the party leaders as representatives of their members. In any case, with the return of divided government, the president is likely to have to engage in more cross-party negotiations. The tax cut extensions deal, although negotiated while Democrats still controlled both houses of Congress, was made after the 2010 elections and in anticipation of Republican control of the House and increased strength in the Senate.

What Is the Regular Process?

The textbook diagram of how a bill becomes a law no longer accurately describes the legislative process on major bills. In the contemporary Congress there are many variations; one can more accurately speak of legislative processes in the plural than of a single cut-and-dried set of steps through which all measures proceed.

While my step-by-step discussion of the legislative process makes the variety obvious, it does not yield any precise sense of the cumulative impact of these procedures and practices. That is best conveyed by a systematic analysis of the legislative process on major legislation. How many of the special process variations characterized the process on major legislation? How frequently did such legislation follow the old textbook process?

For each of the 525 major measures in the Congresses from the late 1980s through 2010 for which I have data, I counted the number of special procedures and practices that the legislation encountered as it worked its way through the House. The procedures and practices enumerated were multiple referral, omnibus legislation, legislation resulting from a legislative-executive branch summit, the bypassing of committees, postcommittee adjustments, and consideration under a restrictive rule.

TABLE 5.1   Special Procedures and Practices in the House and Senate on Major Legislation, 1987–2010

	Percentage of major measures in which the legislative process was characterized by special procedures and practices	
Number of special procedures and practices	House[a]	Senate[b]
0	16	26
1	30	31
2	32	27
3 or more	22	16

[a]The enumerated special procedures and practices that the legislation may have encountered as it worked its way through the House are multiple referral, omnibus legislation, legislation resulting from legislative-executive branch summit, the bypassing of committees, postcommittee adjustments, and consideration under a restrictive rule.

[b]For the Senate essentially the same procedures and practices that were counted for the House, except consideration under a restrictive rule, were enumerated (see note 9). Also counted was whether the bill ran into filibuster trouble and whether it was subject to an amending marathon (ten or more amending roll calls).

Source: Computed by the author.

The House legislative process on the 525 major bills of these recent Congresses displayed at least one of these characteristics in 84 percent of the cases and two or more in 54 percent (see Table 5.1). To talk about the "regular order" in the House as the absence of these characteristics is no longer accurate, at least on major legislation. And these figures—and the comparable ones for the Senate—actually underestimate the prevalence of special or unorthodox practices and procedures, because a number of bills included in the calculations did not get far enough through the legislative process to encounter some of the practices counted.

Another perspective is provided by calculating the proportion of legislation that followed the once regular process: legislation that was reported by one committee, that was not omnibus nor the result of a summit, that was not subject to postcommittee adjustments, and that was considered on the floor under an open rule. In the House the legislative process on less than 5 percent of major legislation—25 out of 525 bills—in these recent Congresses met these criteria.[8] The "regular order" is no longer the norm; on major legislation it has become the rare exception.

---

8. This figure is less than the 16 percent without any of the special process characteristics in Table 5.1 because the table includes measures that did not get to the House floor and measures considered under procedures other than rules—mostly suspension of the rules.

To assess the frequency of the new procedures and practices in the Senate, I counted the same characteristics as for the House, excepting, of course, the use of restrictive rules.[9] In the Senate these special procedures and practices are somewhat less pervasive than in the House; the legislative process on a little more than half (54 percent) of major bills displayed at least one special characteristic, and 14 percent displayed two or more. This measure, which parallels the one constructed for the House, excludes the most notable changes in the legislative process in the Senate: the increase in floor amending activity and the more frequent use of extended debate. When a second Senate measure of special procedures and practices is created by also counting whether the bill ran into filibuster trouble or was subject to an amending marathon (ten or more amending roll calls), 74 percent of major bills display at least one and 43 percent display two or more special process characteristics (see Table 5.1). In the Senate, as in the House, the legislative process on major legislation frequently no longer conforms to what we still tend to think of as the normal process.

In both chambers, then, the legislative process on major legislation has changed; such legislation is now more likely than not to traverse an unorthodox or nonstandard course. How and why this happened is the subject of the next chapter.

---

9. Instead of counting only technical multiple referral, I also counted bills on which more than one committee worked as subject to an unorthodox process or procedure.

Why and How the Legislative Process Changed

W HY DID THE "TEXTBOOK" LEGISLATIVE PROCESS, which seemed so routinized and entrenched, change so much? In this chapter I argue that the modifications and innovations can be seen as responses to problems and opportunities that members—as individuals or collectively—confronted, problems and opportunities that arose from changes in institutional structure or challenges in the political environment.

The story is complex, and its various strands intertwine in intricate ways, but three factors can be analytically isolated as key: internal reforms that changed the distribution of influence in both chambers in the 1970s; the institution of the congressional budget process, an internal-process reform with sufficiently far-reaching effects to deserve separate treatment; and a political environment in the 1980s and early 1990s characterized by divided control, big deficits, and ideological hostility to the legislative goals of the congressional Democratic Party. I discuss each of these briefly and then analyze how the legislative process was affected by them.

Unorthodox lawmaking, I argue, predates the extreme partisan polarization that characterizes contemporary politics. Yet polarization has powerfully affected the form that changes with other origins have taken. I close the chapter with an analysis of how partisan polarization under both Republican and Democratic control has shaped the legislative process since the mid-1990s.

From Decentralization to Individualism in the Senate

In the U.S. Senate of the 1950s and before, influence was decentralized but unequally distributed, with committee chairs and other senior members, who were predominantly conservative, exercising the lion's share. Although Democrats were the majority party (except for the first Eisenhower Congress [1953–1954]), southerners, who were mainly conservative, made up a substantial part of the party membership and, being more senior than their northern colleagues, held a disproportionate share of committee leadership positions. The Senate of this era was a relatively closed and inward-looking institution. Typical senators specialized in the issues that came before their committees and participated meagerly on the floor; they were deferential to their seniors, loyal to the institution, and restrained in the use of the powers that Senate rules confer on the individual (Matthews 1960; Sinclair 1989).

Senate rules then, as now, allowed unlimited debate and, in most cases, unlimited amending activity. The restraint that characterized the Senate of this period was not a function of rules; rather it depended on norms—unwritten rules of behavior—and on a political environment in which acting with restraint was relatively costless to senators.

That began to change in the late 1950s. The 1958 elections brought into the Senate a big class of northern liberal Democrats who had won competitive elections on a platform promising action; succeeding elections through the mid-1960s augmented the number of such members. These senators could not afford to wait to make their mark, as the old norms had demanded; both their policy and their reelection goals dictated immediate and extensive activism.

An activist style based on participation in a broader range of issues and on the floor as well as in committee became attractive to more and more senators as the political environment and the Washington political community changed radically in the 1960s and 1970s. New issues and an enormous growth in the number of groups active in Washington meant that senators were eagerly sought as champions of groups' causes. The news media played an increasingly important role in politics and needed credible sources to represent issue positions and to offer commentary. These developments made the role of outward-looking policy entrepreneur available to more senators. Successfully playing that role brought a senator a Washington reputation as a player, media attention, and possibly even a shot at the presidency.

With this great increase in the incentives to exploit fully the powers that Senate rules confer on the individual, senators began to offer many more amendments on the floor and to use extended debate more often. As a result, the Senate floor became a more active decision-making arena. The proportion of legislation subject to high amending activity (ten or more amending roll calls) was tiny in the 1950s; for the 84th and 86th Congresses of 1955–1956 and 1959–1960, it averaged 3 percent. During

TABLE 6.1   Increase in Filibusters and Cloture Votes, 1951–2010

Years	Congress	Filibusters per Congress	Cloture votes per Congress	Successful cloture votes per Congress
1951–1960	82–86	1.0	0.4	0
1961–1970	87–91	4.6	5.2	0.8
1971–1980	92–96	11	22	9
1981–1986	97–99	17	23	10
1987–1992	100–102	27	39	15
1993–2006	103–109	30	53	21
2007–2008	110	54	112	61
2009–2010	111	54	91	63

Sources: Data for 82nd–102nd Congresses: Congressional Research Service, comp., "A Look at the Senate Filibuster," in Democratic Study Group Special Report, June 13, 1994, app. B; Norman Ornstein, Thomas Mann, and Michael Malbin, *Vital Statistics on Congress 1993–1994* (Washington, D.C.: CQ Press, 1994), 162. Data for 103rd Congress: Richard S. Beth, "Cloture in the Senate, 103d Congress," memorandum, Congressional Research Service, June 23, 1995. Data for 104th–108th Congresses: *Congressional Quarterly Almanac* for the years 1995–2007 (Washington, D.C.: Congressional Quarterly); 108th–111th Congresses: *CQ* online.

the 1960s and 1970s, it rose to a mean of 8 percent per Congress, and in the 1980s it averaged 15 percent (Sinclair 1989, 115).[1]

As senators became much more willing to exploit their prerogative of extended debate, filibusters, both overt and covert, increasingly became a routine part of the legislative process in the Senate. As Table 6.1 shows, filibusters were once rare; in the 1950s a typical Congress saw one filibuster. By the 1970s more than ten filibusters occurred per Congress on average, and by the late 1980s and early 1990s filibusters were taking place at a rate of more than one a month.[2] As the number of filibusters grew, so did attempts to stop them by invoking cloture; cloture votes became an ordinary part of the legislative process. While cloture was successfully invoked fairly often, passing legislation that was at all controversial increasingly required sixty votes.

Reform and Its Legacy in the House

In the House, changes in chamber and majority-party rules during the 1970s transformed the distribution of influence (Dodd and Oppenheimer

---

1. These figures are based on data for even-numbered Congresses from the 88th to the 96th Congress and for all Congresses from the 97th through the 99th.

2. See Chapter 3 and Beth 1995 for cautions about these data.

1977; Sinclair 1983; Smith 1989; Rohde 1991). Even more than in the Senate, legislative influence in the House had been vested in powerful and often conservative committee leaders—often southerners—over whom party leaders and members had little control. Reformers, who were primarily liberal Democrats, objected to the conservative policy this system produced and to the limited opportunities for participation it afforded rank-and-file members.

Elections throughout the 1960s changed the composition of the Democratic Party in the House, as they did in the Senate, increasing the number of northern Democrats, many of whom were liberal reformers, and decreasing the number of conservative southerners. Through a series of rules changes mostly instituted between 1969 and 1975, reformers correspondingly changed the distribution of influence. Powers and resources were shifted from committee chairs down to subcommittee chairs and rank-and-file members and up to the party leadership. For example, the power to appoint subcommittee chairs was taken away from the committee chair and given to the majority-party members of the committee; subcommittees were ensured adequate budget and staff. Rather than securing their positions automatically through their seniority on the committee, committee chairs had to win approval by majority vote on a secret ballot of the majority-party membership. Junior members gained resources, especially staff, that enormously increased their ability to participate actively in the legislative process. The Speaker, the leader of the majority party, was given the power to select the majority-party members of the Rules Committee, a greater say in the assignment of members to other committees, and new powers over the referral of bills.

During the same period, the House adopted "sunshine" rules, which opened the legislative process to greater public scrutiny. Recorded votes became possible—and easy to force—in the Committee of the Whole, where the amending process takes place.[3] Most committee markup sessions and conference committee meetings were opened to the public. The greater visibility of congressional decision making increased members' incentives for activism.

These reforms had far-reaching direct and indirect effects. By reducing the power and autonomy of the committees, the reforms made legislating more difficult for the majority party. To be sure, Democratic reformers had often been unhappy with the sort of legislation conservative-led committees had produced. By the late 1970s, however, the committee

---

3. Before 1971 votes in the Committee of the Whole were either voice votes or teller votes, in which the members voting "aye" and those voting "nay" walked by "tellers," who counted them but did not record who voted how.

chairs and the membership of the most powerful committees were more representative of the Democratic Party than they had been earlier, and Republicans and dissident Democrats had become adept at using floor amendments to make political points and confront mainstream Democrats with politically difficult votes. Compromises carefully crafted in committee were picked apart on the floor, and floor sessions stretched on interminably.

The number of floor amendments decided on a teller or recorded vote had risen gradually from 55 in 1955–1956 to 107 in 1969–1970. With the institution of the recorded teller, it jumped to 195 in 1971–1972, and with electronic voting it jumped again to 351 in 1973–1974 (Smith 1989, 33). During the 94th Congress (1975–1976), 372 such amendments were offered on the floor, and during the 95th, 439. In 1979 floor consideration of the budget resolution took nine days, during which time 50 amendments were offered (Sinclair 1983, 180).

Democrats began to look to their party leaders, the only central leaders in the chamber, to counter these problems. The leaders responded by innovating in ways that led to alterations in the legislative process. The leadership became more involved with legislation before it reached the floor, and this involvement increasingly took the form of negotiating substantive changes in the legislation, often at the postcommittee stage, in order to produce a bill that could pass the chamber. To respond to the barrage of amendments offered on the floor, the leadership developed special rules into powerful devices for structuring floor decision making.

Budget Reform

When President Richard Nixon aggressively challenged Congress's power of the purse, Congress responded by passing the Congressional Budget and Impoundment Control Act of 1974. Presidents had been encroaching on Congress's budgetary powers for decades; lacking a mechanism for making comprehensive decisions, Congress had long used the president's budget as its point of departure for budgetary decision making and usually altered it only marginally. However, when Nixon claimed the right to impound—that is, not spend—congressionally appropriated funds, the Congress had to respond or acquiesce in a severe diminution of its powers. Nixon argued that congressional appropriations were just ceilings and that he was not required to spend any of the money Congress appropriated. In effect, he was arguing that Congress had only negative powers: Congress might be able to prevent the president from doing something by not appropriating funds, but it could not force a president to carry out a policy he opposed.

The Budget Act went far beyond devising a procedure to control impoundments: the budget process that it established provided a mechanism by which comprehensive policymaking in Congress became possible. During its first few years, however, the budget process was not used in that way. In the House the battles over budget resolutions were hard fought and highly partisan; debate did turn on the political parties' different priorities, but the resolutions themselves did not call for significant policy change (Ellwood and Thurber 1981; Schick 1980).

Reconciliation instructions that mandated committees to make changes in legislation under their jurisdiction were first included in the budget resolution in 1980 (Sinclair 1983, 181–190). Frighteningly high inflation in January 1980 convinced President Jimmy Carter and the Democratic congressional party leadership that budget cuts needed to be made, and quickly. The ordinary legislative process, they decided, would take too long and be subject to delay by interests adversely affected by the cuts. Therefore, they decided to use the budget process and to include reconciliation instructions in the first budget resolution. Doing so was highly controversial (in part because the Budget Act envisioned that such instructions would be included in the second budget resolution, which in this and most other cases would be too late), and the committees subject to instructions objected vigorously. Nevertheless, the resolution with the instructions passed, and the committees did comply. To do otherwise was to defy the will of Congress as expressed in its budget resolution.

Although the policy changes required by the 1980 budget resolution were modest by later standards, the experience made clear to perceptive participants that, under certain circumstances at least, the budget process was a mechanism available to central leaders for making comprehensive policy change. David Stockman, a Republican member of the House from Michigan from 1977 to January 1981, was one of those perceptive participants. As President Ronald Reagan's first head of the Office of Management and Budget, he suggested using the budget process to enact Reagan's economic program in 1981 (Stockman 1986). The administration-supported budget resolution included instructions to committees to make substantial changes in policy; supporters forced a single vote on them as a whole and then packaged the policy changes into one massive reconciliation bill, where again the key vote was whether to accept or reject them as a whole. This strategy enabled Reagan and his supporters to achieve major policy change quickly in a system resistant to such change.

The budget process has had wide-reaching effects on the legislative process. In the years since 1981, budget politics have remained at center stage. The attempt to control the big deficits Reagan's economic program created shaped the politics of the 1980s and most of the 1990s. Even more significant, the budget process has become the tool of choice for those attempting to bring about comprehensive policy change.

A Hostile Political Climate as a Force for Innovation: The 1980s and Early 1990s

Both the House and Senate entered the 1980s beset by problems resulting from changes in their internal distribution of influence. The highly individualistic Senate, in which each senator was accorded extraordinary latitude, was very good at agenda setting and publicizing problems, but it was less well structured for legislative decision making. The House, which had greatly increased rank-and-file members' opportunities for participation, also had problems legislating, although its central leadership had begun to develop reasonably effective responses.

The political climate of the 1980s and early 1990s exacerbated the problems of legislating, especially for the Democratic House. Ronald Reagan was a conservative, confrontational president whose policy views were far from those of congressional Democrats, and the policy preferences of his successor, George H.W. Bush, were not much closer. In 1981, Reagan and his congressional allies steamrolled the Democratic House majority and enacted sweeping policy changes over futile Democratic protests. Thereafter, Reagan was never as politically strong again, but he and Bush still had the bully pulpit and the veto.

The growing ideological polarization of the parties exacerbated the conflict. Reagan's nomination had signaled the Republican Party's move to the right. The congressional party, especially the House Republican Party, had begun to change in the mid- and late 1970s. Not only were fewer moderates being elected, but also more hard-edged, ideological conservatives were entering the House. The elections of 1978 brought a Republican freshman from Georgia named Newt Gingrich to the House.

The Democratic Party in the 1980s became more ideologically homogeneous as its southern contingent changed. Republicans won southern seats, often ones previously held by the most conservative Democrats, and the southern Democrats who remained depended for reelection on the votes of African Americans, who tend to be liberal. The Republican Party's increasing conservatism also made any ideological differences that remained among Democrats seem smaller.

The voting cohesion of House Democrats began to increase after the 1982 elections, and in the late 1980s and early 1990s it reached levels unprecedented in the post-World War II era. A member's party unity score is simply the frequency with which the member votes with his or her party colleagues on votes that pit majorities of the two parties against each other.

FIGURE 6.1   Distance between the Parties on Partisan Votes, 1955–2010

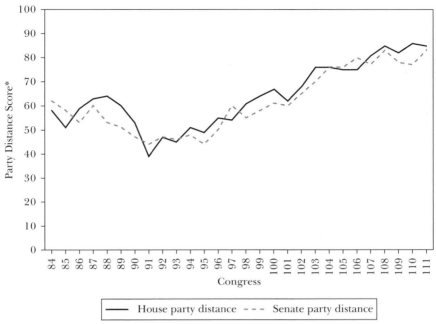

* Party Distance Score = mean Democratic Party voting score − (100 − mean Republican Party voting score)

For the period 1951 through 1970, House Democrats' average party unity score was 78 percent; it fell to 74 percent for the period 1971 to 1982.[4] Then after the 1982 elections the scores began rising again and averaged 86 percent for the 1983–1994 period. During this same period, the proportion of party votes also increased, averaging 56 percent compared with 37 percent during the 1971–1982 period. During the 103rd Congress, a majority of Democrats opposed a majority of Republicans on 64 percent of House recorded votes (Rohde 1991; *Congressional Quarterly Almanac,* various years).

Figure 6.1 illustrates the polarization of the congressional parties since the early 1980s. Party voting scores can be used to construct a measure of the difference or distance between the parties. If, on average,

---

4. Party votes are recorded votes on which a majority of Democrats voted against a majority of Republicans. A member's party unity score is the percentage of party votes on which he or she voted with a majority of his or her party colleagues.

85 percent of Democrats voted against 90 percent of Republicans on party votes, then on average 10 percent of Republicans voted with the 85 percent of Democrats and the difference between these figures (75 = 85–10) provides an indicator of the distance between the parties. As Figure 6.1 shows, that distance increased enormously.

During the 1980s, then, an increasingly cohesive House Democratic majority faced a hostile president, a Republican Senate, and a more aggressive and conservative Republican minority. After 1981 big deficits became chronic and severely restricted feasible policy options. Democrats often found themselves in the position of fighting to protect past policy successes. Partisan conflict and stalemate in Washington fed public cynicism about government's ability to handle effectively the problems facing the country; many citizens concluded that government could not do anything right. Passing legislation that majority Democrats considered satisfactory became very difficult in such a climate. Even enacting legislation to keep the government going was hard, both because of the ideological gulf between congressional Democrats and Republican presidents and because the legislation frequently required making unpalatable decisions. This tough climate forced further innovation in the legislative process, especially in the House.

How Internal Reform and a Hostile Climate Spawned Unorthodox Lawmaking

Internal reforms, the hostile political climate, and other lesser changes in the environment altered the context in which members of Congress functioned. As they and their leaders sought to advance their goals within this altered context, they changed the legislative process. Sometimes changes were brought about by formal revisions in chamber rules; more frequently, they were the result of alterations in practices.

Multiple Referral

As our society and economy evolve over time, the issues at the center of controversy change. In the 1950s and early 1960s, for example, environmental protection was an obscure issue, and congressional attempts to deal with it mostly entailed programs to help municipalities build water treatment plants; by the 1970s the environment had become a highly salient issue, and Congress was considering ambitious legislation to protect endangered species and to force automakers and other polluters to clean up the air. As new issues arise and old ones change, the fit between the prominent issues on the congressional agenda and the committee system becomes increasingly poor. Yet Congress, especially the House, has great difficulty in realigning committee jurisdictions. Taking away jurisdiction from a committee reduces its clout; both committee members and affected interest groups that have established good working relationships with the committee will fight the change. Since committee membership is a considerably more important basis of members' influence in the House than in the Senate, realigning jurisdictions so that they fit better with the issues of the day is harder in the House than in the Senate.

By the early 1970s committee jurisdictions that had last been significantly overhauled in 1946 were seriously outmoded; jurisdiction over a number of key issues—energy, the environment, and health, for example—was spread over a number of committees, leading to a lack of coordination and numerous turf fights. The House attempted to reform its committee jurisdictions in the mid-1970s but largely failed (Davidson and Oleszek 1977). The Senate's attempt at committee reform in the late 1970s was considerably more successful (Davidson 1981).

Unable to realign committee jurisdictions and driven by reform-minded members' desire to increase opportunities for broad participation in the legislative process, the House in 1975 changed its rules to allow multiple referral of legislation (Davidson and Oleszek 1992).[5] In the first Congress with multiple referral, 1975–1976, 6.5 percent of the measures introduced were multiply referred. Over time and driven by the same forces that led to its institution, multiply referred legislation became an increasingly prominent part of the House workload (see Table 6.2). On average 12 percent of measures were multiply referred during the five Congresses between 1977 and 1986; the frequency has risen to an average of 20 percent in Congresses since the mid-1980s.

For major legislation, the increase has been steeper. Multiply referred measures have made up a considerably greater proportion of major legislation than they have of all legislation. Beginning in the late 1980s, about 30 percent of major measures were multiply referred. In the 104th Congress, however, 51 percent of major measures were referred to more than one

---

5. Actually, even before then, something quite similar to multiple referral occurred under specialized circumstances; when legislation referred to a committee other than Ways and Means contained a revenue component, that section would be sent to the tax committee. In the 91st Congress (1969–1970), for example, three bills primarily under the jurisdiction of a committee other than Ways and Means also were referred to Ways and Means for consideration of their revenue sections; thus the Interstate and Foreign Commerce Committee was mostly responsible for the Airport Development Act, but the trust fund and tax provisions were handled by Ways and Means.

TABLE 6.2   Multiple Referral in the House and Senate, 94th–111th Congresses

		House		Senate	
Congress*	Years	Percentage of all bills	Percentage of major legislation	Percentage of all bills	Percentage of major legislation
94th	1975–1976	6.5	8.6	3.2	5.2
95th–99th	1977–1986	12.3	17.9	2.6	5.0
100–108	1987–2004	20.0		1.6	
100–110	1987–2010		33.8		4.1

*For major legislation, selected Congresses

Sources: For all bills, compiled by Thomas P. Carr, analyst with the Government and Finance Division of the Congressional Research Service using the Legislative Information System (LIS). For major legislation, compiled by the author.

committee—despite a rule change intended to rein in multiple referral. Since then the proportion has usually been about a third.

Multiple referral of legislation has always been possible in the Senate through unanimous consent. The Senate, however, did manage to realign its committee jurisdictions during the 1970s, and because senators can more easily influence legislation outside the committee setting than House members can, they have less incentive to insist on a referral (Fenno 1973; Sinclair 1989). As a consequence, the referral of legislation to more than one committee continues to be much less frequent in the Senate.

Major measures are more likely than ordinary bills to be sent to more than one committee, but even on important and controversial bills, formal multiple referral is much less frequent in the Senate than in the House. In keeping with the Senate's tendency toward less formal procedure, several committees sometimes consider different bills on the same topic. This can create complications much like those that stem from formal multiple referral.

Committees as Shapers of Legislation

By reducing the power of committee chairs and increasing the opportunities and incentives for rank-and-file members to participate in the legislative process, the House reforms of the 1970s diminished the capacity of committees to pass their legislation without change. No longer were bills protected by a powerful chair with the weapons to retaliate against members who challenged legislation in committee or on the floor or by voting rules that prevented most recorded votes on floor amendments. Junior committee members and members not on the committee now had the staff and the access to information that made their participation feasible. The increased prevalence of multiple referral lessened committee autonomy; committee leaders were not always capable of resolving the conflicts among their committees, yet unresolved intercommittee conflicts endangered legislation on the floor. The reformers had given Democratic majority-party leaders some new tools, and, as the problems the reforms had wrought became increasingly evident, the now more ideologically homogeneous Democrats began to expect their leaders to use those tools to engineer passage of legislation broadly supported by the Democratic membership.

To respond to their members' demands, the Democratic leadership became more involved in the legislative process in the period before legislation reached the floor. A bill's substance is by far the most important determinant of its fate on the floor. As it became more difficult for the committee or committees of jurisdiction to write a bill that could pass on the floor, the party leaders stepped in more often to help.

Party leaders, of course, may involve themselves informally on legislation during committee consideration; anecdotal and interview evidence indicates that such intervention is much more frequent than it used to be (Sinclair 1995). That kind of involvement is, however, impossible to document systematically across time. Substantive adjustments to legislation after it is reported—whether engineered by the party leadership or others—can be counted with more precision.[6]

Postcommittee adjustments were rare in the prereform era. In the 91st Congress (1969–1970), for example, the House leadership was involved in making an adjustment on one bill but only after a veto. Committees were quite successful on the floor, lessening the need for tinkering after they had finished their work. Even when committees lost on the floor and when that loss was no big surprise, leaders seem to have made no attempt to head off the floor defeat by substantive adjustments in the legislation. Presumably, the committee leaders had done what they could and would in committee and the party leaders lacked the tools to get involved.

In the 94th Congress (1975–1976) there were two clear instances of postcommittee adjustments to major measures; both cases involved the

---

6. I ascertained the presence or absence of a postcommittee adjustment and whether it was directed by the party leadership by doing a case study of each of the major measures for the selected Congresses. The case studies relied primarily on the *CQ Weekly* and the *Congressional Quarterly Almanac*. Thus instances not ascertainable from the public record could have been missed; however, when I had independent information from interviews or participant observation available, they confirmed the coding done on the basis of the written record.

new budget process. In 1975 and again in 1976 it became evident that the budget resolution as reported by the Budget Committee would not pass. In each case the party leadership stepped in and crafted an amendment to the budget resolution to ensure passage in a form acceptable to most Democrats.

In the 1980s and early 1990s the hostile political climate made passing legislation Democrats wanted difficult. Big deficits made it harder for committee leaders to forge broadly acceptable deals; a climate of scarcity begets zero-sum politics in which one group's gain is perceived as a loss by other groups and fewer "sweeteners" to induce support are available. As committee Democrats tried to craft a bill that was passable yet as close as possible to their preferred policy position, they could easily misjudge what was passable. Furthermore, changes in the political environment after the committee had reported—in the salience of the issue or in the public's response to presidential rhetoric—could alter what would pass. Leadership counts of members' voting intentions often showed not enough support for the committee-reported bill. Therefore, major legislation frequently required substantive alterations. As important legislation increasingly involved a number of committees, the compromises that needed to be made among the committees to bring a passable bill to the floor were often beyond the capacity of committee leaders to negotiate. In such a climate postcommittee adjustments, almost always directed by the party leadership, became almost routine (see Table 6.3).

The same forces—internal reforms that decreased the power and autonomy of committees and empowered party leaders, and a hostile political climate that exacerbated the difficulties the reforms had produced— led to committees increasingly being bypassed altogether. To be sure, not every instance of the bypassing of committees is directed by the leadership; occasionally a discharge petition is successful. Most often, however, when a committee is bypassed, it is the party leadership that made the decision, although not necessarily over the committee's opposition. Sometimes a committee is bypassed with its members' full concurrence simply to speed the process—when identical legislation passed in the previous Congress, for example.

In the prereform period and through the 1970s, committees were almost never bypassed in the House. In the 87th and 91st Congresses (1961–1962; 1969–1970), for example, the committee was never actually bypassed in the House, although in one instance in the 91st the committee reported only because of a threat of discharge. (That case, an organized crime control bill forced out of a reluctant Judiciary Committee, is counted as a bypass in Table 6.3.) In the 95th Congress (1977–1978), the House Agriculture Committee was effectively bypassed when the House

TABLE 6.3   The Changing Role of Committees in the Legislative Process, Selected Congresses, 87th–111th

Congress	Years	Percentage of major legislation on which the committee of jurisdiction was bypassed		Percentage of major legislation subject to postcommittee adjustment*	
		House	Senate	House	Senate
87th	1961–1962	0	6	4	4
89th	1965–1966	2	6	8	4
91st	1969–1970	2	4	7	9
94th	1975–1976	0	4	15	4
95th	1977–1978	2	6	13	20
97th	1981–1982	7	2	23	27
100th	1987–1988	19	14	39	20
101st	1989–1990	14	12	39	39
103rd	1993–1994	2	8	31	38
104th	1995–1996	13	28	48	57
105th	1997–1998	10	14	35	30
107th	2001–2002	17	41	22	22
108th	2003–2004	26	31	20	24
109th	2005–2006	21	22	39	31
110th	2007–2008	30	35	48	41
111th	2009–2010	34	45	39	42

*Of bills that were reported from committee

Source: Compiled by the author.

agreed to go directly to conference on a Senate-passed emergency farm bill. As Table 6.3 shows, bypassing the committee has become considerably more frequent since the early 1980s. The circumstances vary widely, but in most cases the decision to bypass the committee is a majority-party leadership decision. Leaders became more willing to use informal task forces or even less formal working groups to work out the compromises necessary to pass legislation and to take a direct hand in the process themselves.

If internal reforms had unintended consequences that made legislating more difficult for the House, the Senate's individualism run rampant made the House's problems look picayune. Furthermore, the Senate, unlike the House, did not give its central leadership new tools for dealing with the problems.

In the Senate as in the House, one response was an increase in postcommittee adjustments to legislation. They were rare in the 1960s and 1970s. In the 1980s and 1990s postcommittee adjustments became much more frequent. The Senate majority leader often engineered or at least oversaw the devising of postcommittee changes in legislation, but committee leaders and even individual senators sometimes took on the task, reflecting the wide dispersion of power in the Senate.

Although the frequency of postcommittee adjustments declined a bit in the 103rd Congress in the House, in the Senate it did not. For the majority-rule House, unified control made legislating somewhat easier; at least amassing large margins to dissuade the president from vetoing the legislation was no longer necessary. The Senate, in contrast, still needed sixty votes to pass most controversial legislation. With the return of divided control in the 104th, postcommittee adjustments became more frequent again in both chambers.

In the Senate the frequency with which committees are bypassed also has increased. Committees were seldom bypassed on major legislation before the mid-1980s, although recalcitrant committees occasionally were bypassed on major bills. In the 89th Congress (1965–1966), for example, the Judiciary Committee was bypassed on a highly controversial open housing bill; nevertheless, civil rights opponents managed to kill it by filibustering the motion to proceed.

The frequency of bypassing increased substantially with the 100th Congress and has remained well above its previous level since then. The first two Congresses of the twenty-first century (the 107th and 108th) saw extremely narrow margins of control in the Senate. When the 107th Congress convened in January 2001, it was split evenly between Republicans and Democrats, and only Vice President Dick Cheney's role as president of the Senate allowed Republicans to organize the chamber. When in June 2001, Sen. Jim Jeffords of Vermont left the Republican Party and began caucusing with the Democrats, Democrats became the Senate's majority party. In the 2002 elections, Republicans won enough seats to reclaim majority status, but just barely, with fifty-one senators. Those difficult circumstances, made more problematic by high partisan polarization, led to the extraordinarily high rate of committees being bypassed, as is evident in Table 6.3. Democrats too faced politically complex circumstances after they narrowly regained the majority in the 2006 elections and then in the first Congress of the Barack Obama presidency, and the rate of committees being bypassed shot up again after a brief drop in the 109th Congress.

Special Rules in the House

In the prereform era most legislation was brought to the House floor under a simple open rule that allowed all germane amendments. Tax bills and often other legislation from the Ways and Means Committee were considered under a closed rule that allowed no amendments (except those offered by the committee itself); tax legislation was regarded as too complex and too politically tempting a target to allow floor amendments. In the 91st Congress (1969–1970), for example, 80 percent of the major legislation was considered under simple open rules; 16 percent—primarily bills reported by the Ways and Means Committee—came to the floor under closed rules. Only two measures were considered under rules with provisions more complex than simply allowing all germane amendments or barring all amendments.

The reforms made legislation much more vulnerable to alteration on the floor. With rank-and-file members having greater incentives and resources for offering amendments on the floor, the number of amendments offered and pushed to a roll call vote shot up. Committee bills were more frequently picked apart on the floor, members often were forced to go on the record on votes hard to explain to constituents back home, and floor sessions stretched on late into the night.

The reformers had given the Democratic leadership the power to name the Democratic members and the chair of the Rules Committee and had thereby made the committee an arm of the leadership. In the late 1970s some Democrats began to pressure their leaders to use special rules to bring floor proceedings under control. Forty Democrats wrote Speaker Thomas "Tip" O'Neill Jr., D-MA, in 1979 to ask that he make more use of restrictive rules in order to curtail frequent late-night sessions (Smith 1989, 40–41).

As Figure 6.2 shows, as late as 1977–1978 (95th Congress) most special rules were still open rules; only 15 percent restricted amendments in some way. As Democratic members began to comprehend the costs of the wide-open amending process fostered by the reforms and to demand that their leaders do something about these costs, the frequency of restrictive rules increased. In the hostile climate of the 1980s and early 1990s, restrictive rules were used more and more often. Holding together compromises and protecting members from political heat became more difficult and more essential, and leaders, in response to their members' demands, developed special rules into powerful devices for shaping the choices members faced on the floor. By 1993–1994 (103rd Congress), 70 percent of special rules restricted amendments to some extent.

The new Republican majority in the 104th Congress had promised during the campaign to pass an ambitious agenda, much of it in the first one hundred days. Before the election, however, House Republicans, including their leadership, had vehemently denounced restrictive rules and also had promised not to use them. And the proportion of all rules that were restrictive did go down in the 104th, although Democrats claimed that Republicans manipulated the figures by considering under open rules some uncontroversial legislation that should have

FIGURE 6.2   Change in the Character of House Special Rules, 1977–2010

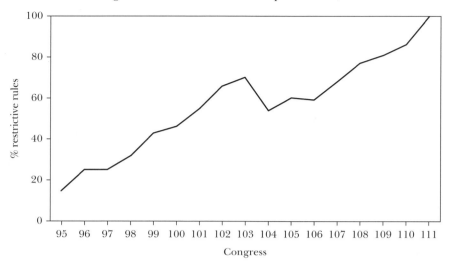

Rules for initial consideration of legislation, except rules on appropriations bills that only waive points of order. Restrictive rules are those that limit the germane amendments that can be offered and include so-called modified open and modified closed, as well as completely closed rules and rules providing for consideration in the House as opposed to the Committee of the Whole.

Source: Compiled by Donald Wolfensberger, formerly minority and then majority counsel, Committee on Rules, now director of the Congress Project of the Wilson Center, from the Rules Committee calendars and surveys of activities and by the author from Rules Committee list of rules at rules.house.gov.

been considered under the suspension procedure. In the next Congress, the use of restrictive rules on all legislation rose, and it has continued to do so ever since, reaching 81 percent in the 109th Congress (2005–2006). When they took the House majority in the 2006 elections, Democrats, like the Republicans in 1994, promised to open up the floor process, but they too continued the trend toward ever-increasing restrictive rules; in the 111th Congress, 100 percent of the rules were at least somewhat restrictive and only one was a modified open rule.

When only major measures are examined, the trend toward restrictive rules is even stronger. Table 6.4 displays the percentage of major measures that were considered under substantially restrictive rules—that is, structured, modified closed, or closed rules (see Chapter 2, page 28 for definitions). These sorts of rules limit the amendments that may

TABLE 6.4   Substantially Restrictive Rules on Major Legislation, Selected
Congresses, 89th–111th

Congress	Years	Percentage structured, modified closed, or closed
89th, 91st, 94th	1965–66, 1969–70, 1975–76	12*
95th	1979–1980	21
97th	1981–1982	18
100th	1987–1988	42
101st	1989–1990	42
103rd	1993–1994	60
104th	1995–1996	63
105th	1997–1998	72
107th	2001–2002	73
108th	2003–2004	87
109th	2005–2006	96
110th	2007–2008	96
111th	2009–2010	99

*Mean percentage for these three Congresses.

Source: Compiled by the author.

by offered on the floor to ones explicitly allowed by the Rules Committee.[7] The frequency of open or modified open rules dropped steeply
between the 1970s and the late 1980s. In the 1990s and early 2000s, substantially restrictive rules became more and more frequent, rising from
60 percent in the last Democratic-controlled Congress of the early 1990s
to 96 percent in the 109th Congress, the last before the GOP lost
control. The figure was also 96 percent in the 110th Congress, after
Democrats won control, and it rose to 99 percent in the 111th, the first
of the Obama presidency.

The power and flexibility of special rules make them a useful tool
under a broad variety of circumstances. Both the uncertainty that the
1970s reforms begot and the problems that majority Democrats faced in
legislating during the adverse political climate of the 1980s and early 1990s
stimulated an increase in the use of complex and restrictive rules (Bach
and Smith 1988; Sinclair 1983, 1995). The election of a Democratic

---

7. The percentage is of those major measures that were considered under rules;
usually a (very) few major measures come to the floor under suspension. In the
first and second editions, I displayed the percentage of major measures considered
under any sort of restrictive rule, including a modified open rule, just as I do for all
legislation. I switched to substantially restrictive in the third and continue that here
so that variation among the later Congresses in the series is evident. Simple open
rules have become an endangered species.

president in 1992 presented congressional Democrats with a great legislative opportunity, but it also put them under pressure to deliver under difficult circumstances. The Democratic leadership responded by intensifying its employment of restrictive rules during the 103rd Congress.

When Republicans won control of the House, they too found restrictive rules to be extraordinarily valuable tools and, on major legislation, increased their use. Even in the 104th Congress, their first, the usefulness of such rules for promoting the Republicans' legislative objectives outweighed any damage from the inevitable charges of hypocrisy that their use provoked. Narrow margins and, after the 2000 election, a president of their party with an ambitious agenda prompted Republican leaders to routinely employ highly restrictive rules. Similarly when Democrats regained control, they too found restrictive rules much too useful to eschew.

The Senate Floor: Amending Activity and Extended Debate

The Senate, unlike the House, has not developed effective tools for coping with the consequences of alterations in its internal distribution of influence and challenges from its political environment. The attractiveness to modern senators of rules that give the individual so much power and the difficulty of changing Senate rules make developing such tools extraordinarily difficult. Since a two-thirds vote is required to cut off debate on a proposal to change Senate rules, an oversized coalition for change must be constructed. To be effective, the tools would have to give more control to the majority-party leadership, as they did in the House, but minority-party senators certainly have no reason to do so, and even many majority-party senators are likely to be ambivalent.

The rules changes the Senate was able to make were modest. Perhaps most important, the Budget Act imposed limits on debate on budget resolutions and reconciliation bills, preventing filibusters on these measures. In 1975 the number of votes required to invoke cloture was lowered from two-thirds of those present and voting to three-fifths of the full membership—usually sixty. (Cloture on changes in Senate rules was exempted and still requires a two-thirds vote, though there is controversy about the threshold for changing rules at the beginning of a Congress.) In response to the postcloture filibuster developed in the late 1970s, rules concerning delaying tactics in order after cloture were tightened. In 1986 floor consideration after cloture was limited to a total of thirty hours.

Although no rules restricted senators' amending activity in the 1950s and 1960s, amending marathons (ten or more amendments offered and pushed to a roll call vote) were nevertheless infrequent. For example, on average, slightly less than 10 percent of major measures were subject to an

TABLE 6.5   The Increasing Frequency of Extended Debate–Related Problems on Major Measures

Years*	Measures affected (in percentages)[a]
1960s	8
1970s–1980s	27
1990s–mid-2000s	51
2007–2008	70
2009–2010	72

*Congresses included

1960s: 87th, 89th, 91st

1970s–1980s: 94th, 95th, 97th, 100th, 101st

1990s–mid-2000s: 103rd, 104th, 105th, 107th, 108th, 109th

Source: Author's calculations.

[a]Figures represent the percentage of "filibusterable" major measures that were subject to extended debate–related problems.

amending marathon in the 87th, 89th, and 91st Congresses. Thereafter, however, an average of 30 percent of major measures considered on the Senate floor encountered such a barrage of floor amendments.

In the 1970s senators often pursued their individual policy interests by offering amendments on the floor. A senator's right to offer unlimited amendments to almost any bill proved as useful to senators in the 1980s, the 1990s, and beyond. The political climate of the 1970s may have been more conducive to policy entrepreneurship, and floor amendments may have been more frequently used as tools toward that end, but amendments also proved to be useful tools in the more ideological and partisan struggles of the 1980s, 1990s, and 2000s.

In the 1960s and before, filibusters were rare although important because of their targets, especially civil rights legislation. Most legislation, however, was unlikely to encounter any sort of extended debate–related problem. As Table 6.5 shows, less than ten percent of major measures in the 1960s Congresses for which I have data encountered any such difficulties. In the 1970s, senators made much more use of extended debate, and they continued to increase their use during the 1980s, the 1990s, and the 2000s. Rules changes may have made imposing cloture easier, but they did not reduce the incentives to use extended debate. Rampant individualism combined with the highly charged political climate to put an increasing share of major legislation under at least a threat of a filibuster.

In the 1990s the filibuster increasingly became a partisan tool. In the 103rd, the first Congress of the Bill Clinton presidency, half of major measures confronted an extended debate–related problem. In that Congress the filibuster was used as a partisan tool to an extent unprecedented in the twentieth century. A Republican filibuster killed Clinton's economic stimulus package, and Republicans used the filibuster or the threat thereof to extract concessions on major legislation—voter registration legislation ("motor voter") and the national service program, for example. Republican attempts to kill or water down legislation via a filibuster were not always successful, of course. For example, the Republican filibuster of the Brady bill, which imposes a seven-day waiting period for buying a gun, collapsed when a number of Republican senators began to fear the political price of their participation.

Time pressure makes extended debate an especially effective weapon of obstruction at the end of a Congress, and the greater the backlog of significant legislation, the more potent any threat of delay is. At the end of the 103rd Congress, Republican filibusters killed campaign finance and lobbying reform bills. Although unsuccessful in the end, Republicans filibustered and tried to prevent passage of a massive crime bill, the California Desert Protection Act, and a comprehensive education bill. In some cases filibusters were waged to prevent legislation from being sent to conference or, more frequently, to prevent approval of the conference report. Republican threats of obstructionist floor tactics contributed to the death of bills revamping the Superfund program, revising clean drinking water regulations, overhauling outdated telecommunications law, and applying federal labor laws to Congress. Succeeding Congresses maintained similarly high levels of filibuster-related problems on major measures through the mid-2000; however, after Democrats regained control in the 2006 elections, the rate shot up again (see Table 6.5). Passing major legislation in the Senate has come to require sixty votes.

Omnibus Legislation and the Budget Process

Omnibus legislation—legislation of great substantive scope that often involves many committees—increased as a proportion of the congressional agenda of major legislation from none in the Congresses of the 1960s to a mean of 7 percent in the 1970s Congresses and a mean of 13 percent in the 1980s. In the 1990s and 2000s (103rd–111th Congresses), an average of 12 percent of major measures were omnibus.[8]

During the 1980s the Democratic majority-party leadership sometimes decided to package legislation into omnibus measures as part of a strategy to counter ideologically hostile Republican presidents, especially Ronald Reagan, who was so skillful at using the media to his advantage. Measures

---

8. In each case, figures are based on those Congresses for which I have data. For a list with dates, see Table 6.3.

the president very much wanted could sometimes be packaged with others that congressional Democrats favored but the president opposed, thus forcing the president to accept legislative provisions that, were they sent to him in freestanding form, he would veto. By packaging disparate and individually modest provisions on salient issues such as trade, drugs, or crime into an omnibus bill, Democrats sought to compete with the White House for media attention and public credit. During the 103rd Congress, congressional leaders no longer needed to coerce the president into signing their legislation, but omnibus measures remained useful for raising the visibility of popular legislation, and the device continued to be employed in that way. When the Republicans took control of Congress, they used omnibus legislation for similar purposes.

Many omnibus measures are budget related. Budget resolutions, reconciliation bills, and massive omnibus appropriations bills have constituted the preponderance of omnibus measures since the passage of the Budget Act in 1974. In both the 94th and the 101st Congresses, for example, all of the omnibus measures were budget related. Budget-related measures, however, were much more important pieces of legislation in the 101st than in the 94th. The Budget Act made omnibus measures a regular part of the congressional agenda, but changes in the political environment made budget measures the focus of controversy. During the 1970s, budget resolutions did not include reconciliation instructions, that is, instructions to committees to make changes in law. The budget process, by and large, accommodated what the committees wanted to do rather than constrained them.

In 1980, as I discussed earlier, the president and congressional Democratic leaders, in response to an economic crisis, used the budget process to make spending cuts, and reconciliation instructions were included in the budget resolution for the first time. Then in 1981 the Reagan administration and its congressional allies not only used the budget process to make significant changes in domestic programs so as to cut spending; they also enacted a huge tax cut. With that, the budget process moved to the center of the legislative process and has remained there ever since. The Reagan administration's use of the budget process to redirect government policy made its potential clear; since then it has remained the tool of choice for comprehensive policy change and was used for that purpose by the Clinton administration in 1993, the new Republican majority in 1995, and the George W. Bush administration in 2001 and 2003.

The budget process's centrality also stemmed from the impact of the big budget deficits of the 1980s and 1990s. The deficits that resulted from the Reagan tax cut powerfully shaped American politics. From the mid-1980s to the late 1990s, efforts to do something about the deficit dominated political debate, if not legislative enactments. The decisions made in the budget resolution and in the reconciliation bill that it usually required became crucial. Decisions on other legislative issues were made within the context of scarce resources, and as discretionary domestic spending shrank, the trade-offs that had to be made among programs became increasingly tough. The Gramm-Rudman legislation, the stated aim of which was to force Congress to balance the budget, complicated the process by adding targets and deadlines that, if missed, would result in substantial automatic spending cuts.[9]

The politics of big deficits thus made unpalatable policy decisions necessary. The deep policy divisions first between Republican presidents and congressional Democrats and, after 1994, between President Clinton and congressional Republicans made reaching agreement between the branches on such decisions excruciatingly difficult. The 1980s and 1990s saw a succession of high-visibility, high-stakes showdowns between the branches and the parties on budget measures. Reconciliation bills, like other omnibus measures, were sometimes used to try to force provisions on an opposition party president that he opposed; such attempts, of course, raised the level of conflict. The existence of the budget process at least made it possible to wrap unpopular spending cuts and, sometimes, tax increases into one big package—often sweetened with provisions that members wanted—and get a single vote on the package as a whole. The congressional leadership frequently could persuade its members to pass such a package because defeating it would be devastating for the party's reputation. Passing the components individually would have been impossible.

Even after deficits briefly turned into surpluses in the late 1990s, partisan and interbranch battles over priorities continued to be fought in the context of the budget process. High partisan polarization and narrow margins of control assured the continued centrality of the budget process, because budget rules in the Senate protect budget resolutions and reconciliation bills from filibusters. In the contemporary climate the sort of legislative changes made via the budget process in the early 2000s certainly would have provoked filibusters had they been possible, and quite likely these filibusters would have been successful. With the return of big deficits, House leaders also found it useful to package many, not necessarily palatable, changes in law into one bill "too big to fail."

---

9. The Gramm-Rudman law was superseded by the Budget Enforcement Act of 1990, which included a "pay as you go" (PAYGO) provision requiring that any tax cuts or increases in entitlement programs had to be offset by either revenue increases or spending cuts of equal total magnitude (see Oleszek 2004, 70–71). PAYGO expired in 2002 and was not renewed until the beginning of the 110th Congress.

Summits

In the 1980s and 1990s the sharp differences in policy preferences between presidents and opposition-party majorities in the Congress and the tough decisions that had to be made sometimes stalemated normal processes. When normal processes, even supplemented by the increasingly active role of majority-party leaders, were incapable of producing legislation, the president and Congress had to find another way—the costs of failing to reach an agreement on budget issues were just too high, especially after Gramm-Rudman, with its automatic spending cuts, went into effect in the mid-1980s. The new device of choice was the summit: relatively formal negotiations between congressional leaders and high-ranking administration officials representing the president. Because summits take place only when the stakes are very high, congressional party leaders have always represented their members in such talks; members are not willing to rely on committee leaders to make such decisions on behalf of the party membership as a whole.

Actually, the first instance of major legislation emerging from a process similar in some respects to the summits of the late 1980s and 1990s was the 1980 (FY1981) budget resolution and reconciliation bill during the Carter administration. The announcement on February 22, 1980, that the consumer price index had increased at an 18 percent annual rate in January created a crisis atmosphere. In early March an unprecedented series of meetings between the Carter administration and the Democratic congressional leadership took place for the purpose of discussing budget cuts. The budget resolution approved by Congress closely followed the agreement that had been reached in those meetings (Sinclair 1983).

The 1983 deal to reestablish the fiscal soundness of the Social Security system emerged from a process that showed some similarities to a summit (Gilmour 1990, 248–250). A commission had been appointed to develop a solution, but the deal was really worked out behind the scenes by a few commission members who directly spoke for President Reagan and Speaker O'Neill. In the mid-1980s attempts at summit negotiations on budget issues were made several times but with limited success.

During the 100th and 101st Congresses (1987–1990), four summits took place, three of which concerned budget issues. In fall 1987 the stock market crashed; in response, Reagan administration officials met with the congressional leadership and worked out a deal that shaped the 1987 reconciliation bill and the full-year continuing resolution. The deal also determined the major outlines of the following year's budget resolution (FY1989). In spring 1989 the new George H.W. Bush administration and the congressional leadership worked out a more modest deal to avert Gramm-Rudman across-the-board cuts; this agreement shaped the 1989

(FY1990) budget resolution and the 1989 reconciliation bill, although it by no means settled all the major issues, especially on reconciliation. The need for action and the inability of normal processes to produce agreement again led to a summit on budget issues in 1990. The highly contentious issue of aid to the Nicaraguan contras was the subject of the fourth summit. In 1989 the Democratic leadership met with Bush administration representatives to work out a final agreement on contra aid. (For details on these cases, see Sinclair 1995.)

An emergency and severe time pressure may create the conditions for a summit, as they did in 1980, but when the congressional majority and the president are of the same party, normal processes supplemented by informal consultation and negotiations almost always seem to suffice. In fact, since that one instance, no summits have occurred when the president and Congress have been controlled by the same party. Thus there were no summits during the first two years of the Clinton presidency or during George W. Bush's first six years in office. (Democrats controlled the Senate during much of the 107th Congress, but they did not gain control until after the budget resolution and the big tax cut bill of 2001 passed.)

Not surprisingly, normal processes are more likely to fail when the president's and the congressional majority's policy and electoral goals are in conflict, as they tend to be under divided government, when the presidency is controlled by one party and the Congress by another. In fact, the increase in partisan polarization and in congressional leadership strength make it less likely that a president can circumvent opposition by House majority-party leadership and pick off enough majority-party members to pass administration priorities. Presidents frequently are forced to deal with opposition majority-party leadership directly. So when Republicans won control of Congress in the 1994 elections, President Clinton and congressional Republicans found they had to resort to summits. The budget summit of 1995–1996 failed to produce an agreement; however, in 1997, Clinton and the congressional Republicans did manage to work out a deal to balance the budget. Differences on appropriations bills also increasingly came to be negotiated in an end-of-the-fiscal-year summit between Clinton administration officials and congressional leaders.

Unorthodox Lawmaking in a Hyperpartisan Era

The 1994 elections brought enormous and unexpected political change to Congress, especially to the House of Representatives. Republicans won majorities in both chambers, taking control of the House for the first time in forty years by picking up fifty-three seats. During the campaign, House

Republicans had promised to change the way Congress works if the voters would give them control. In fact, the rules changes that constitute the reforms of the 1970s were in many cases changes in Democratic Party rules, not changes in the rules of the House itself. Much of the weakening of committees and their chairs and the strengthening of the party leadership was the result of new Democratic Caucus rules concerning committee assignments and the designation of committee and subcommittee chairs (see Sinclair 2006).

One might thus expect that a change in party control would have brought with it major alterations in how the House functions. In fact, the Republican House did operate differently than its Democratic predecessor; however, as the data on special procedures and practices presented in this chapter suggest, Republican control resulted not in a change in direction but rather in an amplification of preexisting trends. An analysis of why this is so illuminates the relationship between the congressional process and the broader political process in which it is embedded.

On the first day of the 104th Congress, House Republicans made some significant but far from revolutionary changes in House rules. Modest committee jurisdiction reform was accomplished by shifting some of the Energy and Commerce Committee's immense jurisdiction to other committees. Three minor committees were eliminated, and committee staffs were cut by a third. Sunshine rules were modestly strengthened, making it harder to close a committee meeting. Committee chairs were subjected to a limit of three terms, a rules change that ultimately would have a major impact on the distribution of legislative influence in the House.

Term limits and staff cuts potentially weakened committee chairs; however, because Republican Party rules pertained, the new Republican committee chairs were in some ways actually stronger than their Democratic predecessors. They controlled the entire majority staff of the committee and had more control over the choice of subcommittee chairs and over the assignment of members to subcommittees.

During the 1980s and early 1990s, House Republicans had in many instances imitated House Democrats by adopting party rules that decreased the autonomy of their committee leaders and strengthened their party leadership. Their committee leaders (ranking minority members when the party was in the minority, committee chairs when Republicans became the majority), after being nominated by the committee on committees, had been made subject to a secret ballot ratification vote in the Republican Conference, the organization of all House Republicans; the Republicans' top leader had been given the power to nominate Republican members of Rules and more say on the party committee that makes

committee assignments. Thus rules strengthening Republican Party leaders were, by and large, not new at the beginning of the 104th Congress,
nor did they give Republican leaders powers that Democratic Party leaders
had not possessed.

Political circumstances, not rules changes, made Newt Gingrich a
powerful Speaker. Gingrich, in the eyes of most Republicans and the
media, was the miracle maker, since he was seen as responsible for the
unexpected Republican victory in 1994. He had worked and schemed to
build a majority for many years (Connelly and Pitney 1994); he had
recruited many of the House challengers who won and had helped them
with fund-raising and campaign advice. The Contract with America, the
policy agenda on which most House Republicans had run, was Gingrich's
idea, and he had orchestrated its realization.

Consequently, the 1994 election results gave Gingrich enormous
prestige. They also provided him with a membership that was ideologically homogeneous and determined to enact major policy change. The
huge freshman class—seventy-three strong—consisted largely of true
believers deeply committed to cutting the size and scope of government
and to balancing the budget. Freshmen and sophomores, who were similar ideologically, made up more than half of the Republican House membership. These members and a considerable number of more senior
Republicans believed themselves mandated to make policy change. Even
moderate Republicans strongly agreed that for the party to maintain its
majority, Republicans had to deliver on the promises they had made in
the Contract.

The combination of an extraordinarily ambitious agenda, a new
majority united behind the agenda, and a leader with enormous stature
made the exercise of strong leadership both necessary and possible.
Without strong central direction, passing the agenda would have been
impossible. Without a membership united in its commitment to swift and
sweeping policy change, no Speaker could have exercised such strong,
central direction of the legislative process.

Relying on his immense prestige with House Republicans, Gingrich,
in the days after the 1994 elections, exercised power well beyond that specified in Republican Conference rules. He designated Republicans to serve
as committee chairs, bypassing seniority in several instances. According to
the rules, the party committee on committees nominates chairs and the
Conference approves them. Gingrich preempted that process, assuming
correctly that his stature would prevent anyone from challenging his
choices.

The 104th Congress saw pervasive party leadership involvement and
oversight on major legislation; committee leaders were clearly subordinate

to party leaders on Contract with America bills and on much of the major legislation that went into the Republicans' attempt to balance the budget. Because most senior Republicans had signed the Contract, Gingrich had a powerful tool for persuading committee leaders to report legislation without making major changes and to do so quickly; he simply reminded them: "We promised to do it in 100 days; we must deliver." In early 1995, and later when balancing the budget was at issue, the chairs knew that the leadership was buttressed by the freshmen's strong support.

The attempt to deliver on the ambitious promises House Republicans had made took the full set of procedural tools available to the majority-party leadership. The need for speed and flexibility, and occasionally the political delicacy of the issues involved, dictated that the leaders sometimes bypass committee. The leadership made extensive use of member task forces on legislative issues ranging from agriculture policy to gun control to immigration reform. By and large, committees were not formally bypassed on the issues task forces worked on, but the task forces did have the purpose and the effect of keeping the pressure on committees to report legislation that was satisfactory to the party majority and to do so in a timely fashion.

Even though political circumstances made committee leaders unusually responsive to the wishes of the party leadership and the party membership, party leaders frequently found it necessary to make postcommittee adjustments in legislation. Multiple referral, the need for speed, and the ambitiousness of the agenda all contributed to producing circumstances in which the legislation as reported had to be altered in order to engineer passage in a form that would accomplish the party's objectives.

As developed by Democratic leaders in the 1980s and early 1990s, special rules had become powerful and flexible tools for the leadership. Given the task Republicans had set for themselves, their leaders could hardly eschew using restrictive rules, despite their preelection promise to use predominantly open rules. In working to pass their ambitious agenda, House Republican leaders continued to use substantially restrictive rules.

The extraordinary political circumstances that allowed such hyperaggressive use of the full set of leadership tools, including the tools of unorthodox lawmaking, waned even before the end of the 104th Congress. The 105th Congress saw leaders retreat a bit from the deep substantive involvement on almost all major legislation that had characterized their role in the 104th. The reversion, however, was to a legislative process still heavily characterized by the practices and procedures I have labeled unorthodox lawmaking. In their attempts to satisfy the party's members by passing the legislation they favored, House party leaders continued to make use of the tools of unorthodox lawmaking. Speaker Dennis Hastert, who had promised a return to "regular order" when he assumed the speakership in 1999, found himself frequently drawn into legislative substance and having to either bypass committees or make postcommittee adjustments, and he routinely employed strategic restrictive rules.

Republican House leaders gained additional leverage over committee leaders when the consequences of chair term limits became evident. In 2000, thirteen chairs became vacant simultaneously, mostly because of term limits, and the Republican Party leadership instituted a new procedure for the selection of committee chairs: chair aspirants were required to appear before the Steering Committee, the committee on committees that nominates chairs to the Conference. There they were put through rigorous interviews about their legislative and communication strategies and their proposed agendas. Given the leadership's influence on the Steering Committee as well as that committee's representative composition, the new procedure made the incentives to show responsiveness to the party and its leadership even stronger for committee chairs and those aspiring to these positions. House party leaders used the clout they gained thereby to ensure that legislation that got to the floor was acceptable to most Republican members and to President Bush.

If passing the Republicans' agenda in the majority-rule House of the 1990s was a task requiring extraordinary means, getting it through the Senate was a considerably more difficult, and sometimes impossible, endeavor. Majority Leader Bob Dole of Kansas and his immediate successor, Trent Lott of Mississippi, used all the special procedures available to them. In the 104th Congress especially, committees were frequently bypassed and great effort went into postcommittee adjustments to bills in an attempt to craft legislation that could amass the sixty votes Senate passage usually requires.

Having had the filibuster wielded against them so effectively in the 103rd Congress, Democrats, now in the minority, returned the favor and made full use of their prerogatives under Senate rules. In the 104th and 105th Congresses, about half of major legislation encountered extended debate–related problems; Democrats killed regulatory overhaul and property rights legislation and forced majority Republicans to make concessions on a number of major bills—product liability legislation, the Freedom to Farm bill, and telecommunications legislation, among others.

Minority Democrats became increasingly adept at using extended debate and the Senate's permissive amending rules in combination to get their issues onto the Senate agenda. By threatening or actually offering their bills as often nongermane amendments to whatever legislation the majority leader brought to the floor and using extended debate to block a quick end to debate, Democrats forced Republicans to consider a number of issues they would rather have avoided—most prominently the minimum wage, tobacco taxes, campaign finance reform, and the patients' bill of rights.

The Republican majority responded with procedural strategies of its own. Majority Leader Lott attempted to impose cloture immediately upon bringing a bill to the floor, because after cloture all amendments must be germane. When cloture failed, he simply pulled the bill from the floor to deprive Democrats of an opportunity to debate and vote on their amendments. Lott also "filled the amendment tree"; that is, he used his right of first recognition to offer amendments in all the parliamentarily permissible slots, thus barring Democrats from offering their amendments. Democratic cohesion on cloture votes, however, limited the effectiveness of such majority-party strategies; so long as the minority party can muster forty-one votes, the majority party may be able to prevent the minority from getting votes on its bills but it cannot pass its own. The result was most often gridlock, and once George W. Bush became president, Senate leaders had to abandon that strategy if they wished to move his program.

Intense partisan polarization is the single most salient characteristic of contemporary politics and one that increasingly shapes the legislative process. From the mid-1990s through 2008, the majority parties' margins of control were narrow—sometimes extremely so; yet the ideological gulf between the parties made bipartisan compromise costly. Even after the waning of the intense sense of mandate that Republicans read into the 1994 elections, congressional Republicans remained unusually ideologically homogeneous for an American party and continued to be dedicated to conservative policy change. In the 1990s, majority Republicans faced a politically adroit president hostile to their policy goals. After Bush became president in 2001, they enjoyed a like-minded ally in the White House, but the pressure on them to produce intensified enormously. Bush offered an ambitious agenda, one that, by and large, Republicans—voters, activists, and members of Congress—supported strongly but, by the same token, one with limited bipartisan appeal.

The period that followed saw a near "replay" but with the two parties' roles reversed. In the 2006 midterm elections, Democrats retook both houses of Congress but with narrow margins. House Democrats had complained bitterly about what they argued was undemocratic Republican leadership that prevented the minority from participating in policy making, often taking effective decision making away from the committees and centering it in the leadership and using highly restrictive floor rules that barred most Democratic amendments. During the campaign Democrats promised less partisan and more open decision making, and many Democrats were eager to return to "regular order" in which the committees would be the primary policy decision makers. Yet House Democrats had also promised to pass a significant domestic policy agenda and to alter the country's course in Iraq. In their attempt to do so, they confronted an adamantly opposed minority party and an opposition-party president who showed little inclination toward bipartisan compromise. The 2008 elections increased the Democratic House majority to 257, almost 60 percent, and brought in a like-minded Democrat as president. But, as was the case in 2001, a new president and the return of unified control immensely increase the expectations of supporters in the electorate for policy change. In the 110th and the 111th Congresses, the House Democratic leaders responded to the complexity of their tasks and the constraints of the political environment by aggressively using the tools of unorthodox lawmaking. As had been the case when the Republicans were in the majority, the House majority leadership's tight control of the floor contributed greatly to the party's legislative success, but it also contributed to the minority party's severe discontent with the legislative process and to the hostility between the parties.

High partisan polarization combined with the Senate's permissive rules spell trouble for the Senate as a legislative body. Contemporary majority leaders usually can count on a more cohesive party membership than could their predecessors of the 1970s and 1980s, but even a totally united party is not usually enough. Major legislation now typically runs into an extended debate–related problem in the Senate. And with the minority party now usually highly cohesive on cloture votes, getting the sixty votes to close debate often requires substantial concessions. Senate rules exert some pressure toward bipartisan compromise even in this highly polarized era when little else does; but, as they are now employed, they often lead to legislative stalemate.

Neither the changes in party control of Congress in 1995 and 2007 nor unified control of government with the George W. Bush presidency in 2001 and then with the Barack Obama presidency in 2009 disrupted the trend toward unorthodox lawmaking. In part, continuity, and often acceleration, in the use of unorthodox practices and procedures can be attributed to the persistence of key conditions: internal rules have not been altered very much and certainly not in a way as to resurrect strong, autonomous committees; the budget process continued to dominate congressional decision making; new congressional majorities faced hostile, opposition-party presidents; and then those congressional majorities confronted the high expectations that unified government in a period of high partisan polarization produce. Perhaps even more important, the frequent employment of these special procedures and practices has continued because, whatever their origins, they have become flexible tools useful to members and leaders under a variety of circumstances. For that reason, we should not expect a return to what once was the regular order, at least not in the foreseeable future.

The case studies in the following chapters illustrate both how the broader political environment shapes the context in which the legislative process occurs and how legislative leaders—and sometimes rank-and-file members—use the various tools of unorthodox lawmaking to take advantage of the opportunities and to cope with the problems that particular political contexts create. They show how House leaders now can tailor the legislative process to the problems that a particular bill raises in ways not available in the past, whereas Senate leaders frequently are confronted with problems derived from the tools being used by opponents to thwart their legislative aims. The cases also demonstrate how the practices and procedures of unorthodox lawmaking combine and interact and thereby illustrate the multiple paths through which bills now do—and sometimes do not—become law.

A Tale of Two Stimuli:
The Bush-Pelosi-Boehner Stimulus
Bill of 2008 and the American
Recovery and Reinvestment
Act of 2009

CONGRESS PASSED SUBSTANTIAL ECONOMIC stimulus legislation in 2008 and 2009; both bills were a response to what were perceived as economic emergencies, and both passed quickly. Despite these similarities, the combination of unorthodox practices and procedures employed on the bills did differ; as the following accounts show, the political contexts differed in important ways and this led key actors to make different choices about the procedural tools they would employ and how they would use them. At the end of this and the following two chapters, tables summarize the chronology of the bills discussed.

The 2008 Stimulus Bill

On January 18, 2008, President George W. Bush called on Congress to pass a $145 billion tax cut stimulus bill. The economy had been weakening with the subprime mortgage crisis, a slump in the housing sector, a decline in the stock market, and poor job growth. Congressional Democrats, who held majorities in both chambers, had begun to talk about a stimulus in 2007. Now the president agreed. In fact, the day before the announcement he had discussed the proposal with congressional leaders in a conference call; administration officials had been talking with key members of Congress, and the bipartisan House leadership had met face-to-face. In his public statement, Bush emphasized tax cuts, but in response to the Democratic leaders' request, he declined to give details, stating that he wanted to work collaboratively with Congress.

To be effective, a stimulus package needed to be enacted quickly. And that would require cooperation between a Republican president and a Democratic Congress that had spent most of 2007 at loggerheads. It would also necessitate a compressed legislative process, and that would require the party leaders to take a central role.

Negotiating the Package

Speaker of the House Nancy Pelosi, Minority Leader John Boehner, and Secretary of the Treasury Henry Paulson undertook the negotiating of a stimulus package. The Bush administration and the congressional Republicans strongly favored a stimulus package consisting solely of tax cuts for individuals and businesses; they would have liked to have made the big Bush tax cuts of 2001 and 2003 permanent as part of the package but knew that was anathema to Democrats. Congressional Democrats strongly favored including extended unemployment benefits and additional funds for the food stamp program in the stimulus. In addition, a number of Democrats also called for the package to include relief for homeowners affected by the subprime mortgage crisis.

Intense talks produced a deal that Pelosi, Boehner, and Paulson announced on January 24. The package consisted of tax rebates to individuals and families and tax breaks for businesses. Pelosi ultimately agreed to drop the Democratic demand for the inclusion of extended unemployment benefits and increased funding for food stamps. In return, she got an income cap on who would be eligible for the tax rebate so as to exclude the most affluent; further, and key to winning the support of her Democratic members, people who made too little to pay income taxes but did pay payroll taxes would be eligible for the rebates. This would provide more relief to low-income people than increasing food stamp funding. A provision that would make it easier to obtain new mortgages or refinance loans in expensive markets also was included.

During the hectic period of negotiating the package, Pelosi and Boehner had kept in touch with their members to make sure the final product would be acceptable. Thus what should be in a stimulus package was the prime topic of discussion during Democratic Caucus meetings; Pelosi talked frequently with Charlie Rangel, chair of the tax-writing Ways and Means Committee and a champion of the poor. Republicans were vehemently opposed to making eligible for tax rebates those who did not pay income taxes; Boehner had to convince them that this was the price of reaching agreement.

Passing the Bill in the House

The House Democratic leadership had planned from the beginning to bypass committee consideration. As Majority Leader Steny Hoyer explained, "We have got to do this in the short term in a timely fashion so that it will have the impact on the economy that is the whole purpose of the legislation. Therefore, to go through the regular process and have hearings and have markups and subcommittee markups, obviously we would be to some degree . . . twiddling our thumbs while the economy burns" (*Roll Call,* January 24, 2008).

On January 28, Speaker Pelosi introduced HR 5140, "To provide economic stimulus through recovery rebates to individuals, incentives for business investment, and an increase in conforming and FHA loan limits." Her fifteen cosponsors included the top party leaders on both sides of the aisle and the chairs and ranking members of the various committees with jurisdiction. As House rules demand, the bill was referred to "the Committee on Ways and Means, and in addition to the Committee on Financial Services, for a period to be subsequently determined by the Speaker, in each case for consideration of such provisions as fall within the jurisdiction of the committee concerned" (Thomas Bill Summary and Status, 110th Congress).

The next day, Ways and Means chairman Rangel moved to suspend the rules and pass the bill. Under this procedure, forty minutes of debate is allowed and no amendments are in order. Because of the importance of the bill, many members wanted to speak. So Rangel asked for unanimous consent to extend debate time to two hours, equally divided between the majority and the minority. (This had, of course, been prearranged.) Most of the members who spoke praised the leaders for expeditiously coming to a bipartisan agreement; the package was not perfect, most conceded, but was good and necessary. Pelosi herself spoke and lavished praise on Rangel, Financial Services chair Barney Frank, and their ranking minority members for their contributions. A few conservative Republicans opposed the package, most arguing that it took the wrong tack and would add to the deficit without stimulating economic growth. But the deal had the blessings of the administration and both party leaderships. To pass a bill under the suspension procedure, a two-thirds vote is required. HR 5140 passed with a 385–35 vote.

Getting to 60 in the Senate

Harry Reid and Mitch McConnell, the Senate majority leader and minority leader, respectively, had acquiesced to the House leaders taking the lead on negotiating with the White House. That would speed up the process, they believed. Nevertheless, when the deal was struck, Senate Democrats criticized it and made clear they wanted to have their say; the package could be "improved," many argued. Finance Committee chairman Max Baucus (D-MT) insisted that his committee would mark up its own version and do so quickly; that would not delay enactment, he contended.

On Monday, January 28, Baucus unveiled his proposal; it included extended unemployment benefits and payments to low-income seniors and disabled veterans, groups that paid no income or payroll taxes and thus were ineligible for rebates in the House bill; in an attempt to pick up Republican votes, it lifted the income cap on the tax rebates. The Finance Committee marked up the bill on Wednesday. An income cap was reinserted; the lifting of the cap had produced a collective "gag reflex" among Democrats, according to Majority Leader Reid, and not much interest among Republicans (*RC,* January 31, 2008). The bill also included expanded business tax breaks, renewable energy tax credits, and tax incentives for oil, natural gas, and coal companies. Finance approved the legislation 14–7, with three Republicans including ranking minority member Charles Grassley supporting the bill.

From the White House, Boehner, and Pelosi, pressure to move quickly and not upset the deal so carefully struck was increasing. McConnell announced that the Senate Republican leadership strongly favored simply passing the House bill. That made it clear that Democrats would need to impose cloture in order to get an up-or-down vote on the Finance bill or other changes to the House package. The Republican leaders began to "whip" their members to stick together against any such attempt. Approval of the Finance bill would necessitate sending the bill to conference, and that would "wreck the balance that was struck" between the White House and House Democrats and Republicans, they argued (*RC,* January 31, 2008).

To keep the package on a fast track, Reid had always planned to put the House-approved bill onto the Senate floor and then offer the Finance Committee version as an amendment. Senate Democrats' vote counts showed, however, that getting to sixty would be very difficult. So Reid began to signal that Democrats expected to have to settle for a stripped-down version of the Baucus plan. But by the beginning of the next week, with the AARP, the powerful seniors group, lobbying intensely for the Baucus version, prospects brightened and Reid began telling Republicans that they would get only one choice—the Baucus plan or the House bill. If they refused to cut off debate on the amendment incorporating the Finance Committee version, he would prevent votes on adding rebates for seniors and disabled veterans. Republicans expected the 2008 elections to be tough for their party, and few really wanted to be seen as responsible for killing these very popular provisions.

On Monday, February 4, the Senate voted 80–4 to impose cloture on the motion to proceed to consider HR 5140. Once cloture has been imposed, thirty hours of debate are in order. Ordinarily little of that time is used because the matter has been decided by the cloture vote but in this case Republicans insisted on using the debate time. They argued they needed the time to study the Finance package; Reid replied that the draft had been available since the previous Wednesday, and, in response to the GOP claim that the Democrats had altered the draft, he said the only change was the addition of Low Income Home Energy Assistance Program (LIHEAP) funds, as Republicans had been advised. Democrats charged that Republicans were actually using up time in order to hold up work on the Foreign Intelligence Surveillance Act (FISA) fix, hoping to run out the clock and force the House to accept the Senate bill, which Bush and the Republicans greatly preferred (*Congressional Record*, February 4, 2008, S583).

On Tuesday the Senate agreed to the motion to proceed and began consideration. Using his right of first recognition as majority leader, Reid then offered amendment #3983, the Finance package, followed by enough other amendments "to fill the amendment tree"; that is, he offered amendments in all of the parliamentary permissible slots, thereby preventing Republicans from offering amendments. Reid then filed for cloture on amendment #3983. If cloture were invoked, a vote requiring only a simple majority for passage would be held on the Finance package and no non-germane amendments to it would be in order.

Reid set the cloture vote for Wednesday so that presidential candidates Hillary Clinton and Barack Obama could be present. Nevertheless, when the cloture vote was held, it failed by one vote. Officially the vote was recorded as 58–41, with Reid voting against cloture. Typically when a cloture vote fails, the majority leader changes his vote for yea to nay so that he can ask for the vote's reconsideration at a later time; this may speed up the process because it means that if the majority leader can find the necessary sixty votes, he does not need to go through the whole cloture process again (see Chapter 3). The Senate Republicans had called Reid's bluff; now he had to decide whether to back down. He immediately began to confer with McConnell.

Under pressure from Speaker Pelosi and House Democrats to act quickly, Senate Democrats agreed to a severely slimmed-down version of the Finance plan. On Wednesday evening, Senate Republicans had consented to the addition of payments to low-income seniors and disabled veterans, as had party leaders in the House. Senior Democrats checked that the White House would accept the addition. On Thursday, Senate Democrats agreed to settle for that and give up on their other add-ons.

Later the same day, on the Senate floor, Reid withdrew amendment #3983 and the others he had offered before the failed cloture vote; he then offered amendment #4010, the narrower amendment that he and McConnell had negotiated. It passed by a vote of 91–6; the bill as amended passed 81–16.

Final Action

Following the script that had been agreed to, at 6:30 p.m. on Thursday, February 7, on the House floor, Ways and Means Committee chair Rangel asked "unanimous consent that it may be in order . . . to take from the Speaker's table the bill with the Senate amendment thereto, and without intervention of any point of order, entertain a motion by the Chairman of the Ways and Means Committee to agree to the Senate amendment . . ." (Thomas). This was agreed to without objection. After forty minutes of debate, as provided for in the unanimous consent request, the House agreed to the Senate amendment by a 380–34 vote. The bill was thus cleared for the president, who signed it on February 13, whereby it became law.

The 2009 Stimulus Package

As 2008 and the Bush presidency drew to a close, the United States was experiencing a severe and deepening recession and a frightening financial crisis. A consensus had emerged among experts that to meet the worst economic crisis since the Great Depression, a very substantial stimulus package was essential. Even conservative economists such as Alan Greenspan and Martin Feldstein concurred. President-elect Barack Obama had been advocating another stimulus since the spring, when he was just one candidate among many, and House Democrats had actually passed stimulus legislation in September. Under veto threat from President Bush, it went no further. Speaker Pelosi had kept economic stimulus on the agenda, asking the chairmen of relevant committees to hold hearings and publicize proposals.

Even before the November elections, congressional Democrats had begun to talk with members of the Obama team about a stimulus package. Pelosi tapped Appropriations chair David Obey as head negotiator for House Democrats; a considerable proportion of a stimulus bill would be within his committee's jurisdiction, and Obey was a politically savvy and tough legislator. By mid-December serious work on a stimulus plan was under way, with Obama transition team members and Democratic congressional staffers meeting almost daily.

The continuing steep economic slide highlighted by harrowing job loss numbers exerted pressure for quick action. Democratic congressional leaders and Obama himself hoped a package could be ready for the president to sign soon after his inauguration on January 20. Republican congressional leaders, however, expressed strong reservations about moving so quickly. Senate minority leader Mitch McConnell and House minority leader John Boehner called for "regular order" with thorough committee hearings and plenty of time for members and the public to study the legislation before floor votes.

There was general agreement that any package would include aid to states, which were being hit hard by the recession; public investment in a variety of areas including prominently infrastructure; and tax relief. The total size of the package and the proportion of the various components, especially the ratio of tax cuts to spending, were in dispute. Most Republicans favored providing stimulus largely through tax breaks; Democrats believed spending would be more effective.

During the campaign, Obama had promised to tamp down the partisan hostility in Washington. He had reached out to Republicans as well as fellow Democrats in Congress in the days after his win. He sent Rahm Emanuel, his chief of staff designate, to meet with the Republican leadership soon after the election and phoned a number of the Republican ranking committee members. Vice President–elect Joe Biden talked to some of his former Senate colleagues, and Obama personally consulted Olympia Snowe (R-ME), a key Senate moderate, on the stimulus package. By his actions and by his own and his team members' statements, Obama put a high premium on getting substantial Republican support for his stimulus package.

On January 5, two days after the new Congress convened, Obama met first with Pelosi and Reid and then with the Republican and Democratic leadership teams. He assured Republicans that he wanted and would take seriously their input. His economic team indicated that 40 percent of the stimulus package would consist of tax cuts.

House Committee Action

On January 15, Speaker Nancy Pelosi unveiled an $825 billion economic stimulus package consisting of $550 billion in new spending and $275 billion in tax cuts. Although the plan was developed in consultation with the Obama team, Pelosi emphasized that the package was a House proposal.

And, as Republicans had demanded, the bill would be marked up by the House committees of jurisdiction rather than being brought directly to the floor. Republicans immediately criticized the package, contending that it spent far too much—and on programs that would not stimulate the economy. "I just took a moment to look over the draft from [Appropriations] Chairman [David] Obey and the outline by [Ways and Means] Chairman [Charlie] Rangel; oh my God," said House minority leader John Boehner at his press conference. "My notes here say that I'm disappointed. I just can't tell you how shocked I am at what we're seeing" (*RC,* January 15, 2009). The Democratic plan calls for "half a trillion dollars in questionable new spending," he charged.

On January 21, the day after Obama's inauguration, the Appropriations Committee marked up in full committee the spending portion of the Recovery and Reinvestment bill of 2009. The draft that Obey had put together served as the mark-up vehicle. The draft included spending for a raft of social and public works programs. Republicans complained bitterly that Democrats had negotiated this draft without Republican input, but Obey retorted that his invitations to ranking Appropriations Republican Jerry Lewis to become involved were rebuffed.

The amending process in committee showed the deep divide between the parties in what they believed appropriate and effective as stimulus. Republicans offered a number of amendments to cut spending, defer spending, and shift money from spending to tax cuts. Committee Democrats stayed unified and voted them down on party-line votes. The committee approved four Republican amendments by voice votes. Then it approved the draft, reporting the bill by a party-line vote of 35–22.

The next day, two more committees marked up their parts of the legislation. Ways and Means approved HR 598 on a 24–13 party-line vote. Included was $303 billion in tax relief to individuals and businesses; the former consisted of a refundable tax credit Obama had proposed for 2009 and 2010 for low- and moderate-income workers, enhancement of the existing refundable earned-income tax credit and child credit to provide more money to low-income people, and a partially refundable $2,500 tax credit for college tuition and other expenses. In addition to direct taxes, Ways and Means has jurisdiction over programs such as unemployment insurance and Medicare. The bill contained spending to promote a swifter shift by health care providers to state-of-the-art computerized record-keeping technology, $46.6 billion in expanded jobless benefits and welfare programs, and $28.6 billion in subsidies to help early retirees or out-of-work employees pay the higher costs for keeping their employer-sponsored health insurance coverage. Although the Republicans mostly supported the business tax breaks, they opposed making workers who did not earn enough to pay income taxes eligible for tax rebates. Republicans offered an amendment to strip that provision out of the bill, but it and more than a dozen other GOP amendments were defeated on party-line votes.

Also on January 22, after a twelve-hour session, the Energy and Commerce Committee approved HR 629, which included about $96 billion in Medicaid expansion, $20 billion in medical technology improvements, and $32 billion in energy transmission modernization. Given the breadth of the committee's jurisdiction and the variety of provisions in the bill, the amendments offered were many and disparate. Democrats voted most of the Republican-sponsored amendments down. Weary and a bit testy, committee members approve the bill on a voice vote.

The PR Battle

On Friday, January 23, President Obama met at the White House with the top nine congressional party leaders from both chambers and parties, his first such meeting as president. Republicans had been ramping up their criticism of the stimulus legislation, and Democrats had responded sharply; Obama hoped to nudge partisans toward a more conciliatory stance. "I know there are differences," Obama said, referring to the objections from Republicans as well as disagreements among Democrats on some of the specifics. "What unites this group is that we recognize we are facing an unprecedented economic crisis," he said (*CQ Today*, January 26, 2009). In the meeting, the House Republican leaders presented Obama with their alternative, which cut out the refundable tax rebate to low-income people, a proposal they knew Obama considered totally unacceptable. In response, the president pointed out that he had won the election! Although the meeting was cordial and afterward Republicans expressed their appreciation to the president, it changed no minds.

Republican criticism, amplified first by the conservative media and then increasingly by other cable television news stations, seemed to be gaining traction. A clever focus on specific items that could be portrayed as frivolous especially resonated in the 24/7 media news cycle: $200 million to resod the National Mall, $50 million for the National Endowment for the Arts, and $360 million to slow the spread of sexually transmitted diseases were singled out. "How you can spend hundreds of millions of dollars on contraceptives; how does that stimulate the economy?" House minority leader John Boehner asked rhetorically after the White House meeting (*Washington Post*, January 24, 2009).

Democrats pressed Obama to use his bully pulpit more aggressively. They wanted to support their new president, and they believed their political future rested on the success of their joint legislative agenda, but he could make it much easer for members from marginal constituencies to support the program if he defended it effectively in the public arena.

In his weekly radio address on Saturday morning, his first as president, Obama laid out more detailed benchmarks of what he expected in the economic recovery package and warned about the consequences of delay. "If we do not act boldly and swiftly, a bad situation could become dramatically worse" (*WP,* January 24, 2009).

On Tuesday, Obama went to Capitol Hill to meet privately with the House and then the Senate Republicans. Even before the meeting Boehner urged his members to vote against the stimulus program. Nevertheless, the unusual meetings garnered Obama heavy and favorable media coverage: he was trying to change the tone, as he had promised.

Passing the Recovery Package in the House

House leaders had scheduled floor debate on HR 1, the combined stimulus bill, for Tuesday and Wednesday, January 27 and 28. On Tuesday, an initial rule for debate was offered. It provided for three and a half hours of debate, an unusually generous amount for the House, reflecting the importance of the bill. After the rule was approved on near party-line votes, the House resolved itself into the Committee of the Whole and debate began.

Appropriations Committee chair David Obey explained what the bill was intended to do:

> Mr. Chairman, this country is facing what most economists, I believe, consider to be the most serious and the most dangerous economic situation in our lifetimes, certainly going back to the early thirties. . . .
>
> We're being asked to use fiscal policy to expand consumer purchasing power to try and stop the slide. And that is what this proposal before us here today will try to do. . . .
>
> This package today that we are considering is an $825 billion package that does a variety of things to try to reinflate the economy. It, first of all, provides tax cuts—which Mr. *Rangel* will discuss—in order to try to put some money in people's pockets.
>
> . . . Secondly, this package attempts to jump-start job creation through infrastructure investments in roads, bridges, sewers, water repair, modernizing our electric power grid and expanding broadband access so that all parts of the country have an opportunity to compete, with Internet access.
>
> Third, this package attempts to help those who are most impacted by the recession, who are losing their jobs, their health insurance, and losing the ability to send their kids to college.
>
> Fourth, this package attempts to modernize the economy—or at least to begin a long process of doing that—by accelerating the development of new technology through key investments in science and energy.
>
> And last, it attempts, also, to save jobs by stabilizing State and local budgets. (*Congressional Record,* January 27, 2009, H557-8)

Republicans responded that the legislation was too expensive and wrongly targeted. Said Rep. Judy Biggert, "We should be enabling families, entrepreneurs, small businesses and job seekers to keep more of what they earn through fast-acting tax relief, not new wasteful government spending on numerous programs that hold little potential for economic stimulus" (*CR*, January 28, 2009, H613).

In the meantime, the Rules Committee was meeting to decide on a rule governing the amendment process. Members of the House had filed 206 amendments that they wanted to offer. After a marathon hearing, during which members went before the committee to make their case, the committee on a party-line vote approved a rule that allowed eleven amendments—one with bipartisan sponsorship, six sponsored by Democrats, and four, including a substitute, sponsored by Republicans. In addition, the rule "self-executed" an amendment making several last-minute changes to the bill; these postcommittee adjustments included provisions striking the money for resodding the Mall and the family-planning funds. Democratic leaders had decided that these provisions had become lightening rods that were not worth the pain they were causing their members. Better to remove them than try to explain in the face of the conservative onslaught. In fact, Obama had privately urged House Democrats to remove the funds for contraception because they had become a distraction. At 9:30 p.m., the Rules Committee reported H. Res. 92, the rule, to the House.

The next morning the House took up the rule and passed it on a near party-line vote. On the four roll calls to that point—three related to the two rules and one on a question of consideration, a roll call forced by Republicans and made possible by the fact that the stimulus bill of necessity waived the pay-as-you-go (PAYGO) rule—not a single Republican had voted with the majority. Once the rule passed, the House again resolved itself into the Committee of the Whole and commenced the one additional hour of debate the rule provided. Just before 2:00 p.m., the amendment process began. The rule had stipulated the length of debate time on each amendment, ten minutes for each, except for the Republican substitute, which was given sixty minutes.

Eight amendments were agreed to by voice vote; all were relatively minor. On two others, a recorded vote was demanded after the chair had declared that the "nays have it" following a voice vote. The chair postponed those votes, as the House allows the chair to do in order to save members time. An hour of debate on the Camp substitute then ensued. Dave Camp, the ranking minority member on the Ways and Means Committee, introduced the Republican substitute, which consisted of tax cuts only. Shortly before 5:00 p.m. the House began voting on the amendments, with the first vote a normal fifteen-minute vote and the subsequent votes reduced to five minutes. All the amendments were defeated. Significant numbers of

Republicans voted with Democrats against the two amendments that sought to cut parts of the stimulus funding, but on the substitute only nine Republicans and two Democrats crossed the aisle.

The Committee of the Whole then rose and reported to the House. Jerry Lewis, the ranking minority member of the Committee on Appropriations, offered a motion to recommit with instructions. The instructions consisted of some increased spending for highways and the Army Corps of Engineers and a large cut in other programs. The motion was defeated on a 159–270 recorded vote that mostly fell along party lines, though 31 Republicans and 13 Democrats voted against their party colleagues. HR 1 then passed the House by 244–188; 11 Democrats, mostly more conservative Blue Dogs, voted against the bill; not a single Republican supported it. The Republican whip system was aggressively employed to keep any Republican members from straying; even Joseph Cao, newly elected from a poor, majority-black district, was pressured into opposing the stimulus bill (*The Hill*, December 13, 2009).

Senate Committee Action

Two Senate committees approved stimulus provisions on January 27. The Finance Committee legislation consisted of tax cuts and health care spending, primarily aid to states for Medicaid. During the markup the committee added a $70 billion provision shielding middle-class households from the alternative minimum tax, which was originally aimed at the wealthy but had not been indexed to inflation. Republicans offered a series of amendments, most of them aimed at cutting the Medicaid funds or increasing tax cuts. Democrats defeated them all, fourteen on recorded votes. However, the biggest battle in the markup took place among Democrats over an amendment on the targeting of Medicaid aid; at base this was a fight between rural and urban states, a not unusual line of cleavage in the Senate. Chairman Max Baucus talked the contestants into deferring the debate. He persuaded several other members to withdraw their amendments by promising to negotiate about them. The committee approved the legislation on a vote of 14–9, with only one Republican, moderate Olympia Snowe, voting with all the Democrats in favor.

The Senate Appropriations Committee also approved its portion of the economic recovery bill despite Republican objections that the committee was moving too fast. As is often the case in the Senate, Chairman Daniel Inouye urged his members to refrain from offering their amendments in committee but rather to wait and offer them on the Senate floor. Three were offered in committee, but all were withdrawn. The committee voted to report the legislation on a 21–9 vote. Four Republicans joined all seventeen Democrats on the pro side, but three of the four made it clear they reserved the option of opposing the bill once it reached the floor (*CongressDaily,* January 27, 2009).

Getting to Sixty in the Senate

With the recovery bill having passed the House and having been reported out of the Senate committees, the focus shifted to the Senate floor. The PR battle to define the bill continued unabated. On the Sunday morning interview shows, Democrats and Republican dueled over the likely impact of the stimulus.

During the weekend, Senate moderates Ben Nelson, Democrat of Nebraska, and Susan Collins, Republican of Maine, began talks about possible revisions to the committee-reported bill. "My goal is to come up with a more targeted package," Collins explained. Majority Leader Harry Reid encouraged their effort; he knew he would need sixty votes to pass the bill in the Senate and that he did not as yet have them.

On Monday, February 2, HR 1 was put before the Senate by unanimous consent. Reid and McConnell had reached a unanimous consent agreement (UCA) to that effect at the end of the previous week. Republicans could have forced Democrats to offer a motion to proceed to consider the bill and to muster sixty votes to cut off debate and get a vote on the motion, but seeming to block debate on the new president's top priority in an economic emergency would send the wrong message. Republicans were arguing that they too wanted to stimulate the economy but that they had a better way. That did not mean, however, that Republicans were prepared to let the bill itself pass by a simple majority vote.

Reid offered, for Senators Inouye and Baucus, Senate amendment #98 in the nature of a substitute. That is, this "amendment in the nature of a substitute" was the combined Appropriations- and Finance-reported legislation. This would now serve as the text to which amendments would be offered.

For the next six days, the Senate debated and amended the bill. By Friday evening, February 6, as Reid reported, 450 amendments had been filed, 46 amendments offered, 19 agreed to, and 25 subjected to a recorded vote (*CR,* S1856).

Off the floor, furious negotiations and persuasion efforts were proceeding. On Monday evening President Obama met with the Democratic congressional leaders to urge them on. On Wednesday he met with Collins and Nelson separately, explaining that he believed it essential that the package be big enough to accomplish its purpose. Collins, who had wanted to cut it back to about $650 billion, came away convinced that a price tag around $800 billion was necessary.

Lawrence Summers, director of the White House National Economic Council, and White House budget director Peter R. Orszag had been assigned by Obama to work with the moderates on what funding could be cut. "We're trying to find a way to reach 60" votes, Majority Whip Richard J. Durbin, the Senate Democrats' chief vote counter, told reporters. "A number of Democrats have said they want to see changes to the bill before they can vote for it" (*Washington Post*, February 4, 2009).

Obama continued to put on the pressure. On Thursday in an op-ed in the *Washington Post,* he reiterated the urgency of passing a stimulus program. After new data showing huge job losses were released, Obama said, "These numbers demand action. It is inexcusable and irresponsible for any of us to get bogged down in distraction, delay or politics as usual while millions of Americans are being put out of work. Now is the time for Congress to act" (*WP,* February 6, 2009).

On Thursday, Collins and Nelson, who had been talking intensively with a group of fifteen to twenty moderates, gathered the group twice for collective deliberations. And, in the evening, a draft of a compromise began to circulate.

In the end, it took until Friday evening to reach a deal that could get the necessary sixty votes. After a meeting in Reid's office with the negotiators and the leadership, Reid took the tentative deal to the entire Democratic caucus to get a sign-off. At that meeting, White House chief of staff Rahm Emanuel told Senate Democrats that the president supported the deal. The agreement cut $83 billion in spending and $25 billion of the tax provisions out of the bill. All fifty-eight Democrats and at least three Republicans—Susan Collins (MA), Arlen Specter (PA), and Olympia Snowe (MA)—indicated they were prepared to vote to invoke cloture.

Passing the Bill in the Senate

Reid had hoped that Republicans would agree to a truncated procedure to save time: Democrats would stipulate that sixty votes were necessary to pass the compromise amendment and the bill itself, and Republicans would not force the time-consuming cloture procedure. Although this shortcut is now often used by the Senate, in this case Republicans were unwilling to consent. So the cloture process would have to be gone through. As is so frequently the case in the Senate, Reid and McConnell did reach a unanimous consent agreement governing that process and the remainder of the Senate's initial deliberations on the bill. The UCA stipulated:

> . . . providing for further consideration of the bill at 12 p.m., on Saturday, February 7, 2009, and that the Collins-Nelson (NE) Amendment be called up, and that cloture be filed on the amendment, and that no further

amendments or motions be in order for the duration of the bill; provided further, that on Monday, February 9, 2009, the time from 1 p.m. until 5:30 p.m., be equally divided and controlled in the same manner and at 5:30 p.m., Senate vote on the motion to invoke cloture on the amendment offered by Senator Reid for Senators Collins and Nelson (NE); that if cloture is invoked on the amendment; then post-cloture time run during any recess or adjournment of the Senate on Monday, February 9, 2009; and that all post-cloture time be considered expired at 12 noon, on Tuesday, February 10, 2009; that on Tuesday, February 10, 2009, the time until 12 noon be equally divided and controlled as provided above; and that if a budget point of order is raised against the amendment, then a motion to waive the applicable point of order be considered made; that if the waiver is successful, the amendment be agreed to; that if there is no point of order against the amendment, then adoption of the amendment be subject to a 60 affirmative vote threshold, and Senate vote on final passage of the bill, that upon passage of the bill, Senate insist on its amendment, request a conference with the House on the disagreeing votes of the two Houses, and the Chair be authorized to appoint conferees, with the ratio agreed upon by the two Leaders. (*Daily Digest* Friday S 1859)

In order to meet the deadlines of the cloture process, the Nelson-Collins amendment, that is, the compromise bill, had to be filed before midnight on Saturday. That proved to be a challenge. All the details had to be agreed to and then turned into legislative language. The size of the bill and the necessity of getting it all right required many of the staff involved to work all Friday night and almost up until the deadline on Saturday night. At just before midnight on Saturday, Reid withdrew S.A. 98, the committee bill, and submitted and then called up S.A. 570, the compromise, on behalf of Senators Nelson and Collins; he then immediately filed for cloture.

The UCA controlled Senate floor proceedings when the body returned to work on Monday, February 9. In the late afternoon, the Senate voted to invoke cloture on the Nelson-Collins amendment by a 61–26 vote; every Democrat and three Republicans—Collins, Snowe, and Specter—voted to cut off debate. The next day, the Senate passed the bill by an identical vote.

Obama, in the meantime, continued to promote the stimulus package vigorously; he endorsed the compromise in his Saturday radio address and advocated quick completion of the process. "The time for action is now," Obama said. "If we don't move swiftly to put this plan in motion, our economic crisis could become a national catastrophe" (*New York Times,* February 8, 2009). He traveled to Indiana, Virginia, and Florida for forums and meetings to push the plan. And on Monday evening, in prime time, he held his first formal White House news conference.

Reconciling Differences

With Obama pressing for swift action and the Democratic Party leaders having promised to finish a bill before the mid-February Presidents' Day recess, the pressure to reach a House-Senate agreement was intense. Pelosi had, in fact, vowed to keep the House in Washington until the process was complete. Yet, the bills passed by the two chambers differed in significant ways. House Democrats, including specifically Speaker Pelosi, were unhappy with cuts to education and aid to the states in the Nelson-Collins compromise.

As soon as it passed its bill on Tuesday, the Senate insisted on its amendment, asked for a conference, and appointed as conferees Inouye, Baucus, Reid, Thad Cochran, and Grassley. Unusually, in addition to the expected inclusion of the chairmen and ranking members of the Senate Appropriations and Finance committees, Majority Leader Reid appointed himself. By serving on the conference committee himself, he could speed up the process and assure that any agreement reached was one that could pass the Senate. Reid knew he had to keep the three Republicans who had voted for passage on board, as the conference report could also be filibustered. Later the same afternoon, the House by voice vote disagreed to the Senate amendment and agreed to a conference. The Speaker appointed as conferees Obey, Rangel, Energy and Commerce chair Henry Waxman, Appropriations ranking minority member Jerry Lewis, and Ways and Means ranking minority member Dave Camp. Thus the Speaker also kept the House conference delegation small in order to make quick action possible.

As is often the case, the serious bargaining took place behind closed doors before a formal meeting of the conference committee. Although the Obama administration had left much of the detailed drafting to Congress, at this point the administration was deeply involved with Emanuel and Orszag acting as point men. Pelosi too was a key negotiator. And the Senate moderates had to be consulted. When talks seemed to hit a wall over funding for school construction, the president phoned Pelosi and House majority whip James Clyburn to make sure that negotiations moved ahead.

The agreement reached by House and Senate negotiators was for a stimulus plan costing about $789 billion. The open conference committee meeting was tightly controlled by Democrats intent on holding together the package they had so painstakingly crafted; no amendments were allowed. At 10:25 p.m. Thursday night, the nearly 1,000-page, two-part bill was filed in the House.

The next day, Friday, the House considered the conference report. After several procedural motions and ninety minutes of debate, the House approved the conference report by a vote of 246–183; seven Democrats voted against the bill, down from eleven on the initial House passage vote; again not a single Republican supported it.

The bill was immediately sent to the Senate, which considered it the same day. By unanimous consent, the Senate agreed to raise the majority required for adoption of the conference report to sixty votes and to take one roll call on two motions—to waive the Budget Act, necessary for any stimulus bill and requiring sixty votes, and to adopt the conference report. These shortcuts would enable the Senate to finish work on the bill on Friday and leave town for the Presidents' Day recess. Getting to sixty took some fancy footwork by the Democratic leadership. Ted Kennedy, who had been diagnosed with brain cancer, was unable to participate, so every other previous "yea" vote was needed. The Democratic leaders held a several-hours-long roll call. They began it early enough to allow Joseph Lieberman (I-CT), an Orthodox Jew, to cast his vote before sundown. And they kept the roll call going late into the evening so that Democrat Sherrod Brown could fly back to Washington from Ohio, where he was attending a memorial service for his mother, who had recently died (*CQW*, February 16, 2009). The conference report passed 60–38 with no one changing their vote.

That cleared the bill for the president. Obama signed it into law on February 17, less than a month after his inauguration.

Two Unorthodox Paths to Stimulus Legislation

The similarities and differences in how these two bills became law illuminate both the aspects of "unorthodox" lawmaking that have become standard operating procedure and the continued variation in the paths that seemingly similar bills may follow from initiation to enactment. Both bills were high priority and, as responses to economic emergencies, needed to be passed quickly. Those factors dictated pervasive party leadership involvement in the legislative process. In the House, the majority-party leadership brought both bills to the floor under highly restrictive rules that assured swift and predictable action. In contrast, Senate extended-debate rules were employed—to somewhat different ends, in the two cases—but with the effect that sixty votes were needed for passage.

The 2008 stimulus bill bypassed committee in both chambers, and the differences between the two chambers' versions were resolved without a conference committee; thus much of what once was the regular order was circumvented. In circumstances that might well have led to what would have been labeled a summit in the recent past, the negotiating group consisted of only the Speaker of the House, the House minority leader, and the secretary of the Treasury, a group too small seemingly for the media to label it a summit. With the increasing concentration of decision-making authority in the party leaders, especially on the majority side, those leaders may take on an even more prominent negotiating role and such very small groups may succeed the larger summits. Of course, the consensus that speed was essential contributed to making those leadership decisions palatable.

The 2009 bill traversed a somewhat more orthodox course, at least on the surface. In both chambers, committees drafted and reported bills. Several committees were involved in each chamber, though in neither case was legislation formally multiply referred. Although the stimulus bill was a top priority of President Obama's, White House involvement in drafting the legislation was less formal than was the case in 2008. Partly this was because Obama did not actually become president until after the drafting process was well under way; in addition, when one party controls both branches, informal processes generally suffice. By early 2009 it had become clear that the economic crisis was much greater than it had appeared to be in early 2008. The 2009 bill was a great deal larger than the 2008 bill, and it was a true omnibus bill in contrast to the 2008 legislation, which was really simply a tax bill. The complexity of the 2009 bill and, even more, the complexity of the political context made postcommittee adjustments in both chambers critical to passage.

In 2008 a Republican president called for a stimulus bill, and congressional Republicans, though in the minority in both chambers, knew that they had to cooperate with the majority or make their president, and therefore their party, look ineffectual. In 2009, by contrast, Republicans quickly concluded that cooperating offered no electoral benefit, while opposition might well pay off. Furthermore, with Democrats having the upper hand in drafting the legislation, the bill would include much that most Republicans disliked. This change in political context had its greatest impact in the Senate. In 2008 minority Republicans used Senate extended-debate rules and the sixty-vote threshold to force Senate Democrats to accept—with minor changes—the deal worked out by Pelosi, Boehner, and Paulson. In 2009 they used those rules to extend the process in a way that gave their conservative media allies more time to revile the bill and, in the end, forced Democrats to decrease significantly the size of the stimulus in order to amass the sixty votes to pass it.

TABLE 7.1   HR 5140 Economic Stimulus Bill: A Chronology

Date (all 2008)	House action	Senate action	Postpassage action
January	*Pelosi, Boehner, and the White House negotiate stimulus package*		
1/28	Pelosi introduces HR 5140		
1/29	Bill referred to the Committee on Ways and Means, and in addition to the Committee on Financial Services		
1/29	Bill brought up under suspension of the rules and passed, 385–35		
2/4		Cloture on motion to proceed to consideration of HR 5140 voted 80–4	
2/7		Passed with an amendment, 81–16	House agreed to Senate amendment, 380–34
2/13			President signs bill

Note: Official actions are in roman type; behind-the-scenes, unofficial actions are in italics.

TABLE 7.2 American Recovery and Reinvestment Act: A Chronology

Date (all 2009)	House action	Senate action	Postpassage action
Dec–early Jan	*Obama advisers discuss components/size of a stimulus package with congressional party and committee leaders and their staffs*		
1/21	Appropriations marks up draft bill		
1/22	Ways and Means approves HR 598		
	Energy and Commerce approves HR 629		
1/26	Appropriations reports HR 679		
	Obey introduces HR 1 (combination bill)		
1/27		Appropriations reports S 336	
		Finance approves S 350	
1/28	HR 1 passes, 244–188		
Late Jan/early Feb		*Nelson and Collins negotiate compromise*	
2/9		Cloture invoked	
2/10		Bill passes, 61–37	
2/12			Conference report filed
2/13			House approves conference report, 246–183
			Senate approves conference report, 60–38
2/17			President signs bill

Note: Official actions are in roman type; behind-the-scenes, unofficial actions are in italics.

Making Nonincremental Policy Change through Hyperunorthodox Procedures: Health Care Reform in 2009–2010

HEALTH CARE REFORM was at the pinnacle of Barack Obama's and the Democratic Party's agenda. All the major Democratic presidential candidates had strongly advocated health care reform throughout the lengthy campaign, and many congressional Democrats had been working on the issue for years. Once the stimulus package was enacted, focus could turn to health care. Although some commentators and many Republicans argued that reform should be postponed until the economy recovered, the administration retorted that rising health care costs were a major threat to the economy and so needed to be tackled right away and that the only way of doing so was through comprehensive reform. Many Democrats also believed that the prospects for reform were never likely to be better; certainly, putting the effort off until 2010, an election year, would be a mistake.

The failed attempt to reform health care in the early Bill Clinton administration informed the strategies of both the president and the congressional leaderships. Unlike Clinton, Obama would not send legislative language to Congress; he would set out general principles and let Congress fill in the details. He would not draw lines in the sand that would make later compromise difficult. And he would attempt to preempt the opposition by drawing into the process the major interest groups that had killed Clinton's reform attempt; getting and keeping those groups at the table and negotiating deals when possible were major administration aims from the beginning.

The First Phase: Consultation and Drafting

In the House three committees have significant health policy jurisdiction: Energy and Commerce, Ways and Means, and Education and Labor. To avoid the turf fights that had hindered the Clinton effort, Speaker Nancy Pelosi, D-CA, asked the chairmen of the three committees to negotiate a single bill that then could be introduced in all their committees, a decision announced March 18, 2009. The two Senate committees with jurisdiction, Health, Education, Labor, and Pensions (HELP) and Finance, had been working together since June 2008. Sen. Edward Kennedy, D-MA, chairman of HELP, had been promoting health care reform for decades and considered it his top priority; Max Baucus, D-MT and chair of the Senate Finance Committee, was also committed to avoiding an intercommittee impasse and passing significant legislation. The staffs of the two committees met regularly to plan strategy; a series of discussions with representatives of groups with a stake in the results took place during the same months and into the new year.

Allowing for Reconciliation

Congress yearly passes a budget resolution that sets the framework for spending and tax decisions for the upcoming fiscal year. The budget resolution may call for passage of a reconciliation bill to reconcile legislation with the specifications of the budget resolution. By law, a reconciliation bill is protected from a filibuster in the Senate. A key decision in spring 2009 and a major point of controversy was whether the budget resolution would allow health care reform to be accomplished through a reconciliation bill. House leaders strongly favored that approach, and the House resolution included the provision. Senate Budget Committee chair Kent Conrad, D-ND, opposed it, arguing that it was not a realistic way of handling health care reform, and the budget resolution the Senate passed and sent to conference did not provide for using reconciliation. In conference negotiations the White House vigorously advocated including the provision, arguing that it would serve as a prod to get Republicans involved and a last-resort fallback. Conrad acquiesced, and the conference report approved by both chambers on April 29 allowed health care reform to be done as a reconciliation bill. Little noticed at the time, the budget resolution also allowed reform of the student loan program to be included in a reconciliation bill.

HELP Reports a Bill

Senate majority leader Harry Reid, D-NV, was more inclined than Pelosi to give his chairmen considerable running room, even on top party priorities.

In the Senate the two committees would be expected to produce bills, and then Reid would step in to try to put them together into a product that could pass the Senate. In late April, the Finance and HELP committees began holding a series of working-group discussions. Their aim was to produce bills that could be marked up in June and be ready for a floor vote before the August recess.

In early June, Chris Dodd, D-CT, who had taken over the chair's duties from an ailing Ted Kennedy, unveiled a draft bill that he and his fellow committee Democrats had negotiated in weeks of meetings. Formal markup began on June 17; it stretched over thirteen days and sixty hours, during which almost 500 amendments were considered. On July 15 the HELP Committee reported the bill on a party-line vote. It included the public option, a government health insurance program to compete with private insurance. This proposal had become the center of controversy, with Democrats arguing it was essential to keep the private insurance companies honest and Republicans claiming it would drive private companies out of business and represented a government takeover of health care. For activists the public option became *the* key decision.

Bill Drafting and Committee Action in the House

In the House, the three chairmen, now dubbed the "three tenors" by Pelosi, produced an outline of a bill by early June and took it to the Democratic Caucus for discussion; it included a public option. Pelosi and Majority Leader Steny Hoyer, D-MD, had met frequently with the chairs and with various party subgroups. The Blue Dogs and the New Democrats were particularly concerned that their more moderate points of view be heard. "We will continue to seek input and work closely with our colleagues, outside stakeholders, and the administration and are on track to introduce legislation shortly," the three chairs stressed at the Caucus meeting on June 9 (*CQ Today*, June 9, 2009).

On June 19, after Pelosi held another series of meetings, House Democrats released a discussion draft. Another intense set of negotiating sessions followed, and on July 14, Pelosi, Hoyer, and the three chairs unveiled their bill. Getting to that point had been difficult. The Blue Dogs continued to express concern about a number of provisions. A letter expressing "strong reservations" about the bill that forty Blue Dogs sent to Pelosi and Hoyer delayed the bill's unveiling. "We've had ongoing conversations; and yet then, when they're going to unroll something, that input from Blue Dogs wasn't in it," Heath Shuler, D-NC, a junior Blue Dog, complained (*CQW,* July 13, 2009). On the other end of the spectrum, the Progressive Caucus warned that if the public option were dropped, its members would oppose the bill. A large majority of the House Democratic members supported the public option, as did the House leaders themselves, and it remained in the bill. To pay for the reforms, as Obama and the Democratic leaders had promised they would, the leaders decided on a surtax on high-income tax payers. The bill, HR 3200, was referred to the three committees.

The Ways and Means committee approved HR 3200 on July 17 after a sixteen-hour markup. The vote was 23–18, with all of the Republicans and three Democrats voting no. The Education and Labor Committee's markup was even longer; the committee met through the night of July 16–17 before approving the bill, 26–22. Again all of the Republicans and three Democrats voted against it. A number of amendments were adopted; most expanded the scope of coverage. HR 3200 emerged from the two committees still largely similar.

The Energy and Commerce Committee began its markup on July 16 as well, but it soon became evident that the Blue Dogs, unless appeased, might bring down the bill. Chairman Henry Waxman, D-CA, suspended the markup after a second session on July 20. On the 21st, the Blue Dogs sent Waxman a list with ten changes they wanted made. The top issues, according to Mike Ross, D-AK, a committee member and the Blue Dogs' spokesman on health care, included "greater efforts to lower health care spending, a more generous exemption for small businesses from requirements that they provide insurance, and changes to the proposed government-run plan that would compete with private insurers" (*CQ Today*, July 27, 2009). In response to the evident danger to the effort, Obama called Energy and Commerce Democrats to the White House for a meeting; a "verbal agreement" on the cost issue was reached, but other problems remained. Negotiations continued, with the leaders playing a major part. As Waxman explained on July 24, Speaker Pelosi had convened "extensive negotiations and invited everyone with concerns to participate." The result, he said, was "a significant breakthrough in resolving the outstanding issue of regional disparities in Medicare" (*CQ Today*, July 27, 2009).

Talks continued by fits and starts. At one point Waxman threatened to bypass his own committee and bring the bill directly to the floor. Meetings continued in both Pelosi's and Hoyer's offices, and the leaders kept their rank and file informed by frequent Caucus meetings. Finally on July 29, "after two weeks of very long and intense negotiations" as Ross said, a deal was reached (*Politico*, July 29, 2009). In return for concessions on their major issues, four committee Blue Dogs agreed to vote to report the bill from committee. The markup resumed on July 30, and on the 31st the committee voted 31–28 to report the bill. The Blue Dogs' concessions were incorporated through an amendment, as were several changes agreed to in order to placate liberals upset at the concessions granted the

Blue Dogs. All the Republicans, joined by five Democrats—four Blue Dogs and Bart Stupak (D-MI)—voted against the bill.

As a final concession to the Blue Dogs, the leadership agreed to put off the floor vote until after the August recess. Many moderate Democrats did not want to vote before they saw what the Senate Finance Committee produced; why take a tough vote on a liberal bill, they reasoned, when the end result may be much less ambitious.

Finance Chairman Baucus's Negotiations

Finance Committee chairman Max Baucus persisted in his effort to reach a bipartisan deal. Since early in the year, he had been negotiating with ranking member Charles Grassley, R-IA; he later expanded the group, pulling in other Finance members from both parties. By July the primary negotiators—soon known as the Gang of Six—were Republicans Grassley, Mike Enzi (WY), and Olympia Snowe (ME) and Democrats Jeff Bingaman (NM), Kent Conrad, and Baucus himself. The deadline of having a bill to mark up in committee before the July 4 recess slipped, and Baucus took to responding to questions about when the bill would be marked up by saying, "We're ready when we're ready."

Reid had been checking in with both Dodd and Baucus several times a week and presumably encouraging Baucus to move the process along; in early July he let it be known that he had told Baucus to give up on bipartisanship and just get a bill out (*RC*, July 7, 2009). Liberals were increasingly unhappy with the delay and concerned about the concessions Baucus might make to pick up a few Republican votes; the Obama administration wanted the Senate bill passed before the August recess; Finance Committee Democrats excluded from Baucus's talks were beginning to express their discontent. Despite this pressure, Reid the next day seemed to retract. After a meeting with Grassley, Enzi, and Snowe, who had all along complained vociferously about "artificial deadlines," Reid reiterated his support for a bipartisan agreement.

As is so often the case for contemporary Senate majority leaders, Reid found himself caught between his party colleagues' expectations and the Senate imperative to get sixty votes. Democrats, especially the liberal bulk of the membership, were increasingly frustrated with the process. As Sheldon Whitehouse (D-RI) said, "I do think that a point comes when it just becomes time to pack up and move on because the business of the country is more important than what may be an elusive appearance of bipartisanship" (*Politico*, July 19, 2009). Yet Reid knew that without some Republican support, passing the legislation would be difficult; although Democrats now had sixty members, two were often absent because of illness, and some moderates were leery of supporting such major legislation without the cover provided by a least a few Republican votes. Reconciliation was still an option but one fraught with severe procedural complications and possible grave political consequences.

On Thursday, July 30, Baucus announced that there would be no Finance markup before the August recess. Despite weeks of near daily and often hours-long negotiations and continuing claims of progress, no deal had been reached. In fact, when several members had intimated that a deal might be close, Enzi and then Grassley heatedly denied it. Rumors that the GOP members of the Gang of Six were under intense pressure from their leadership to not reach a deal picked up steam, fueled by Grassley's and Enzi's talk about the need to write a bill that would command seventy-five or eighty votes. Many Democrats were now convinced that Republicans were simply slowing down the process and had no intention of actually cooperating (*RC*, August 22, 2009). Reid reportedly threatened Baucus with taking over the bill. The next day, July 31, Baucus set a September 15 deadline for reaching a bipartisan deal; the group would continue to negotiate over the August recess, but Baucus promised his Democratic colleagues that on September 15 he would move forward with a markup whether a bipartisan deal had been achieved or not.

The August Recess and Its Aftermath

August proved to be a public relations debacle for Democrats, as many had feared. Since neither chamber had produced one bill and especially since the Finance bill's outlines remained so unclear, Democrats lacked a proposal to defend, and wild rumors about the reform gained currency. Opponents staged rowdy protests at some Democratic House members' town hall meetings, and the media gave the most disruptive demonstrations enormous play. Republican leaders endorsed the protests and slammed the entire Democratic reform endeavor as an outrageously expensive big-government power grab. Efforts by congressional leaders, the White House, and the media themselves to counter the wildest rumors—death panels for senior citizens, for example—had some effect, but the overall impact appeared dire. When Grassley, home in Iowa and under considerable pressure from conservative constituents, gave credence to the death panel claim, congressional Democrats took that as irrefutable proof that Republicans had no intention of agreeing to any bipartisan deal. Reporters and pundits came close to declaring the entire reform effort dead.

The congressional Democratic leaders pressed Obama to respond more forcefully. During the summer of negotiations, Obama and his closest aides had repeatedly talked privately to various groups of members in an effort to keep the process moving forward; Obama himself had invited to the White House the Blue Dogs, the Gang of Six, together and individually, various other Republican senators, and, right before the recess, the entire Democratic Senate membership. At both the staff and the principal levels, information sharing and discussion of strategy between the White House and leadership offices were continuous (*Politico,* November 2, 2009). Obama had also promoted health care reform publicly through statements and appearances. Yet the Washington consensus was that he had failed to convey a "clear and coherent" message.

On September 9, Obama delivered a speech on health care to a joint session of Congress. His three goals, he emphasized, "were providing security and stability to individuals who already have coverage, extending coverage to those who don't, and slowing the growth of health spending" (*CQW,* September 14, 2009). The plan would cost $900 billion over ten years and, he promised, would be entirely paid for. The speech was well received by Democrats; the decline in public support for health reform stopped, and Democratic members responded positively. "Everybody in the Caucus loved the speech," a moderate Democrat reported. "He made people feel a lot better."

Finance Reports a Bill

Shortly before the speech, Baucus gave the other members of the Gang of Six a draft of a plan, and on September 11 he called a final meeting to wrap up their negotiating sessions. No agreement was reached. As Baucus later reported, "We met 31 times for 63 hours over the course of 4 months" (*CR,* March, 23, 2010, S1824).

With a bipartisan agreement clearly out of reach and obligated to deliver on his promise, Baucus on September 16 publicly unveiled his bill. Criticism from both the right and the left—and some from the center as well—followed quickly. Liberals objected to the lack of a public option, though that was hardly a surprise. Since early in 2009, Republicans had moved en mass to unyielding opposition, and the Baucus proposal changed no minds. Some moderates, including Republican Olympia Snowe—as well as most liberals—argued that the subsidies were too meager to make health insurance affordable for middle-class families. Reid emphasized that the bill was just a starting point.

On September 22 the Finance Committee began its markup. Baucus had made some revisions in response to criticisms from Democratic members. On October 2, after seven days of debate and amendment, the markup finished. The committee defeated two major amendments to provide for a public option. All of the Republican killer amendments also lost. No final vote was taken because a number of members wanted to see the Congressional Budget Office (CBO) report on the cost first. On October 7 the CBO reported that the bill as amended would cost $829 billion, well below the president's $900 billion figure, and would be paid for by the fees and cost cutting in the legislation.

When the Finance Committee met on October 13 to vote on approving the bill, the only suspense was over whether Olympia Snowe would vote for the bill; but that suspense was intense. She did but warned that she still had concerns and would not necessarily support it later in the process. Snowe was the only Finance member to cross party lines and the committee approved the bill 14–9. Democrats were thrilled to get Snowe's vote; but it was clear that the votes of some of their own members were not assured.

Building Winning Coalitions to Pass Health Care: Postcommittee and Floor Action

With bills reported out of all the relevant committees, the next step was getting legislation ready for floor consideration. That required merging the multiple bills in each chamber into a single bill in each and, in the process, creating a bill that could pass that chamber. Here the party leaders would play the central role.

Merging the Bills in the House

The House party leadership had begun the process by the August recess, but the lack of a Finance bill hampered the effort. The leaders knew they could expect no Republican votes at all, so they could lose at most thirty-nine Democrats. That meant they would have to get a considerable number of moderate to conservative Democrats on board, and such members were leery of committing on the most contentious issues until they saw the Finance bill.

Because health care reform is so complex, the House leadership made a serious and continuing effort to educate the membership; so in late July, the leaders held a five-hour tutorial on HR 3200, with the first half devoted to briefings from expert staff—with no questions allowed until the second half (*WP*, July 29, 2009). Caucus meetings devoted to specific aspects of reform—the public option, for example—followed in the fall.

The core negotiating group included the top party leaders and the three chairmen. But, as a Pelosi spokesman insisted, "Everyone is going to be in discussions on health care. . . . People are going to continue to offer input" (*Politico*, August 4, 2009). A number of major disputes needed to be settled. Whether the bill would include a public option and, if so, what its form would be received the most media attention. Progressives, including Pelosi herself, strongly favored the so-called "robust" public option, a public insurance plan that would pay providers at the Medicare rate plus 5 percent. Many Blue Dogs preferred no public option at all; some were, however, willing to support the version contained in the Education and Commerce compromise, which called for a public insurance plan with rates negotiated by the secretary of Health and Human Services. The cost of the bill and how to pay for it were contentious issues. Blue Dogs worried about the total cost; junior Democrats from wealthier suburban districts opposed the Ways and Means bill's surtax on the wealthy to pay for a good part of the cost. When Obama in his September 7 speech called for a bill with a maximum cost of $900 billion dollars, the Democratic leaders knew they would have to reduce the price tag on HR 3200, but doing so created other problems, including assuring that subsidies for the middle class remained high enough to make coverage affordable. Antiabortion Democrats insisted on strong language to prohibit any federal funding from being used for elective abortions; pro-choice Democrats were outraged, claiming that this was an effort to make antiabortion language more draconian than at present. In August the Tea Party protesters and right wing bloggers claimed that the Democrats' health care bill would provide benefits to illegal aliens; Texas Republican Joe Wilson's infamous shout of "You lie" at Obama during his health care speech was in response to the president's assertion that this was not the case. Latino Democrats were concerned that, in attempting to assure that undocumented workers would not receive benefits, the bill would place onerous conditions on legal immigrants. Each of these controversies threatened, if not adeptly handled, to drain away crucial votes.

For weeks Pelosi and Hoyer met almost daily with the chairmen, other party leaders, and various groups of members who had problems with the legislation. Numerous Caucus meetings were held to brief all Democrats and to hear still more opinions and complaints. The Progressive Caucus claimed it had the votes for a robust public option, and the Blue Dogs claimed they had the votes to stop it; at one point, the two caucuses produced dueling whip counts. Pelosi tried hard to get the votes for a robust public option; regular whip counts and open Caucus questioning of members indicated a majority was close. CBO scoring concluding that the robust public option would cut the deficit more than other versions gave it a boost. In the end, however, Pelosi found she could not get the necessary 218 votes. She decided the public option with negotiated rates would be included in the compromise bill. To pick up other votes, the level at which the surtax on high-income tax payers went into effect was raised and more small businesses were exempted from a requirement to provide coverage (*NYT,* October 20, 2009).

On October 29, 2009, the House leadership called a Caucus for a final briefing of the membership, and then Democrats, with Speaker Pelosi at their head, proceeded to the west front of the Capitol for an unveiling of their bill (*WP,* October 30, 2009). "We are about to deliver on the promise of making affordable, quality health care available for all Americans," Speaker Nancy Pelosi said (*NYT,* October 30, 2009). "It reduces the deficit, meets President Obama's call to keep the costs under $900 billion over 10 years and it insures 36 million more Americans" (*Politico,* October 29, 2009).

The Democratic leadership had not yet solved the abortion dilemma and could not yet count to 218. The leaders continued negotiations even as they moved toward a vote. On the night of Tuesday, November 3, they filed a manager's amendment aimed at ensuring that insurance companies would not rapidly increase premiums in the period before most of the reforms take effect. Pelosi had promised that members would have seventy-two hours to review the legislation before floor action, so with this filing a vote could take place on Saturday evening. The abortion language continued to be problematical, and the immigration issue also was a problem. "We are continuing to discuss this legislation with our members, and I will bring it to the floor once we have consensus and in keeping with our 72-hour pledge," Hoyer reported after yet another leadership meeting (*CD,* November 4, 2009). Asked whether she had the votes to pass the bill, Pelosi responded, "We will" (*The Hill,* November 5, 2009).

The AARP (formerly the American Association of Retired Persons), the huge senior citizens' group, and the American Medical Association (AMA) endorsed the House bill, providing an important boost. Opponents staged a loud and intense protest outside the Capitol, and many House Republicans including the leaders spoke to the protestors.

Marginal Democrats, spooked by right-wing attacks, mounted a last-minute effort to get the leadership to include language excluding undocumented immigrants from buying insurance in the exchange with their own money—a provision included in the Senate Finance Committee bill. Members of the Congressional Hispanic Caucus were outraged and threatened to vote against the rule for bringing the bill to the floor if that was done. Pelosi asked Democratic Congressional Campaign Committee (DCCC) chair Chris Van Hollen to coordinate negotiations with Democratic Caucus vice chairman Xavier Becerra on the issue. Obama also met with Hispanic Caucus members at the White House (*CD,* November 5, 2009).

Lois Capps, a pro-choice Democrat, had attempted to come up with language to satisfy the antiabortion Democrats led by Bert Stupak, but they considered her language not restrictive enough. Brad Ellsworth, an anti-abortion Democrat, working with Hoyer, then made an attempt with more restrictive language. Pro-choice Democrats indicated they could go along, but again Stupak argued it was not enough. Stupak's language would block any subsidies from being used to purchase plans that cover abortion, and it became increasingly clear that the U.S. Conference of Catholic Bishops would not settle for anything less. For many of the vulnerable antiabortion Democrats, the Bishops' endorsement was key. If the vote was to occur on Saturday, as planned, the Rules Committee needed to report the rule for floor debate on Friday, and that meant a decision on abortion needed to be made. Pelosi held a series of meetings on Friday—with leaders of the Pro-Choice Caucus, with staff members from the Bishops' Conference, and with Stupak, Ellsworth, and Mike Doyle, another Roman Catholic Democrat who had worked on the issue. Whip counts indicated that with the Bishops' Conference actively against the bill on the basis of abortion, the votes to pass it were not there. Pelosi decided that the rule would have to allow Stupak to offer his language as an amendment. With almost all the Republicans likely to vote for it, it would pass. Members of the Pro-Choice Caucus were furious and denounced the decision but grudgingly acknowledged that they would nevertheless support the bill.

Passing the House Bill

The top leaders, the whip system, and the administration continued to focus on undecided members. One member reported that on Friday alone he received calls from Obama; Pelosi; Rahm Emanuel, the White House Chief of Staff; Health and Human Services Secretary Kathleen Sebelius; and Education Secretary Arne Duncan (*WP,* November 7, 2009). The leadership had promised Latino members that the language they opposed would not be added; now they met with Pelosi seeking assurances that were Republicans to attempt to add it through the motion to recommit with instructions, their last parliamentary opportunity to change the bill, the leadership would go all out to defeat it. Pelosi promised that the leaders would, but she asked them to promise in return that they would support the bill whatever happened. Obama came to Capitol Hill on Saturday to talk to the Democratic Caucus. He argued that this was a historic opportunity, perhaps the most important of their careers. He also warned them, a participant reported: "If you think the Republicans are not going to go after you if you vote no, think again."

Debate had started on Saturday morning. The first order of business was approving the rule for consideration of what was now HR 3962, the Affordable Health Care for America Act. The rule provided for four hours of debate "to be equally divided and controlled by the chair and ranking minority member of the Committee on Energy and Commerce, the chair and ranking minority member of the Committee on Ways and Means, and the chair and ranking minority member of the Committee on Education and Labor." The manager's amendment and a "perfecting" amendment to it "shall be considered as adopted"; that is, the manager's amendment with some last-minute changes the leaders had negotiated would be adopted without a separate vote by virtue of the rule being adopted. Only two amendments were made in order: the Stupak abortion amendment to be debated for twenty minutes and the amendment "in the nature of a substitute printed in part D of the report of the Committee on Rules if offered by Minority Leader Boehner or his designee" to be debated for one hour. As is now routine, the Rules Committee had required the Republicans to submit their substitute to the committee, thus depriving them of any element of surprise. Pelosi, who makes the final decisions on rules for such critical legislation, decided to go back on a promise she had made to Anthony Wiener, a liberal Democrat from New York, to allow him to offer an amendment establishing a single payer plan. Although disappointed, Weiner realized that, given how difficult and delicate putting together a majority was proving to be, Pelosi needed to keep floor consideration as streamlined as possible, and thus uncertainty as low as possible.

After a contentious debate marked by Republican attempts to delay the process, the previous question on the rule was moved successfully by a vote of 247–187; then the rule was approved 242–187; on the first vote ten Democrats voted with all the Republicans in opposition; on the second, fifteen did so. Next came the four hours of general debate, an unusually long time for the House. Debate on the Stupak amendment followed. A rumor had circulated that Republicans might vote "present" rather than "yea"; without Republican votes the Stupak amendment would almost certainly be defeated and then enough antiabortion Democrats would likely vote against the bill, as they had threatened, to bring it down. The Democratic leadership had, however, assured that the Bishops' Conference would impress on Republicans their strong opposition to that tactic, and most of the major antiabortion groups also opposed it vigorously. The result was unanimous Republican support for the Stupak amendment, which passed 240–194; sixty-four Democrats voted for it. Little drama attended the vote on the Republican substitute; the CBO scored it as costing little but also providing coverage for few additional people. No Democrats voted for the substitute, and it was defeated 176–258.

One potential obstacle did remain before the final vote. By House rules, the minority has the right to offer a motion to recommit with or without instructions before the passage vote. A motion to recommit with instructions is essentially a motion to amend the bill, and the only limit on what the minority can offer is that it must be germane to the bill. There is no requirement that the minority inform the majority of the contents before it makes the motion. Since House Republicans lost the majority in

2006, they had used the motion to recommit with instructions to confront vulnerable Democrats with tough votes. Democrats feared that on the health care reform bill the Republican motion to recommit with instructions would focus on immigration and likely include stringent identification requirements for legal immigrants and bar undocumented workers from buying insurance through the exchanges with their own money. This would be politically dicey for red-district Democrats to vote against, but if it won, it would endanger the votes of Latino Democrats for passage. Democrats—the leadership and the membership—were surprised and relieved when the Republican leadership offered a motion to recommit with instructions on medical malpractice. "I was very pleased I didn't have to worry about that one [immigration] tonight," said Majority Whip James Clyburn (D-SC). "I don't know if it was a mistake or not because I don't know exactly why they did it" (*RC,* November 8, 2009). Democrats easily defeated the motion 247–187, with thirteen Democrats and three Republicans crossing party lines.

John Dingell (D-MI), the longest serving member of the House and a longtime proponent of health care reform, closed the debate. At about 6:00 p.m., as planned, the vote on passing the bill began. The leaders were confident they had the votes; this was not the sort of bill they would bring to the floor on spec. As Chris Van Hollen explained the day before, "You don't want to roll the dice on this" (*CD,* November 6, 2009). Nevertheless tension filled the House chamber. Votes went up on the electronic board quickly at first and then more slowly; when the "yea" vote reached 218, a cheer went up from the Democratic side. Pelosi, however, had one more chore to perform; she went to a room off the floor to persuade Loretta Sanchez, D-CA, to come in and cast the 219th vote. With more than a bare majority, vulnerable Democrats could not be attacked as having cast the decisive vote. Toward the end of the voting period, a lone Republican cast his vote for the bill; Joseph Cao, who had defeated disgraced Democrat William Jefferson in a majority-black district of Louisiana, voted for the bill but only after passage was assured. The vote was 220–215; thirty-nine Democrats voted against the bill; of those thirty-one represented districts McCain had won in 2008; twenty-four of fifty-three Blue Dogs voted against the bill (*NYT,* November 8, 2009).

Mike Lux, a former Clinton staffer involved in the 1993–1994 effort, said admiringly, "On the final vote, the whipping process was intense and impressive. Democratic leaders I have known in the past have rarely played this kind of hardball, but some kneecaps were broken Saturday night to get these votes, and the Speaker did a masterful job of doing every little thing that needed to be done. She gave no passes to people, and she was very clear there would have been consequences to all who voted no. She got the job done" (*Huffington Post,* November 9, 2009).

"That was easy," Pelosi joked at the news conference following House passage. Compared with what would be required to pass a bill in the Senate, it was.

Merging the Bills in the Senate

As soon as Finance had reported its bill, Senate majority leader Reid began the arduous task of merging the bills from the two committees. The bills differed in several significant respects: the HELP bill included a public option; the Finance bill did not; the HELP bill provided substantially more generous subsidies to middle-income people than the Finance bill did. Constructing one bill to take to the floor, however, entailed much more than simply finding a compromise between the two committees. To get a health care reform bill onto the floor would require imposing cloture on the motion to proceed to consider the bill—and that takes sixty votes. With Republicans adamantly opposed, Reid would need to hold all the Democrats plus the two independents who caucused with them.

The core negotiating group consisted of Reid; Baucus; Dodd, who continued to represent the HELP committee; and, for the White House, Rahm Emanuel and Nancy-Ann DeParle, the president's top health care adviser. OMB director Peter Orszag also sometimes participated. Reid kept the group small with the hope that would speed action. Nevertheless, the need for sixty votes required Reid to consult widely with his members. He, Baucus, and Dodd held daily meetings with various Democratic senators and occasionally with Olympia Snowe as well (*RC*, October 22, 2009).

Pressure from various factions of the party was intense, as was that from interest groups. Liberals demanded that a public option be included. "There are 52 solid Democrats for the public option," said Sen. Tom Harkin. "Only about five Democrats oppose it. Should the 52 give in to the five? Or should the five go along with the vast majority of the Democratic caucus?" Moderate Democrats pushed back, declaring they might not even vote for bringing to the floor a bill with a public option. An unusually heated argument broke out at a regular Democratic senators' lunch. It was only a little less raucous than the August tea party protests, Sen. Ben Nelson joked. Reid's task, according to Sen. Evan Bayh, "requires the wisdom of Solomon and the patience of Job" (*NYT*, October 19, 2009).

Even before Finance reported its bill, a possible compromise version of the public option was floating around Washington; the proposal was for a national public health insurance plan but with a provision that allowed any state to opt out of the plan if it so wished. This built on a proposal that Tom Carper (D-DE) had been promoting but Charles Schumer (D-NY), third ranking in the Democratic leadership, altered it to make it more attractive to liberals—Carper originally had an opt-in rather than an opt-out—and then became its most visible champion.

On October 25, on NBC's *Meet the Press,* Schumer declared that Reid was close to reaching the sixty votes needed. "I'm becoming increasingly optimistic that we will have a health care bill," said Sen. Russell Feingold (D-WI), another liberal, on CBS's *Face the Nation.* "I'm frankly getting excited that we may have some momentum for something very positive" (*WP,* October 26, 2009). Moderate Ben Nelson, D-NE, on CNN's *State of the Union,* however, reiterated that he was not yet on board.

The next day at a press conference, Reid announced, "I've concluded with the support of the White House and Sens. Dodd and Baucus, that the best way to move forward is to include a public option with the op-out provision for states" (*The Hill,* October 26, 2009). After talking with almost every Senate Democrat over the weekend, Reid found fifty-six or fifty-seven votes for a proposal to create a national insurance plan with an opt-out and decided to move ahead (*Politico,* October 27, 2009). Democratic proponents of the public option, such as Schumer, had argued that given that a large majority of congressional Democrats and of the public favored a public option, Reid should put the public plan in the bill and force opponents to try to strip it out (*NYT,* October 23, 2009). That would advantage the public plan.

Getting the Bill onto the Senate Floor

Reid now needed a CBO cost estimate of the merged bill and sixty votes to bring it to the floor. While all the players waited for the CBO, a number of moderates publicly expressed their unhappiness with Reid's public option. Mary Landrieu (D-LA) and Ben Nelson both said they could not support it. Joe Lieberman (I-CT) vowed to filibuster the final bill if it contained any form of public option. Reid and his lieutenants worked to persuade Democrats to vote for cloture on the motion to proceed. They had been arguing since midsummer that Democrats needed to stick together on procedural votes. "I have urged all my colleagues to stick with this process and realize that the first vote is not the last vote and that we want to come together procedurally to keep this process moving," Democratic whip Dick Durbin explained in July. "The Republican [minority] wants to filibuster us into failure, and we can't let that happen. We have to move forward" (*RC,* July 29, 2009). Now the Democratic leadership intensified its efforts to cast the vote as a procedural—not a policy—vote; it was a vote to let the Senate debate and amend a bill. The Republican leadership responded with the counterargument; this was, in effect, a vote for the Reid bill and his version of the public option, Minority Leader Mitch McConnell contended.

With the CBO scoring taking considerably longer than expected, Democrats worried about the schedule. Obama continued to press for final action before the end of the year. Republicans signaled that they would do everything they could to drag the process out, believing that the longer it went on, the more likely they would be able to kill it. Sen. Tom Coburn, R-OK, declared he would demand the reading of the entire bill, a step usually dispensed with by unanimous consent. Although Coburn is a maverick on the far right of the Senate GOP membership, the consensus assumption was that he had cleared that step with his leadership.

Reid believed he had to get the bill onto the floor before any Thanksgiving recess so that the lengthy amending process could be finished before Christmas. At Reid's invitation, Bill Clinton spoke at the Senate Democrats' regular Tuesday lunch on November 10; Clinton reminded them of what had happened in 1993–1994 and urged them to pass a bill. Late that afternoon, Reid filed a motion necessary to make the motion to proceed in order on Monday, November 16, after the Veterans Day break.

On Wednesday, November 18, Reid finally received the CBO report; it contained good news; the cost was below the president's $900 billion mark and, counting new fees, taxes, and savings, it actually reduced the deficit over ten years by more than the Finance bill did—and it would cover 94 percent of the population. Anticipating the report, Reid had scheduled a Democratic Caucus meeting for late afternoon to brief his members on the bill. Before that meeting, he met separately with Nelson, Landrieu, and Blanche Lincoln of Arkansas; the three Democratic moderates had concerns about the bill and had not yet promised to vote for the motion to proceed. "He is walking through the particulars with them," said Reid's spokesman, Jim Manley (*WP,* November 18, 2009). At the Caucus meeting, Democrats generally reacted favorably to the bill. Reid and his team then unveiled it publicly at a press conference. Still, they were uncertain if they had the votes. "We're still counting. Harry is still counting and working," said Majority Whip Durbin (*Politico,* November 19, 2009).

The White House sent Interior Secretary Ken Salazar, former Senate majority leader Tom Daschle, and Vice President Joe Biden, all former senators, to the Hill to help Reid work the bill. Salazar ate lunch with moderate Mark Pryor (D-AR) in the Senate dining room, and Biden spent three hours talking with moderates—including Lincoln—one on one (*Politico,* November 18, 2009).

Reid decided that rather than using the House's health care bill as the vehicle, HR 3590, a noncontroversial House-passed tax bill to extend a home-buyer tax credit to members of the armed forces, would be employed. The procedure would be the same: the House-passed bill (HR 3590) would be brought up, and the Senate version would then immediately be inserted; that is, HR 3590 would serve as the "shell." By using HR

3590, Senate Democrats would never have to cast a vote that could be represented as favoring the House's bill, with its unqualified public option, and Republicans would have to vote against a popular bill helping soldiers. This maneuver would not, however, obviate the need for sixty votes (*RC,* November 18, 2009).

On Thursday afternoon Reid filed a motion to close further debate on the motion to proceed to the consideration of HR 3590 and announced that the cloture vote would take place on Saturday at 8:00 p.m. Reid proceeded to spell out the unanimous consent agreement (UCA) he had reached with the Republican leadership. The Senate would continue to debate the motion to proceed on Friday from 10:00 a.m. to 11:00 p.m. and on Saturday from 10:00 a.m. to 8:00 p.m., when the vote would occur. The UCA further stipulated that "if cloture is invoked on the motion to proceed to consideration of the bill, then all postcloture time be yielded back, and the motion to proceed be agreed to; that after the bill is reported, the Majority Leader be recognized to call up his amendment, and that it be reported by number only" (quoted from the *Daily Digest,* November 19, 2009). That meant that if the Democrats got the sixty votes, the UCA called for no postcloture debate, no separate vote on the motion to proceed itself, and no reading of the health care bill (i.e., the majority leader's amendment). Republicans had decided that in return for a lengthy debate before the cloture vote, they would not insist on further drawing out the first phase of the process. And, of course, agreeing to the UCA meant they could go home for Thanksgiving.

Now all that Reid needed was sixty votes. The effort to woo the last few Democrats went into overdrive. On Friday, Ben Nelson announced he would vote to begin debate. On Saturday morning, Mary Landrieu promised to do the same; Reid agreed to add a provision that would result in more Medicaid funds for Louisiana and that presumably helped her decide. Now only Blanche Lincoln was uncommitted. When she finally declared she too would vote to begin debate, the suspense was over. Democrats had the sixty votes; Max Baucus had to fly back from Montana, where he had been called because his mother had taken ill, but the vote and its aftermath played out as expected. The bill was now on the floor.

Senate Marathon: Passing the Bill

The Senate returned from Thanksgiving on Monday, November 30 and began considering health care. Democrats knew that the legislation as Reid had put it together—now on the floor as Reid amendment #2789 in the nature of a substitute to HR 3590—could not command sixty votes. Four Democrats—Lincoln, Landrieu, Nelson, and Lieberman—had emphasized when they cast their vote for cloture on the motion to proceed that they did not support the bill as written and would not vote for cloture on the bill itself if it were not changed; all had problems with the public option, and Nelson also objected to what he considered too lenient abortion language. "I've already alerted the leader, and I'm promising my colleagues, that I'm prepared to vote against moving to the next stage of consideration as long as a government-run public option is included," Lincoln said before the vote (*CD*, November 21, 2009).

On the Monday the Senate returned, Reid met in his office with top Democrats and administration officials to begin the process of finding a compromise acceptable to sixty senators. Participating were Rahm Emanuel, Interior Secretary Ken Salazar, Health and Human Services Secretary Kathleen Sebelius, former Senate majority leader Tom Daschle, and health reform director Nancy-Ann DeParle (*Politico,* November 30, 2009). Reid pulled in various Democrats and, after a few days, tapped a group of ten Democrats—five liberals and five moderates—to negotiate a deal. The moderates initially invited, "the Caucus's squeakiest wheels," were Blanche Lincoln (AR), Mary Landrieu (LA), Mark Pryor (AR), Ben Nelson (NE), and Joe Lieberman (CT) (*RC,* December 8, 2009). Ominously Lieberman did not attend, though he did send staff. Tom Carper (DE) was then invited to fill out the moderate group.

Rahm Emanuel conferred with Reid daily; Nancy DeParle essentially moved to Capitol Hill, meeting with the Group of Ten and various other participants in the process, including Snowe and Susan Collins (R-ME), the two Republican senators considered possible yes votes (*CD*, December 7, 2009). Former senators Salazar and Daschle as well as an assortment of White House aides continued their efforts, working at Reid's direction and for his bill. On December 7, at Reid's request, Obama went to Capitol Hill to give Democrats a pep talk.

As negotiations and persuasion played out behind the scenes, health care reform was being considered on the Senate floor. Democrats knew that the Republican strategy would involve stretching out the process as long as possible. Other elements of GOP strategy soon became evident. In terms of substance, Republicans would concentrate on what they argued were debilitating cuts to Medicare; in terms of process they would offer many of their proposals as motions to commit the bill to the Finance Committee with instructions. Republicans believed that this procedure more clearly made their point that they wanted to start the process over again. And, were they to actually win such a vote, the Democrats would be faced with the time-consuming process of bringing the bill back to the floor—a process that would again require sixty votes. Republicans blocked votes for the first several days the bill was on the floor, but on Wednesday, the leaders reached a UCA to vote the following day on the two pending matters—an amendment by Democrat Barbara Mikulski (MD) and a motion to commit by Republican John McCain (AZ). The UCA also made it in order for Republican Lisa Murkowski (AK) to call up her amendment, which was on the same subject as the Mikulski amendment, and for Democrat Michael Bennet (CO) to call up "Amendment No. 2826, a side-by-side amendment with respect to the McCain motion to commit" (*Daily Digest,* December 12, 2009). ("Side-by-side" amendments are first-degree amendments on the same subject considered simultaneously, which cannot be done except by unanimous consent. See Chapter 3.) The UCA further specified that sixty votes would be required to prevail on any of the votes.

This set the pattern for the following days. Debate would be extended, but eventually the leaders would agree on a unanimous consent agreement for votes. Usually two matters would be on the floor at the same time—typically a Democratic amendment and a Republican motion to commit. Most of the Democratic amendments were intended to provide "cover" to Democrats on the changes to Medicare proposed, though the Mikulski amendment was on assuring women would have access to mammograms. One purpose of this amendment was also to provide cover; Republicans had used an advisory committee report suggesting that most women did not need regular screening mammograms until age fifty to argue that the Democrats' bill would lead to rationing and second-class health care. (The Murkowski amendment attempted to up the ante in terms of guaranteed testing.) Sixty votes would be needed for any of these motions to prevail. All of the Republican motions to commit were voted down, with none even commanding a majority. Democrats largely stuck together in opposition.

Reid kept the Senate in session on both Saturday and Sunday, December 5 and 6; he was making clear that if Republicans wanted a lengthy debate, it would not be painless. On Tuesday, December 8, Nelson offered his amendment with the same antiabortion language as the House-passed Stupak amendment. Democrat Barbara Boxer (CA) moved to table the amendment, a nondebatable motion and one that requires only a simple majority to prevail; the amendment was tabled by a vote of 54–45, with fifty-two Democrats and two Republicans voting to table and seven Democrats and thirty-eight Republicans voting against.

On Wednesday, December 9, the Group of Ten sent its product to the CBO for scoring. Although the participants were unwilling to provide much detail until the CBO had made its determinations, some aspects had been leaking out over the previous days. Instead of a public option, the Office of Personnel Management (OPM), which administers the health insurance program for federal workers, would negotiate private but non-profit plans available to those without employer-provided insurance and some people fifty-five to sixty-four years old would be allowed to buy into Medicare.

As Democrats awaited the CBO report, debate on the floor continued. Consideration of North Dakota Democrat Byron Dorgan's amendment to allow importation of prescription drugs began on December 10. The amendment presented Reid with a conundrum; a majority of Democrats, including Obama, had a history of supporting drug importation, a proposal the pharmaceutical drug industry vehemently opposed. Yet earlier in the year the White House had made a deal with the industry that called for it to offer discounts worth $80 billion to Medicare patients as its contribution to reform. The Dorgan amendment threatened the industry's support of reform, and the last thing Senate Democrats needed was more opponents. Reid was unsure he had the votes to defeat the amendment and needed time to figure out how to handle it.

Reid thus decided to move to some important unfinished business. He brought up the conference report on HR 3288, which carried six of the seven appropriations bills that had not been separately enacted. Because conference reports are privileged, Republicans could not filibuster bringing it to the floor, but they could filibuster the conference report itself and did force Democrats to impose cloture. Thus the Senate spent another weekend in session; cloture was successfully imposed on Saturday, and the conference report was passed on Sunday.

Also on Sunday, December 13, Joe Lieberman announced on CBS's *Face the Nation* that he would join Republicans in filibustering the health care bill if it contained any form of public option—or the Medicare buy-in provision. The first was no surprise, but Lieberman had seemed to back a Medicare buy-in as recently as September. Reid called Lieberman into his office Sunday afternoon and found he would not budge. Reid saw no alternative but to accede to Lieberman's demands, and rumors were rife that the White House was pushing him to do so.

Democrats were furious at Lieberman, many seeing his stance as a betrayal. "The two outstanding issues are: Will Senate progressives be forced to surrender the Medicare buy-in to get Lieberman and, if so, will Lieberman honor that deal," said one senior Senate Democratic aide anonymously. "It would be good if the next personal commitment [Lieberman] made to vote for the bill was made to the president, because it would be a lot harder for him to break that one" (*RC*, December 15, 2009).

Reid called a Democratic Caucus meeting for late afternoon on Monday to see if his members would go along with dropping both the public option and the Medicare buy-in. The meeting was tense and many liberals were unhappy, but they too saw no real choice. Not all committed to voting for such a bill, but none declared their unequivocal opposition.

In contrast, many Democratic activists and liberal bloggers were outraged to the point of calling for killing the bill. Howard Dean proposed that on television. But the more politically savvy and many of those with the best grasp of the policy details responded that killing the bill would be folly; even without those provisions, the bill represented a major step forward and another chance was unlikely to come soon.

On December 14, Reid and McConnell reached a unanimous consent agreement to vote on the following day on the Dorgan amendment, a Frank Lautenberg (D-NJ) alternative on drug importation, a Crapo motion to commit the bill to the Finance Committee (with instructions that it be reported back with changes that would provide that no provisions of the measure could result in a federal tax increase for individuals with adjusted gross incomes of less than $200,000 and married individuals with adjusted gross incomes of less than $250,000), and a Baucus side-by-side amendment with Crapo. The UCA read, in part,

> "It be in order for Senator Baucus to offer a side-by-side amendment to the Crapo motion to commit; and Senator Lautenberg be recognized to offer Amendment No. 3156, as a side-by-side to Dorgan-McCain Amendment No. 2793, as modified. . .; that upon the use or yielding back of all time, Senate vote on or in relation to the aforementioned amendments and motion in this order: Baucus, Crapo, Dorgan, and Lautenberg; with each subject to an affirmative 60 vote threshold, and that if they achieve that threshold, then they be agreed to; that if they do not achieve that threshold they then be withdrawn" (*Daily Digest*, December 14, 2009).

The UCA also stipulated that, after those were disposed of, the Bernie Sanders (I-VT) amendment establishing a single-payer system as well as a Kay Bailey Hutchison (R-TX) motion to commit would be in order.

On the 15th, Obama called all the Senate Democrats to the White House for another "pep talk." He also telephoned and met one on one with a number of senators, mostly Democrats but also Olympia Snowe. His message was we need to get this done; it is an opportunity to make historic progress, and we cannot let it slip by. By the end of the day, most liberal Democrats had indicated they would vote for the bill, and even Lieberman seemed on board.

The Senate defeated the Dorgan amendment 51–48, thus preserving the White House deal. The Baucus amendment, another amendment to provide cover, passed 97–1; Lautenberg and Crapo were defeated.

On December 16, Sanders called up amendment #2837 (National Single Payer System) and, as is customary, asked consent that the clerk dispense with the reading. Coburn objected, making clear that the Republicans were ratcheting up their delaying tactics further. The Sanders amendment was more than 700 pages long, and the clerks estimated that it would take approximately ten to twelve hours to complete the reading. To thwart that effort, Sanders agreed to withdraw his amendment and was allowed to do so, itself a controversial decision by the parliamentarian. Republicans argued that once the reading had started, Sanders's request was no longer in order.

Time was growing short to finish the bill before Christmas. The staff of Majority Whip Durbin estimated that if Republicans took full advantage of all their rights under the rules, as they were likely to do, six days would be needed after Reid filed the final compromises as a manager's amendment. Yet the deal was not yet complete; Ben Nelson, the last Democrat, was still not on board.

In a surprise move, Republicans on December 17 blocked quick action on the defense appropriations bill. The bill itself was not controversial, and it had to be finished before the Senate adjourned for the year. By forcing Reid to invoke cloture on "the motion to concur in the House amendment to the Senate amendment" to the bill and then insisting on the full the postcloture thirty hours of debate, Republicans hoped to make it that much harder for Democrats to meet their pre-Christmas target on health care reform. Reid filed for cloture on December 17. Antiwar Democrat Russ Feingold had been telling Reid for weeks that he would not vote for cloture on the Department of Defense (DOD) appropriations bill, but with the fate of the health care bill in the balance, he relented. On December 18, the Senate imposed cloture; the DOD bill was finally cleared on Saturday, December 19.

Meanwhile Democrats focused on persuading Ben Nelson. Obama met personally with him three times, and Reid met with him daily. Pete Rouse, a senior White House adviser, was assigned specifically to address Nelson's concerns (*NYT,* December 18, 2009). Former senators Tom Daschle and Bob Kerrey, the latter of Nebraska, talked with him. Fellow senator and antiabortion stalwart Bob Casey (PA) worked on compromise language on that issue.

Late on Wednesday afternoon, December 16, Reid and Schumer met with Nelson and, setting aside the abortion issue for the time being, discussed Nelson's other problems with the legislation. Nelson provided a list of the "fixes" he wanted to see, and Reid and Schumer took it to Rouse and White House deputy chief of staff Jim Messina. Together they came up with a series of options to address Nelson's concerns. On Friday morning, Reid, Schumer, Rouse, and Messina met with Nelson in Reid's office, and by noon they had worked out a deal on those issues.

The abortion issue still loomed as a possible insurmountable obstacle. Nelson personally felt strongly about the issue, and in conservative Nebraska his political future might depend on his hanging tough. Yet Senate liberals felt just as strongly that reproductive choice should not be abridged in the legislation. After lunch, the negotiating group moved to the abortion issue. By 4:30 p.m. Friday, the group had made considerable progress, but they needed to be sure that any deal they came up with was one that liberals could accept. Thus Barbara Boxer, a strongly pro-choice senator and chief deputy whip was brought into the talks. Rather than bringing the two camps together face-to-face, always a touchy proposition on such a volatile issue, Reid and Schumer shuttled between Reid's office, where Nelson and his staff worked, and a nearby office housing Boxer and her people. On this issue exact language had to be worked out, so the leaders took proposals for legislative language back and forth, trying to whittle down the differences. By early evening a deal seemed near. Nelson went to confer with anti–abortion rights organizations, and when he was more than a hour late returning, Reid and Schumer worried that the deal was falling though. When Nelson did return at 9:30 p.m., however, he was ready to cut a deal, and within an hour the final details were hammered out. Reid had his sixtieth vote. At about 10:30 p.m., Obama called Reid's office to congratulate Reid, Schumer, and Boxer for their efforts. (Account based on the excellent article "Three Days of Negotiations Delivered Nelson's Vote," December 19, 2009, 10:31 p.m., by John Stanton, *Roll Call* Staff.)

The next morning, Saturday, December 19, Reid introduced his 383-page manager's amendment that reflected the final round of compromises and concessions. The manager's amendment dropped the public option but provided for a new system of national, private insurance plans supervised by the OPM, one of which would have to be a nonprofit plan. To make the lack of a public option easier for liberals to accept, Reid increased the new financial requirements for private insurers. Beginning in 2011, insurers covering employees of large businesses would have to spend at least 85 percent of their revenue from premiums on medical claims. Insurers covering employees of small businesses or selling policies to individuals would be required to spend at least 80 percent on claims. Bernie Sanders won an expansion of government-funded community health centers and of the National Health Service Corps, which provides doctors for underserved areas. Additional Medicaid payments for three states—Nebraska, Vermont, and Massachusetts—to help them cover people who would be newly eligible for the program were included. So, of course, was the abortion deal worked out with Nelson. (See *CQW,* December 28, 2009.)

The Congressional Budget Office estimated that the changes in Reid's manager's amendment would bring the bill's ten-year cost to $871 billion—up from the $848 billion cost estimated for the version Reid had released in November but still below the $900 billion mark Obama had set.

With the DOD spending bill cleared at 8:00 a.m. on Saturday, the Senate moved back to health care. Minority Leader McConnell insisted that clerks read, word-for-word, Reid's manager's amendment, a process that took almost seven hours. By then, Washington was in the midst of a major snowstorm.

Reid's manager's amendment, S.A. 3276, was offered as an amendment to the Reid substitute amendment, S.A. 2786, to HR 3590, the "shell." Passing the health care bill required an affirmative vote on the manager's amendment, then on the substitute amendment, and finally on the bill itself as amended. Republicans could and clearly would filibuster at each stage, so three cloture votes needed to be won. And if Republicans insisted, each successful cloture vote would be followed by thirty hours of debate. This is why the process was expected to take so long even after the Democrats had their sixty votes.

After the manager's amendment was read, Reid filed for cloture on it, on the substitute amendment, and on the bill itself. He then filled the amendment tree; that is, using his prerogative of first recognition, Reid offered amendments in all the parliamentarily permissible slots. This move meant that no further amendments would be in order until Reid's were disposed of, and if cloture were invoked, he could run out the clock—that is, prevent his amendments from coming to a vote until the postcloture time had expired and so no other amendments could be offered. To this point, twenty-one amendments or motions to commit had been offered and pushed to a roll call vote.

A cloture motion needs to "ripen"; the rules specify that the vote take place one hour after the Senate meets on the second day after the introduction of the cloture motion. Thus the first cloture vote could not be held until 1:00 a.m. on Monday, December 21. Assuming that the thirty hours of postcloture debate were used in each case, the second cloture vote would occur at about 7:00 a.m. on Tuesday, the third about 1:00 p.m. on Wednesday, and the vote on passage of the bill at 7:00 p.m. on Christmas Eve.

A little after 1:00 a.m. on December 21, Democrats won the first of the three crucial cloture votes when they imposed cloture on the manager's amendment by a strict party-line vote of 60–40. Senators voted from their desks, a formality observed only for the most important bills. Watching from the gallery despite the hour were Vicky Reggie Kennedy, widow of Sen. Edward M. Kennedy, who had died in August, as well as Health and Human Services Secretary Kathleen Sebelius, Jim Messina, and Nancy-Ann DeParle.

On December 22 the manager's amendment was adopted, 60–39, and on an identical vote cloture was invoked on the underlying substitute. (Retiring Republican senator Jim Bunning had gone home.) On December 23 the substitute was adopted and cloture was invoked on the underlying bill. In each case Republicans had insisted on the full thirty hours of postcloture debate and had made a number of motions and points of order intended to further their message. Thus several senators made "constitutional points of order," arguing that the bill violated the Constitution.

All these parliamentary actions counted against the thirty hours, so they could not delay the final vote, but they did show the GOP's strongest supporters that Republicans were fighting to the bitter end.

The thirty hours of debate on the third cloture motion would not run out until 7:00 p.m. on Christmas Eve, and Washington was in the grips of a snowstorm projected to get even worse. With senators and their staffs desperate to get home for the holiday, the Republican hard core relented and their leadership cut a deal. The vote on passage of the bill would take place on December 24 at 8:00 a.m. (later moved to 7:00 a.m.), followed by a vote to extend the debt limit for two months. As part of the agreement, Republicans received a guarantee that they would be able to offer specific amendments to a long-term extension of the debt limit on January 20: a rescissions package by Tom Coburn, a set of spending caps by Sen. Jeff Sessions (R-AL), an amendment by Sen. John Thune (R-SD) sunsetting the Troubled Asset Relief Program (TARP), an amendment on the Environmental Protection Agency's regulation of carbon dioxide emissions by Sen. Lisa Murkowski, and a fiscal task force amendment by Sen. Judd Gregg (R-NH). Reid would also offer a pay-as-you-go (PAYGO) budgeting amendment (*RC*, December 22, 2009).

With Vice President Joe Biden presiding and Vicky Kennedy again in the gallery, the Senate passed the health care bill in the early morning of December 24. An exhausted Harry Reid initially voted no by mistake, providing one of the few notes of levity in what had been a bitter and truly extended process. The Senate had debated the bill for twenty-five days, without breaks for weekends, since early December. It had taken thirty-eight roll call votes, some in the middle of the night, some at the crack of dawn. Provisions that a large majority of the Democratic membership strongly supported had been dropped to get the requisite sixty votes. But the majority party had eked out a victory.

A Long and Convoluted End Game

Work on resolving the differences between the House and Senate versions of the legislation started before the end of 2009. With members of Congress at home and after a well-deserved but abbreviated rest, health care staff began reviewing documents and preparing for negotiations.

Democrats were eager to finish up health care so that they could move on to more popular jobs legislation. Although Congress would not officially go back into session until mid-January, President Obama and congressional leaders hoped to have a deal in place by then. The party leaders would have to decide on the formal procedure to be used. Until the recent past, a conference committee would certainly have been appointed to resolve differences on such a major piece of legislation. In December, however, Senate Republicans had objected to Majority Leader Reid's request to go to conference and appoint conferees; since three motions are necessary for the Senate to go to conference and all are subject to extended debate, Democrats realized that the conference route might be too prolonged. And other routes, such as amendments between the chambers, were available.

Although the House and Senate bills had much in common, some provisions were at odds and highly controversial. The Senate had included a tax on high-priced health insurance plans, both to finance the expansion of health care to the uninsured and to rein in the cost of health care over time. Organized labor and many House Democrats vehemently opposed this tax on so-called "Cadillac plans," arguing that many workers had given up pay raises in return for generous health care coverage. The House bill included a public option, and the Senate bill did not; the House's bill also included more generous subsidies for the middle class than did the Senate's. The abortion language in the two bills differed, and the Senate bill included a number of "sweeteners" for particular senators that had become notorious. Republicans were blasting Democrats for the "Cornhusker Kickback" and the "Louisiana purchase." Because Senate Democrats had no votes to spare, everyone knew that the final bill would have to be quite similar to the Senate bill, but House Democrats were anxious that their leaders get the maximum possible concessions.

House party and committee leaders began meeting the first week of January and on January 7 held a conference call with their members—175 participated—to assure them they had no intention of just accepting the Senate bill, as had been suggested.

The White House ramped up its involvement, as it had always planned to do at this stage. Obama met with Pelosi twice during the week and also with Majority Leader Hoyer and Chairmen Baucus and Dodd. Reid and Durbin participated by telephone. Obama made clear that he wanted some form of the tax on Cadillac plans included as a cost-control measure.

The next week, with Reid back in town, negotiations at the White House intensified. On Wednesday, January 13, Obama met with Pelosi and Reid and then with all the major players—Speaker Pelosi, Majority Leader Hoyer, Majority Whip Clyburn, and Chairmen George Miller, D-CA, Charles Rangel, D-NY, and Waxman from the House; Majority Leader Reid, Assistant Leader Durbin, and Chairmen Baucus, Dodd, and Harkin from the Senate; White House aides Rahm Emanuel, Phil Schiliro, and Nancy-Ann DeParle—in a session that lasted from 10:30 in the morning until 6:40 p.m. (*WP*, January 14, 2010). No cell phones or BlackBerrys were allowed. The group went through the health care package section by section (*RC*, January 15, 2010).

On Thursday the marathon of meetings continued. After separate meetings between administration officials and labor leaders, Obama announced that an agreement on the Cadillac tax had been reached; the tax would be made less onerous but would remain in the bill. On Thursday evening Obama addressed the House Democratic Caucus, giving members a pep talk on health care (*NYT,* October 16, 2010). "I know that some of the fights we've been going through have been tough," he said. "I know that some of you have gotten beaten up at home. But," he continued, "fighting for a cause we believe in is why each of us got into public service in the first place" (*RC,* January 14, 2010). Once the bill becomes law, he predicted, Americans will learn what is really in it and it will become more popular.

Obama then returned to the talks, which continued until 1:00 a.m. On Friday afternoon negotiators, including Obama himself, holed up once again in the Cabinet Room from 1:00 p.m. to 3:45 p.m. The White House then announced no further meetings were scheduled, suggesting that the outlines of a deal on the cost and coverage issues had been reached and sent to the CBO for scoring. Participants were careful but optimistic in their public comments. "We did well today. We agreed on some things," Senate majority leader Harry Reid said. "We're pretty close" (*Politico,* January 15, 2010).

On Tuesday, January 19, Scott Brown, R-MA, running on an anti–health care reform and anti-Washington platform, won the Massachusetts Senate seat vacated by Ted Kennedy's death. This upset win in a heavily Democratic state sent a chill through Democratic ranks. The preelection polls in Massachusetts had looked increasingly ominous for Democrats and had spurred efforts to finish up health care quickly. The reality of the loss came close to provoking panic among Democratic members. Many commentators and Washington insiders declared health care dead.

Debate raged on concerning what Democrats should do about health care legislation. Pass one or more stripped-down bills, including only the more popular elements, some urged. The House should pass the Senate bill and declare it a victory, others—especially Senate Democrats—advocated. Move on to issues of more immediate concern to voters and therefore more popular, still others advised, implicitly suggesting that health care reform be abandoned. Congressional Republicans unanimously called on Democrats to abandon their handiwork and "start over" on a modest, bipartisan bill.

Speaker Pelosi never contemplated any of these courses of action. As she saw it, both policy and politics dictated passing a comprehensive bill. It was the right thing to do for the American people and the smart thing to do politically, she believed. Having experienced the dire electoral consequences of the failed health care effort during the early Clinton administration, she believed that if the Democratic Congress failed again, it would show it could not govern. Democrats who had voted for a health care bill would not escape GOP attacks just because it had not become law; and all Democrats would suffer if the party showed itself unable to legislate. After some confusing signals from the White House, Obama also firmly came down on the side of pushing ahead with comprehensive reform; he had already bet his presidency on its success; pulling back might lessen the damage of a failure but not by much. In his State of the Union address on January 25, 2010, Obama said, "Here's what I ask of Congress, though: Do not walk away from reform. Not now. Not when we are so close. Let us find a way to come together and finish the job." When, in early February, Anthem Blue Cross of California announced big rate increases for health insurance for its individual customers—some as large as 39 percent—Obama found a perfect example to drive home his message that reform was needed, and he used it effectively throughout his public campaign to sell the bill.

Procedural Choices

The Republican victory in Massachusetts had complicated the procedural landscape. Democrats had lost their sixty-vote Senate margin and, without at least one Republican vote, an unlikely prospect, could not pass a compromise bill through any of the customary procedures. The Brown win, explained a House Democrat, "took any 60-vote options off the table." The decision to avoid a conference had already been made; but using amendments between the chambers would also require sixty votes in the Senate. Pelosi stated publicly on January 21 what she had been telling all concerned: the House would not simply pass the Senate bill; the votes were not there. Her members opposed the tax on "Cadillac plans," they believed the subsidies for the middle class were too meager, and they would never vote for the various sweeteners that had become so unpopular.

A route already bruited about now increasingly looked like the only path: the House would pass the Senate bill but also a bill with the compromises agreed to by the two chambers' negotiators; this latter bill would be a reconciliation bill and so would be protected from a filibuster in the Senate. Thus Reid would have to amass only fifty votes—not sixty. A barrier to this procedure was House Democrats' suspicion of the Senate; they wanted assurance that the Senate would actually pass the reconciliation bill.

Obama's Summit

The leaders understood that members needed breathing space. Democrats moved on to jobs legislation. Behind the scenes, however, discussions on health care continued. Right after the Massachusetts special election,

Pelosi and her leadership team held a series of meetings—for "temperature taking" with the freshmen and sophomores, with the Blue Dogs and the Progressive Caucus (*RC,* January 21, 2010). These were just the first of a marathon series of meetings and caucuses over the following weeks. Reid too talked continuously with his members. Discussions between negotiators for the two chambers continued as well, attempting to resolve the remaining substantive differences and agree on a procedural path.

In a television interview with Katie Couric on February 7 right before the Super Bowl, President Obama invited congressional Republicans to a health care summit. "I want to consult closely with our Republican colleagues," Obama said. "What I want to do is to ask them to put their ideas on the table. . . . I want . . . Republicans and Democrats to go through, systematically, all the best ideas that are out there and move it forward" (*NYT,* February 8, 2010). It would take place February 25, last half a day, and be televised.

Congressional Democrats' responses ranged from head scratching ("What does Obama think this is going to accomplish?") to dismissive ("He's just stretching out a painful process with no hope of getting any GOP votes"), but the invitation and the subsequent summit accomplished a number of useful things. It put a focus back on the issue but not on congressional maneuvering and deal making; it provided some breathing room for the congressional leaders to work with their members but also put pressure on members to come up with an agreement by the time of the summit; and it focused on the Republicans and their lack of health care solutions.

On February 23, in preparation for the summit, Obama released an eleven-page blueprint of what he wanted to see in a final health care bill. It made clear that he continued to press for comprehensive reform, largely following the bills that had passed both chambers; it also provided guidance for resolving the remaining differences between the chambers and addressed some of the most serious House concerns (*WP,* February 27, 2010). Republicans cried fowl and again called for starting over. Democrats were encouraged by the administration's stronger public posture, and a pleased Pelosi asserted it would accelerate the process of reaching a final bill.

The summit, held at Blair House on February 25, lasted for seven hours. It was substantive, serious, and civil but, as expected, led to no breakthroughs. Republicans argued that Congress was incapable of making comprehensive policy effectively and that only small, incremental reforms should be attempted. Obama responded that given the complexity of the health care system and the interdependence of the problems it faced, only comprehensive change had a chance of working. Congressional Democrats responded favorably, bucked up by the strong case the president had made.

In a White House speech to an audience of medical professionals on March 3, Obama urged Congress to "finish its work" on health care and said that Congress "owes the American people a final vote on health care reform." The legislation, he continued, "deserves the same kind of up-or-down vote that was cast on welfare reform, the Children's Health Insurance Program, COBRA health coverage for the unemployed, and both Bush tax cuts—all of which had to pass Congress with nothing more than a simple majority." As all those bills had passed using the reconciliation procedure, Obama was clearly endorsing its use (*WP,* March 4, 2010). Senior White House aides made it clear that the administration would make an energetic public push for health care reform during the next several weeks beginning with presidential trips to Philadelphia and St. Louis in the following week. "Whatever it takes to get health care done," White House press secretary Robert Gibbs said of the president's schedule (*WP,* March 4, 2010).

Putting Together the Reconciliation Bill

Putting together a final deal that could pass was a complex multifaceted process. It needed to meet cost estimates, it had to be able to withstand parliamentary (Byrd rule) challenges in the Senate, and both the substance and the procedure had to be acceptable to majorities in both chambers. Republicans tried hard to paint the use of reconciliation as an underhanded, undemocratic trick, but their own use of the procedure in the past undercut their claims. (All of the instances Obama had cited had occurred when Republicans controlled Congress.) In the House, Majority Leader Hoyer had worked quickly and effectively in the wake of the Brown victory to forestall panicky Blue Dogs from coming out against the use of reconciliation (*Huffington Post,* April 9, 2010). Although the House leaders had quickly figured out that reconciliation was the only viable procedural path, they did not "cram it down [their members] throats" but used the "endless meetings and Caucuses" to encourage members to realize it themselves. The president's arguments for an up-or-down vote won the day with the public and so with centrist Democratic senators. A senior Senate Democratic aide said: "I think that the battle to define the reasonableness of an up-or-down vote on health care has largely already been won by the White House. A good bellwether of whether we're winning that message war is the level of comfort of 51 or more [Democrats]. If Republicans were breaking through . . . you would see a lot more skittish Members" (*RC,* March 9, 2010).

Obama's signing on to a number of fixes House Democrats wanted as well as the united push by progressive and Democratic-leaning groups went a considerable way toward persuading liberal House Democrats to get on board. Although disappointed about many provisions, they realized that the choice was between an imperfect product and nothing. Even Dennis Kucinich, D-OH, an ardent single-payer supporter who had voted against the original House bill from the left came around. Obama had flown with Kucinich to his Cleveland district; after a health care rally there and much face-to-face persuasion on Air Force One, Kucinich agreed to vote for the bill.

Obama had promised the bill would be paid for—and, in any case, many moderate Democrats would be unwilling to vote for a bill that was not—so making the substantive adjustments necessary to get the votes of liberals while not loosing those of moderates required a delicate balancing act. Congressional Democrats consulted repeatedly with the Congressional Budget Office's analysts and the bipartisan staff of the Joint Committee on Taxation as they fine-tuned the bill's various provisions, adjusting them when necessary to meet the targets (*NYT,* March 18, 2010).

The bill with the compromises would, of course, have to be approved by the Senate after it passed the House. As a reconciliation bill, it could not be filibustered but it did have to conform with the Byrd rule (see Chapter 4). That rule requires that anything included in a reconciliation bill must have a budgetary impact but, beyond that, is extremely complex. Because the presiding officer follows their advice, the Senate parliamentarians are the customary arbiters of what does and does not comply. If the presiding officer rules that a provision does not comply with the Byrd rule, waving the rule requires sixty votes. If the motion to waive is not passed, the provision at issue is struck from the bill. Democrats were, of course, attempting to avoid the sixty-vote threshold by using reconciliation, and also they wanted to avoid having the bill sent back to the House for another vote, as would be required if provisions were struck; so they needed to be sure their bill did not run afoul of the Byrd rule. Senate Democrats and their Republican opponents conferred with the parliamentarians about whether various provisions passed the test, with Republicans arguing that key provisions did not and Democrats arguing the opposite. Democrats also worked to "scrub" their bill of language the parliamentarians seemed to indicate might not pass the test.

Byrd rule strictures limiting what could be included in the reconciliation bill complicated the process of getting a deal acceptable to enough House Democrats. Thus stronger antiabortion language and national rather than state health care exchanges, both changes which groups of House Democrats wanted to see, were ruled out. The budget resolution that allowed a reconciliation bill had, however, included a reform of the student loan program as well as health care as possible subjects of reconciliation. Student loan reform had passed the House as an ordinary bill but, as with so much else, seemed stuck in the Senate. Now both the administration and House Democrats urged that it be included in the reconciliation bill. Senate Democrats were wary. By Friday, March 13, negotiators were getting close to a final deal.

Passing the Bills in the House

President Obama and the House leadership had been working on House members for days. Obama had met with the Progressive Caucus, arguing that the bill was a good start on the more ambitious program the group favored. "He told us, 'This is not the end of the road. This is the beginning,'" said Rep. Lynn Woolsey, D-CA, cochair of the Caucus (*Los Angeles Times*, March 8, 2010). Obama had other groups of members to the White House as well and made innumerable calls. The House leadership arranged another series of intensive staff briefings to make sure no members could claim to not know what was in the bill. Pelosi, Hoyer, and Clyburn talked with members individually, in small groups, and in the frequent Caucus meetings. They argued on substance and on politics, emphasizing that failing to pass health care would inflict "severe damage" on the Democratic Party; they worked out individual, often constituency-related problems that certain members had with the legislation, to the extent they could. They also coordinated their efforts with allied interest groups. So Pelosi, in a meeting she called in early March, asked the leaders of national hospital associations for help. Hospitals are "influential employer[s] in most congressional districts, particularly in rural areas represented by many of the wavering House Democrats." According to National Association of Public Hospitals and Health Systems president Larry Gage, the Speaker said, "I don't have the votes . . . I think we can get there, but I'm going to need help from any place I can get it" (*LAT*, March 8, 2010).

On the Sunday talk shows on March 14, the rhetorical battle intensified. Republicans continued to vow to defeat the bill. Democrats expressed varying amounts of optimism. Obama senior adviser David Axelrod asserted that Democrats "will have the votes to pass this." House Democratic whip James Clyburn more cautiously said, "We don't have them as of this morning, but we've been working this thing all weekend." He added, "I'm also very confident that we'll get this done" (*WP*, March 15, 2010).

On Monday, March 15, by a vote of 21–16, the House Budget Committee approved a reconciliation bill, as the budget process required. Under reconciliation rules, the measure has to originate in the Budget Committee but that committee may not amend it. The committee used health care legislation approved by the House Education and Labor and Ways and Means Committees as the base text, but this would only serve as a vehicle for the "fixes" that had been negotiated. They would be inserted by the Rules Committee (*National Journal*'s *Markup Reports,* March 15, 2010). All the Republicans and two Democrats voted against the bill.

On March 17 the CBO released its estimates; the package of legislation would cost about $940 billion over ten years, would reduce deficits by $138 billion during that period and $1.2 trillion over the following decade (*NYT,* March, 17, 2010). Thus the bill met Obama's criteria and provided assurance to moderate Democrats. The negotiators had worked closely with CBO throughout the process of putting together the package of "fixes," making sure all along the way that the deals proposed would pass muster with the CBO.

The CBO's report signaled that the countdown to the House vote had begun. The president, who had been scheduled to travel to Indonesia and Australia, postponed his trip to concentrate on passing the legislation.

The bill was filed late on Thursday, March 18. It included the student loan reforms as well as a number of other provisions House Democrats wanted. It generally followed the contours of the Obama proposals, which had largely followed the preliminary agreements that the administration and congressional Democrats had agreed to before the Massachusetts election. The actual language had been worked out in a long series of meetings that included the House and Senate Democratic leaders and senior White House staff, including Chief of Staff Rahm Emanuel.

Pelosi had promised House members a seventy-two-hour period between the filing of the bill and the vote, so a vote would not take place before Sunday, March 21. Much work still needed to be done.

The bill would, of course, be brought to the floor under a special rule. On March 16, Pelosi had suggested the possibility of using a self-executing rule to allow her members to avoid a direct vote on the Senate bill. Essentially, the rule would specify that upon the adoption of the rule, the Senate bill would be adopted. The debate and final vote would thus be on the package of "fixes" to the Senate bill. Most House Democrats really did not want to vote for the Senate bill with its tax on Cadillac plans and now politically toxic sweeteners for individual senators. By not requiring a direct vote on the Senate bill, a self-executing rule would provide members with a bit of cover against the sort of opposition campaign ads they feared.

Once the countdown to the vote got under way, cable news focused almost exclusively on the health care battle to come, and this procedure became a cause célèbre of conservatives on the airwaves. Although congressional Republicans had used such rules themselves when they controlled the House, they now argued this was an abuse of power, and right-wing commentators echoed and amplified their message. By the time the decision on the rule actually had to be made, it was clear the procedure no longer provided cover—the opposite, in fact—and Pelosi dropped the notion. During the week of March 15, she reiterated what she had been telling her members: the rule could not allow votes on amendments changing the Senate abortion or immigration language because they would not pass the Byrd rule test.

The week saw an intensification of the whipping that had already been intense in the preceding weeks. In what became an emblematic and often quoted anecdote, the *New York Times* described Pelosi's effort: "With a vote drawing near and dozens of House Democrats still wavering . . . House leadership aides arrived at Ms. Pelosi's office with a list of 68 lawmakers to lobby, turn or bolster. The aides presumed the Democratic leadership would divvy up the names. 'I'll take all 68,' Ms. Pelosi declared" (*NYT,* March 20, 2010).

The White House political operation also went into high gear, gathering information and tracking member voting intentions, working with allied groups, and getting influential constituents to lobby their members. Obama involved himself deeply in the effort, and congressional Democrats who had criticized him for not committing completely gave him much credit for the eventual victory. "Taking it out into the country, the speeches, the rallies, taking on the insurance companies has been important," said Rep. Raul Grijalva, D-AZ, cochair of the Progressive Caucus. "That button had been on mute in the White House" (*NYT,* March 20, 2010). The president spent countless hours on the telephone and in face-to-face encounters at the White House, attempting to persuade Democrats to vote for the bill; in the week before the House vote, he talked to sixty-four members (*NYT,* March 20, 2010). Brian Baird (D-WA), for example, had a personal meeting with President Obama and talks with Vice President Biden and Commerce Secretary Gary Locke, former governor of Washington. He also went through the bill point by point with OMB chief Peter Orszag, and discussed it with a top health care adviser to Pelosi, before committing on Sunday to voting yes (*RC,* March 23, 2010).

On Saturday, March 20, President Obama came to the Hill to speak to the Democratic Caucus. "Every once in a while a moment comes where you have a chance to vindicate all those best hopes that you had about yourself, about this country," he said. "This is one of those moments" (March 21, 2010). The president laid it out: "We have been debating health care for decades. It has now been debated for a year. It is in your hands." The atmosphere was rallylike and, when he recognized for their courage two junior, marginal-district Democrats who had committed to voting yes, both received a standing ovation (*RC,* March 20, 2010). Health and Human Services Secretary Kathleen Sebelius, OMB Director Peter Orszag, and former House members Interior Secretary Ken Salazar and

Transportation Secretary Ray LaHood also attended the Caucus (*RC,* March 20, 2010). Speaker Nancy Pelosi told her Caucus that they were "on the verge of making great history" (*RC,* March 20, 2010).

Harry Reid attended the Caucus to reassure Democrats that the Senate would, in fact, pass the reconciliation bill. House Democrats, upset at the number of bills they had passed, sometimes on tough votes, that had gone nowhere in the Senate, worried that the same might happen with the reconciliation bill. They would then be stuck with having cast a vote for a Senate health care bill that they loathed on both policy and politics grounds. To help persuade her members to vote for the Senate bill, Pelosi had attempted to get Senate Democrats to commit to passing the reconciliation bill publicly and in writing. "We're in the process of actually contacting every single Democratic Senator," Senate majority whip Dick Durbin said on Sunday on NBC's *Meet the Press.* "When Nancy Pelosi goes before her House Democratic Caucus, it will be with the solid assurance that when reconciliation comes over to the Senate side, we're going to pass it" (*RC,* March 16, 2010). But without final legislative language, Democratic senators were unwilling to commit. At the Caucus, Reid said he was "happy to announce" that a significant majority of senators had officially committed to use reconciliation to pass the overhaul. "I have the commitments of a significant majority of the United States Senate to make that good law even better," he said (*NYT,* March 21, 2010). Reid released a letter to that effect signed by more than fifty Senate Democrats but did not make the names public.

Throughout the week House Democrats had been announcing how they intended to vote, and media whip counts proliferated. The Democratic leadership's count was edging up but not enough to make them confident of victory. The biggest problem proved to be the Senate abortion language. The Stupak group considered it not strong enough even though it was the handiwork of staunchly antiabortion senators, and Stupak threatened to bring down the bill if his stronger language was not somehow incorporated. Pelosi and her team knew that any abortion language would not pass the Byrd rule test and so was out of the question. They worked on members of the Stupak group and managed to peel away some of them; a number were, after all, longtime committed supporters of health care reform. Help came from a group of more than fifty nuns from various religious orders who sent a letter to all House members in support of the bill (*NYT,* March 17, 2010). The Catholic Health Association, a large organization of Catholic hospitals and other health care facilities, also endorsed the bill. The United States Conference of Catholic Bishops, on the other hand, remained adamantly opposed to the bill without the Stupak language. The leadership considered giving Stupak a vote in some other form but decided against it when pro-choice Democrats threatened to defect. Even without Stupak himself and the few sticking with him, the leadership might well have had the votes. However, Republicans would be able to offer a motion to recommit with instructions on the reconciliation bill and those instructions would almost certainly contain the Stupak language. Without a deal, that motion to recommit might well pass.

On Sunday afternoon the White House and the House leadership announced that after the House passed health care reform, President Obama would sign an executive order to make it clear that no federal funds would be used for abortions (*RC*, March 21, 2010). The executive order would reaffirm the measure's "consistency with longstanding restrictions on the use of federal funds for abortion" (*NYT*, March 21, 2010). At a press conference right afterward, Stupak and several other holdouts announced their support for health care reform. "I'm pleased to announce we have an agreement," Stupak said. With these members on board, the leadership had the votes.

The House had convened at 1:00 p.m. on Sunday afternoon, March 21. The session began with ten one-minute speeches that foreshadowed the debate to come. Democrats hailed the historic moment and trumpeted the benefits of the legislation. "Today we have an historic opportunity, more than a century after President Teddy Roosevelt first raised this subject, to establish the foundation for health care reform," Oregon Democrat Earl Blumenauer declared (*CR*, H1820). "Mr. Speaker, today we will act on a uniquely American solution to health care reform. Our action will bring down health care costs for middle-income families, will help small businesses afford coverage for their employees, will improve coverage for our seniors, will rein in wasteful spending, and will provide access to 32 million uninsured Americans," said Pennsylvania Democrat Allyson Schwartz (*CR*, H1819). Republican Marsha Blackburn (TN) responded, "Mr. Speaker, my colleagues are celebrating the birth of a great new entitlement program today; only they see dependency on the Federal Government and the death of freedom as a cause for celebration. . . . My colleagues are overjoyed that soon their goal of having Americans dependent on the Federal Government for mortgages, student loans, retirement, and health care will be realized. That is a chilling goal. . . . Freedom dies a little bit today. Unfortunately, some are celebrating" (*CR*, H1820). Many Republicans too saw it as a momentous choice. "Mr. Speaker, today is a defining moment in this Nation's history. Will we choose the path of individual liberty or will we choose the path of government tyranny?" Republican Ted Poe of Texas asked (*CR*, H1821).

The actual work of the session began with some noncontroversial unfinished business, giving Democrats more time to finish up the abortion deal. Shortly after 2:00 p.m., Louise Slaughter, D-NY, chair of the Rules Committee, called up H. Res. 1203, the rule for the health care legislation. The committee had had met for thirteen and a half hours, considered eighty amendments from sixty-five Republicans, and finished its work on the rule shortly after midnight. The rule provided "for consideration of the Senate amendments [the Senate health care bill] to the bill (HR 3590) [the base bill the Senate had used] . . . and for consideration of the bill (HR 4872) to provide for reconciliation pursuant to section 202 of the concurrent resolution on the budget for fiscal year 2010" (Thomas). The rule provided for "two hours equally divided and controlled by the Majority Leader and Minority Leader or their respective designees" on "the topics addressed by" the two measures; in other words, the debate would be on both together. After the debate "a single motion offered by the Majority Leader or his designee that the House concur in the Senate amendments" shall be in order. If that motion passes, it is then in order to consider in the House [not the Committee of the Whole] the reconciliation bill (HR 4872), that is, the bill reported by the Budget Committee. The "fixes" that had been so painstakingly negotiated were incorporated into HR 4872 by the following provision of the rule. "The amendment in the nature of a substitute printed in part A of the report of the Committee on Rules accompanying this resolution, modified by the amendment printed in part B of the report of the Committee on Rules, shall be considered as adopted." The rule continued: "The bill, as amended, shall be considered as read. All points of order against provisions in the bill, as amended, are waived." Both are typical provisions foreclosing delaying tactics by opponents. The rule then specified: "The previous question shall be considered as ordered on the bill, as amended, to final passage without intervening motion except one motion to recommit with or without instructions" (Thomas). This provision barred amendments but did allow a motion to recommit and so a means for opponents to try to change the bill.

Republicans attempted to delay proceedings by making several points of order that required twenty minutes of debate for each. They also used parliamentary inquiries of the Speaker pro tempore to stretch out the proceedings. At the insistence of Republicans, the House took two recorded votes on whether the House would consider the rule despite points of order that the rule would waive certain points of order; both won on party-line votes. When those motions were disposed of, the usual hour of debate on the rule commenced. Democrats largely argued substance. Republicans argued process as well as substance. They objected to the rule because it barred amendments. A number also attempted to spook Democrats by raising the specter that the Senate would fail to pass the reconciliation legislation. Thus, Rules Committee ranking member David Dreier, R-CA, stated:

The Democratic leadership has tried to claim that the reconciliation package will fix all of the problems in the Senate bill. That claim is far from accurate. The fundamental approach to health care reform put forth by the Senate bill, which is fatally flawed, will remain intact. Putting aside that hard truth for just a moment, the more immediate issue is that the reconciliation package will not become law today. It will merely be sent to our friends, our colleagues in the other body, where it will be slowly picked apart like everything else that is sent to the other body. Maybe the Senate will amend it and send it back here for further action, Mr. Speaker. Maybe it will fail to act at all. No matter what anyone says in this institution, Mr. Speaker, no one knows. No one has any idea what takes place those many, many miles away, it seems, down that hallway. The only thing that can be sent to the President for signature today is the Senate bill that virtually no one supports. (*CR*, H1835)

Although Dreier argued for defeating the previous question so he could offer an amendment to the rule requiring actual roll call votes—rather than electronic votes—on the legislation, a time-consuming process, the motion to order the previous question on the rule passed by a vote of 228–202. The rule itself passed 224–206. If there had been doubt before, these votes suggested Democrats had the votes to pass health care.

The two hours of debate on the legislation itself started at 6:43 p.m. and became increasingly bitter and intense. Republicans called the bill a "fiscal Frankenstein," claimed it was the result of "dirty deal after dirty deal" and extorted their House colleagues to "Say no to totalitarianism!" (*WP*, March 22, 2010). They argued the bill allowed government funding for abortions, raised taxes and insurance premiums, cost too much, and cut Medicare; it entailed a government takeover of one-sixth of the U.S. economy, they claimed. "Mr. Speaker, the simple truth is this health care bill is a killer," Paul Broun of Georgia intoned. "It kills over 5 million jobs in future job creation with $52 billion in mandates and taxes. It kills economic freedom and the American entrepreneurial spirit. It kills the family budget with over $17 billion in more mandates and taxes primarily aimed at the poor and at seniors. It kills our future by allowing taxpayer-funded abortions" (*CR*, H1839).

Confident they would win, Democrats were more measured. "[A]s an old friend said to me today, there are not too many times in politics that you get to do something monumental, and this is the day," Doris Matsui of California said. "We have the opportunity today to vote for a health insurance reform bill to improve the quality of life for millions of American families. It will also control costs, improve Medicare, and reduce the deficit" (*CR*, H 1836). David Price of North Carolina, in an eloquent statement, also emphasized the historic nature of the occasion:

Mr. Speaker, "once to every man and nation," wrote the great abolitionist poet James Russell Lowell, "comes the moment to decide."

Mr. Speaker, there are moments in history when it becomes clear that we simply cannot wait any longer to do what is right. When we have the opportunity to take a significant step to make our country better, the sort of opportunity that comes only a few times in a lifetime. We face such a moment tonight.

Our health insurance system is falling far short of the American peoples' basic needs. . . .

Reform will save money for employees, business owners, and taxpayers. It will end insurance company abuses. It will let young people stay on their parents' policies until age 27. It will extend coverage to 95 percent of Americans. It expands community health centers and increases the number of primary care doctors and nurses. And it will end the hidden tax that the insured pay every month in the form of higher premiums. . . .

Mr. Speaker, the American people have waited long enough. We face an historic decision tonight, one that will resonate throughout our country, as have Social Security and Medicare, for decades to come. Let us seize the moment for the people we were elected to serve, and for future generations. (*CR*, H 1907)

Many told the stories of the people they had met or who had written to them, people who had lost insurance when they had gotten sick, who could not get insurance because of a preexisting condition, who, thought they had adequate insurance but found that when they did get sick that their policy covered very little. Robert Andrews of New Jersey challenged the Republicans' arguments:

Mr. Speaker, our friends on the other side of the aisle have asked frequently tonight what kind of country are we. They've asked exactly the right question. Tomorrow when a person is denied a job because she has breast cancer or is charged higher premiums because he has asthma, what kind of country will we be? Tomorrow when a senior citizen has enough money in her checking account to pay the utility bill or her prescription bill but not both, what kind of country will we be? When a person who tonight is scrubbing floors or pumping gas or waiting on tables tomorrow tries to go to buy a health insurance policy for herself or her children, what kind of country will we be?

For Social Security, we gave decency for seniors. In Medicare, we gave compassion for seniors. In the Civil Rights Act, we gave equality for all Americans. Tonight, we will give justice and decency. That's the kind of country that we will be. (*CR*, H 1896)

Minority Leader John Boehner and Speaker Pelosi closed debate, as is customary on the most controversial and consequential legislation. Their diametrically opposed perspectives highlighted just how far apart the two parties were on the issue. To cheers from his side of the aisle, Boehner gave an angry address:

Look at this bill. Ask yourself, do you really believe that if you like the health plan that you have that you can keep it? No, you can't. You can't say that.

In this economy, with this unemployment, with our desperate need for jobs and economic growth, is this really the time to raise taxes, to create bureaucracies, and burden every job creator in our land? The answer is no.

Can you go home and tell your senior citizens that these cuts in Medicare will not limit their access to doctors or further weaken the program instead of strengthening it? No, you cannot.

Can you go home and tell your constituents with confidence that this bill respects the sanctity of all human life and that it won't allow for taxpayer funding of abortions for the first time in 30 years? No, you cannot.

And look at how this bill was written. Can you say it was done openly, with transparency and accountability? Without backroom deals and struck behind closed doors hidden from the people? Hell, no, you can't.

Have you read the bill? Have you read the reconciliation bill? Have you read the manager's amendment? Hell, no, you haven't.
. . .

[W]hat [Americans] see today frightens them. They're frightened because they don't know what comes next. They're disgusted because what they see is one political party closing out the other from what should be a national solution. And they're angry. They're angry that no matter how they engage in this debate, this body moves forward against their will.

Shame on us. Shame on this body. Shame on each and every one of you who substitutes your will and your desires above those of your fellow countrymen. . . . (*CR,* H 1895)

Pelosi responded:

Mr. Speaker, it is with great humility and with great pride that tonight we will make history for our country and progress for the American people. Just think, we will be joining those who established Social Security, Medicare, and now tonight health care for all Americans. . . .

This legislation will lead to healthier lives, more liberty to pursue hopes and dreams and happiness for the American people. This is an American proposal that honors the traditions of our country. . . .

With this action tonight, with this health care reform, 32 million more Americans will have health care insurance and those who have insurance now will be spared of being at the mercy of the health insurance industry with their obscene increases in premiums, their rescinding of policies at the time of illness, their cutting off of policies even if you have been fully paying but become sick. The list goes on and on about the health care reforms that are in this legislation: insure 32 million more people, make it more affordable for the middle class, end insurance company discrimination on preexisting conditions, improve care and benefits under Medicare and extending Medicare solvency for almost a decade, creating a healthier America through prevention, through wellness and innovation, create 4 million jobs in the life of the bill and doing all of that by saving the taxpayer $1.3 trillion. . . .

I urge my colleagues to join together in passing health insurance reform, making history and restoring the American Dream. I urge an "aye" vote. (*CR*, H 1897)

At 10:30 p.m. John Spratt, D-SC, as Majority Leader Hoyer's designee, moved that the House agree to the Senate amendments. When that motion passed, the House had approved the Senate health care reform bill and it would next go to the president for his signature. The vote was 219–212; thirty-four Democrats joined all the Republicans in opposition. Although a number of the marginal Democrats who supported the bill might have preferred to vote against it but still have it pass, voting against it and having it fail was unacceptable.

Despite their cheers and hugs when the gavel came down, for House Democrats their business was only partially done. Consideration of the reconciliation bill containing the fixes began at 10:49. No debate was in order, as the earlier two hours had been for both bills. Republicans, as expected, offered a motion to recommit with instructions that would have amended the bill with strict abortion language. During the ten minutes of debate allotted to motions to recommit, in a coup for proponents of the bill, Bart Stupak spoke against the motion to recommit, giving even the staunchest abortion opponent cover to vote against it. As he was speaking, a shout of "baby killer" could be heard in the chamber. The next day, Texas Republican Randy Neugebauer admitted to having been the shouter, though he claimed it had been directed at the bill, not at Stupak. That comment did encapsulate the acrimony of the battle. "Tea Party" protestors had been loudly demonstrating outside the Capitol, and many GOP members had egged them on. The motion to recommit was defeated 199–232 and the reconciliation bill passed 220–211 without a single Republican vote. Using the gavel employed when Medicare passed in 1965, Pelosi gaveled the vote closed.

Obama watched the roll call with Vice President Biden at the White House. Shortly before midnight, he spoke to the press in the East Room. "This isn't radical reform, but it is major reform," he said, implicitly answering the opposition's arguments. "In the end what this day represents is another stone firmly laid in the foundation of the American dream. Tonight, we answered the call of history as so many generations of Americans have before us. When faced with crisis, we did not shrink from our challenges. We overcame them. We did not avoid our responsibilities, we embraced it. We did not fear our future, we shaped it" (*NYT*, March 21, 2010). The vote, he said, "proved that we are still capable of doing big things. We proved that this government—a government of the people and by the people—still works for the people" (*WP*, March 22, 2010).

The Senate Passes the Reconciliation Bill

The action now pivoted to the Senate; it was up to the Senate to pass the reconciliation bill, as Senate Democratic leaders had promised House Democrats they would. Yet because the bill the Senate had passed in December would now become law, Senate action was something of an anti-climax. If Republicans were able to stop the reconciliation bill, the most this would do is embarrass Democrats. Nevertheless, Republicans were committed to fighting strenuously, as their base voters demanded. Their strategy depended on the Byrd rule. Because under reconciliation Democrats would need to muster only fifty votes—Vice President Biden could provide the tie-breaking vote if necessary—GOP chances of defeating the bill on an up-or-down vote were unrealistic. However, if they could get the parliamentarian to find Byrd rule violations in the bill, waiving the Byrd rule would require Democrats to muster sixty votes, also a completely unrealistic possibility. If the Byrd rule could not be waived, any provisions that were found to violate the rule would have to be dropped. Consequently, a Byrd rule violation that went to the heart of the bill could bring the bill down entirely; more peripheral violations would at least require the bill to go back to the House for another vote.

Senior staff from both parties had been conferring with the Senate parliamentarian, and Democrats had drafted their reconciliation bill so as to avoid successful Byrd rule challenges. Still, nothing was certain, as Sen. Kent Conrad explained. "Although we've spent many, many hours with the Parliamentarian, some things he has not yet rendered a conclusion on. He wants to hear from both sides before he does" (*RC*, March 18, 2010). At a meeting with the parliamentarian on Monday, March 22, Republicans argued that the tax on "Cadillac" health insurance plans affects Social Security and so is a Byrd rule violation (*The Hill*, March 23, 2010). Having to drop that provision would kill the reconciliation bill. Late Monday the parliamentarian ruled against the Republicans on that point, as Democrats had been fairly confident he would. Democrats knew that Republican staffers would continue to comb through the bill looking for other provisions to challenge.

On Tuesday morning, March 23, President Obama signed the Senate health care bill into law. The Senate parliamentarian had ruled in early March that the president had to sign the original health care reform bill before the Senate could act on the reconciliation package amending that bill (*RC*, March 11, 2010). When, in the wake of the Republican win in Massachusetts, the Democratic leaders had sought a path forward, having the Senate pass the reconciliation bill before the House voted on the original Senate bill had been suggested. With most House Democrats detesting the Senate bill and mistrusting the Senate's capacity to actually pass legislation "fixing" it, that would have made getting the votes in the House much easier. However, the parliamentarian's ruling made that impossible.

With the president's signature and the bill now law, Senate majority leader Reid moved that the Senate proceed to consider HR 4872, the health care reconciliation package; because no filibuster was possible, the motion was expeditiously voted on, and it passed 56–40 along strict party lines. That started the twenty-hour debate limit clock. Finance Committee chairman Max Baucus began the debate, pointing out that the president had signed the big bill into law and what was at issue in the Senate now was a modest set of improvements. "Today, we have before us a bill to improve the new law. We do not have before us the whole health care reform bill. We do not have to reopen every argument we had over the last 2 years. We do not have to say everything we said about health care one more time . . ." (*CR*, March 23, 2010, S1824).

Baucus's plea was in vain, and the debate was a rehash of now familiar arguments. Republicans offered a stream of amendments, many, Democrats charged, crassly political. Democratic whip Dick Durbin said of an amendment by Tom Coburn to prohibit prescription coverage of erectile dysfunction drugs for child molesters and rapists: "I'm not making this up. There is a fertile mind somewhere on the staff of the other side of the aisle dreaming up gotcha amendments. . . . Viagra for child molesters" (*CR*, S1850).

The Senate debated the bill for more than seven hours on Tuesday. When junior Democrat Sherrod Brown of Ohio closed the Senate for the night, he warned his colleagues, "Senators should expect a very long day [Wednesday] with votes occurring throughout the day" (*RC*, March 23, 2010).

On Wednesday, March 24, the Senate convened at 9:00 a.m. Majority Leader Reid reminded senators that the twenty hours would expire in the afternoon and the "vote-a-rama" would then begin. Although the Budget Act specifies time limits for debate on reconciliation bills, it does not limit amendments; thus senators may offer an unlimited number of amendments. Once the debate time has expired, however, no debate on them is allowed unless agreed to by unanimous consent. The resulting series of recorded votes has been dubbed the "vote-a-rama."

The Democratic leadership had worked hard to persuade its members that all the Republican amendments had to be defeated and that no Democrat should offer amendments. Their pact with the House Democrats entailed no changes to the deal encapsulated in the reconciliation bill. When voting on amendments began, Baucus reminded his colleagues, "each amendment offered here is intended to kill health care reform, and that is why each amendment should fail" (*CR,* March 24, 2010, S1992). No Democrat offered an amendment.

Before the House vote, Senate Republicans had threatened to filibuster by amendment, as the rules permitted; however, once the House had passed both bills, most Senate Republicans realized doing so would accomplish little and so, although they offered a slew of amendments, they no longer vowed to continue indefinitely. Reid was thus willing to be accommodating. As he explained concerning debate during the "vote-a-rama":

> [W]e do not have to agree to 1 minute, but we want everyone to understand we have tried to be as fair as we can through this whole process. . . . In recent years, we have agreed by unanimous consent to have 1 minute to explain the amendment and 1 minute to disagree with the amendment. I think that is the appropriate thing to do. We want to make sure everyone is treated fairly.
>
> But I alert everyone: The Chair is going to enforce . . . that to the letter of the law. . . .if this consent agreement is agreed to—there will be 1 minute to explain the amendment and 1 minute to disagree with the amendment. (*CR,* March 24, 2010, S1992)

After propounding the unanimous consent agreement he had reached with Minority Leader Mitch McConnell, Reid continued:

> Mr. President, I also note that with just the amendments that have been proposed, if we are fortunate, it will probably take 9 hours or so, maybe more than that, to get rid of those. There will be continuous votes without any breaks. We are not going to have any breaks unless something untoward happens. Senators should be advised that they should remain close to the floor during this process. If people are not here at the end of the time, we are going to close it up. We need to move on. We have other things we have to do prior to the recess. I have to work with the Republican leader. It has taken an enormous amount of time to do this. Everybody stay here. It works a lot better if my colleagues stay close to their seats and, hopefully, we will have an orderly process as much as possible during the vote-a-rama. (*CR,* March 24, 2010, S1992)

The Senate took twenty-nine roll call votes during the session that started March 24. Republican amendments were called up. In most cases Democrats moved to table; a majority made up entirely of Democrats voted to table and so kill the amendment. Because only a simple majority was needed, some Democrats could defect on amendments that were particularly difficult for them, but never enough to approve the amendment.

During the vote-a-rama, the leadership learned that the parliamentarian intended to rule in favor of at least one Republican point of order concerning the Byrd rule. It was minor, but that made it clear that the bill could not be finished that night. So, after conferring, Reid and McConnell reached an agreement for finishing up. Reid explained:

> [A]fter having had long discussions with my friend, the distinguished Senator from Kentucky, I ask unanimous consent that we are going to adjourn in a few minutes; that we will convene at 9:45 a.m. this morning, resume the bill, consider amendments up to 2 p.m., we will dispose of points of order that have been determined—and one is still under review—by 2 p.m. There will be no further amendments after 2 p.m., and the third reading will occur after points of order are disposed of after 2 p.m.
>
> I ask that in the form of a unanimous consent agreement. (*CR*, S 2012)

At 2:56 a.m. the Senate adjourned.

The session of March 25 played out as expected. The vote-a-rama continued with votes on another bunch of amendments; all were defeated. In all, the Senate took recorded votes on forty-one amendments; all were decided by party-line votes. Two Byrd rule points of order were sustained, but both were minor. The Senate leaders had conferred with Speaker Pelosi, who told them they would not cause a serious problem. Democrats did not contest the rulings of the chair on either one. The bill passed on a vote of 56–43; fifty-six of fifty-nine Democrats voted for the bill; no Republicans did.

The House took up the slightly changed bill the evening of March 25. The rule was approved at 8:23 p.m.; it provided for ten minutes of debate. At 8:24, George Miller, chairman of the House Education and Labor Committee, moved that the House agree to the Senate amendments; by 9:02 the House had approved the motion—and thereby the second piece of the health care bill—220–207.

On March 30, President Obama signed the bill, the Patient Protection and Affordable Care Act, into law.

Making Nonincremental Policy Change in a Partisan Era

Passing complex legislation that makes nonincremental policy change is seldom easy, and in a period of high partisan polarization it is truly difficult indeed. That the legislative process was characterized by all sorts of unorthodox procedures is thus hardly surprising. The stakes were enormous, and both proponents and opponents had every incentive to use all the tools at their disposal.

The president and his administration played a central role as agenda setters, negotiators, and motivators, as the enactment of nonincremental legislation always requires. Our division of powers system makes that a necessity. The contemporary hyperpartisanship did raise the stakes for the Democratic Party; most Democratic members of Congress did perceive their fate as tied closely to that of their president. The argument that the failure of health care reform, the signature Democratic priority, would deal a major if not lethal blow to the Obama presidency but also to the congressional Democratic Party was frequently used and often effective.

The complexity of the task, the high stakes, and the partisan polarization all dictated pervasive congressional leadership engagement throughout the legislative process. Members have grown accustomed to a more centralized leadership direction of the legislative process, especially on the bills of highest priority. Thus Speaker Nancy Pelosi could task the chairs of the three committees with negotiating a single bill, and she could not only oversee the process throughout but also involve herself in negotiations whenever she believed it necessary. Senate majority leader Harry Reid deferred to his committee chairs more than Pelosi, but he too was deeply involved in the negotiations that led to a bill passing in December 2010. Because legislative strategy and policy substance were so closely intertwined throughout the arduous process of drafting bills that could pass, the party leaders often made major substantive decisions. In both chambers, the period between the committees reporting out their bills and floor consideration involved the party leaderships' orchestrating "the mother of all postcommittee adjustments." Although Pelosi and Reid and their leadership teams played crucial central roles in the process, the Democratic committee leaders in both chambers also were continuously engaged. And both party and committee leaders consulted widely with their members, often finding ways to accommodate their special concerns. Even in a period of unusual leadership strength, congressional leaders are not like army generals who can give orders to their troops and expect them to be obeyed without question. Unlike soldiers, members of Congress can just say no.

In the House the creative use of special rules aided in passing—quickly and without amendments—the bill Democrats had so painstakingly negotiated among themselves. In the Senate, in contrast, rules aided the minority. Minority Leader McConnell unified his members in opposition, and although, with only forty GOP senators, he could not block enactment, he compelled the Democrats to hold every one of their sixty members. Furthermore, by insisting on all their rights under the rules, minority Republicans forced majority Democrats to jump through all the hoops the cloture process imposes four separate times—five if the defense appropriations bill is counted. Imposing cloture requires a cloture petition to be filed and a layover period of a full day. If cloture is invoked, opponents may insist on thirty hours of debate. Only on the very last postcloture debate did Republicans relent and not insist on the full thirty hours; this made it possible to have the passage vote on Christmas Eve morning rather than at 7:00 p.m. in the evening! Reid used the tactics available to him to protect the bill; for example, at the end of the process, he "filled the amendment tree" to bar GOP amendments that might split his coalition and drag on the process still longer. The Senate majority leader's procedural weapons are meager, however, when faced with an adamant opposition. Even a minority of fewer than forty-one can, in effect, shut down the Senate for extended periods of time.

Procedurally the budget process proved to be crucial to the enactment of health reform legislation. Given the extreme partisan polarization, when Democrats lost their sixtieth vote in the Senate, they lost any real chance to pass health reform through another procedure. A conference report or amendments between the chambers would require sixty votes in the Senate, and House Democrats were totally unwilling to just accept the Senate bill. Those participants who had insisted on including reconciliation instructions concerning health care in the budget resolution proved to be prescient, though even they probably had not anticipated how the process would play out.

Major policy change had been effectuated through the budget process before, Reagan's economic plan in 1981, Clinton's in 1993, and the George W. Bush tax cuts in 2001 and 2003 being prominent examples. (See Chapter 9 for an account of the Bush tax cuts.) Over time, however, the rules governing what could be included in reconciliation bills had tightened, most notably with the institution of the Byrd rule. Given extant parliamentary rulings, the entire health care bill could not have been enacted as a reconciliation bill; too much of the structure set up by the legislation would not have passed the Byrd rule test of being directly budget related. Despite that, enough of what House Democrats needed to make the Senate bill acceptable could be passed as a reconciliation bill. In fact, a number of health care supporters have argued "the fix" included in the reconciliation bill made the end result better than either the Senate or the House bill (Jacobs and Skocpol 2010). In the end, then, it was the budget process that made enactment of the health care reform bill possible.

TABLE 8.1 Patient Protection and Affordable Care Act

Date	House action	Senate action	Postpassage action
March 2009	*Pelosi charges three chairmen with drafting one bill*	*Baucus negotiates with Grassley*	
June–July	*Informal negotiations*	*Bipartisan Gang of Six, members of Finance, negotiate*	
7/14	Pelosi and leadership team and three chairs unveil HR 3200		
7/15		HELP approves draft bill	
7/17	Ways and Means approves HR 3200		
	Education and Labor approves HR 3200		
7/31	Energy and Commerce approves amended version of HR 3200		
9/22–10/2		Finance markup	
10/13		Finance approves bill	
Sept.–Oct.	*Party and committee leaders negotiate with members to craft bill that can pass*	*Reid and committee leaders negotiate with members to craft bill that can get sixty votes*	
10/29	HR 3962, negotiated bill, unveiled by leaders and introduced		
Early Nov.	*Pelosi negotiates rule*		
11/7	Rule for HR 3962 debated and approved; bill debated, amendments considered, bill passes 220–215		

TABLE 8.1 (Continued)

Date	House action	Senate action	Postpassage action
11/19		Motion to proceed to HR 3590 (shell bill) made	
11/21		Senate votes cloture on motion to consider HR 3590 amendment S.A. 2786 in the nature of a substitute proposed by Reid	
11/30–12/24		Debated, amendments considered, cloture motions passed	
12/24		HR 3590 as amended passes 60–39	
Jan.–March 2010			*Obama and House and Senate leaders negotiate final bill*
3/21	HR 4872, reconciliation bill, passes 220–211		
			House agrees to the Senate amendments to HR 3590 219–212
3/23			President signs HR 3590
3/25		HR 4872 passes with amendments 56–43	
			House agrees to Senate amendments to HR 4872
3/30			President signs HR 4872

Note: Official actions are in roman type; behind-the-scenes, unofficial actions are in italics.

c h a p t e r   n i n e

The Republican Tax-Cutting Agenda and the Budget Process: The Bush Tax Cuts of 2001 and 2003

GEORGE W. BUSH MADE BIG TAX CUTS a centerpiece of his 2000 presidential campaign. However, any claim that the voters had given Bush a mandate for his program ran up against the murky outcome of the 2000 elections. Bush received fewer popular votes than his chief opponent, Democratic nominee Albert Gore; his narrow electoral college majority depended on questionable counts in the state governed by his brother and on a 5–4 decision by an ideologically split U.S. Supreme Court. His party lost seats in both chambers of Congress. Republicans held on to control of the House of Representatives by a razor-thin majority of 221 to 211;[1] the Senate, which before the elections was 54–46 Republican, emerged from the 2000 elections with an even split.

After barely squeaking into office, Bush was advised by most Democrats, many unaffiliated commentators, and even some Republicans to cut back the size of his proposal so as to make it more broadly acceptable. A majority of Democrats had opposed much of the tax-cutting agenda in the past. Getting their support would probably require considerable compromise.

Yet despite the weakness of any mandate claim, other political circumstances were more favorable. Bush enjoyed unified partisan control of

1. There was one vacancy and two independents, who usually split their votes between the parties.

235

both chambers of Congress, something no Republican president since Eisenhower in 1953–1954 had had. And big tax cuts were the number one priority of a great many Republicans; congressional Republicans had passed large tax cut packages several times in the late 1990s, only to see them vetoed by President Bill Clinton. Furthermore, the budget surplus seemed likely to make selling a sizable tax cut easier.

Bush and his political advisers decided that paring down his proposal would be seen as an admission of weakness and would alienate his core supporters. Bush therefore determined to stick with his full package of across-the-board income-tax rate cuts, repeal of the estate tax, alleviation of the "marriage penalty," new charitable-giving deductions, and some lesser provisions estimated to cost in total $1.6 trillion over ten years.

Everyone took for granted that the budget process would be used. Although the big deficits of the 1980s and much of the 1990s had led many casual observers to associate the budget process with spending cuts and tax increases, the process itself is neutral and reconciliation instructions can dictate tax cuts. Republicans knew that in the Senate the protection from filibusters that the budget process afforded would be indispensable to enacting the Bush tax cut.

In fact, as this account shows, the budget process and some of the other practices and procedures of unorthodox lawmaking—restrictive rules and close and continuous leadership involvement in the process, for example—were essential; in order to get Republican tax-cut legislation through Congress in 2001 and again in 2003, Republican House leaders even extended the boundaries of unorthodox lawmaking.

Delivering: Cutting Taxes in 2001

Before Bush even formally presented his proposal, congressional Republicans began pushing for quick action, and they and business lobbyists began to lay out their own preferences for possible add-ons to the package. In a January 9 memo to all House Republicans, Majority Leader Dick Armey, R-TX, wrote that Congress should push Bush's entire plan, plus a few additions, and should make the cuts retroactive to January 1, 2001. Trent Lott, R-MS, the Senate majority leader, endorsed making the cuts retroactive and urged Bush to settle soon on a proposal—and a timetable for selling it (*Congressional Quarterly Weekly,* January 13, 2001, 100). Lobbyists swarmed across Capitol Hill touting their clients' preferred tax breaks. A coalition of business and trade associations, whose formation was announced on February 6, said it aimed to amend Bush's plan to benefit "all U.S. taxpayers" by adding tax breaks for business (*CQW,* February 10, 2001, 318).

Concerned that the package could get out of hand, the administration responded. "Some in Congress view this as an opportunity to load up the relief plan with their own vision," Bush said at the White House on February 5. "I want the members of Congress and the American people to hear loud and clear: This is the right-size plan, it is the right approach, and I'm going to defend it mightily" (*CQW,* February 10, 2001, 318).

On February 8, Bush formally sent Congress his tax cut proposal, and on February 13, Treasury Secretary Paul O'Neill testified before the Ways and Means Committee, urging its swift adoption. The Bush camp, which had been arguing that the large budget surplus made their tax cut not just possible but necessary, now argued that it was the best response to a slowing economy.

The softening economy had led Democratic congressional leaders to signal that they were willing to accept a tax cut—but not such a huge one and not one so heavily targeted to the well-off. Democrats faulted Bush's proposal as unfair to working people. To make their point in dramatic fashion, House minority leader Richard Gephardt of Missouri and Senate minority leader Tom Daschle of South Dakota appeared with a black Lexus sedan and a battered replacement muffler. The car, Daschle charged, was "just like the Bush tax cut—fully loaded. If you're a millionaire, under the Bush tax cut, you get a $46,000 tax cut, more than enough to pay for this Lexus. But if you're a typical working person, you get $227, and that's enough to buy this muffler" (*New York Times,* February 9, 2001). Democrats also argued that such a big tax cut would endanger Medicare and Social Security by using up too much of the surplus.

Early Action in the House

The normal budget process requires that first both chambers pass a budget resolution to set guidelines for future legislative action, including any tax cut. Then the chambers would be expected to pass a reconciliation bill that actually enacts into law the instructions included in the budget resolution. Bush and House Republican leaders, however, decided to pass the first and biggest part of the Bush tax cut—the across-the-board cut in income tax rates—in the House before the budget resolution was passed. They wanted to establish momentum and feared the budget resolution might highlight less popular elements of Bush's budget plan, such as spending cuts.

On February 27, in his first address to a joint session of Congress, President Bush promoted his agenda to members of Congress and to a large television audience. Although he also discussed his spending priorities, the tax cut was front and center. Bush then undertook a campaign-style tour across the country to sell the tax cut, but the effort seemed to have little impact on Democrats. "When members were home last week, they were feeling no pressure on tax cuts," an aide to a Blue Dog (conservative) Democrat reported. A Gallup poll showed that Democrats in the electorate opposed the Bush plan by more than 2 to 1 (*CQW,* March 3, 2001, 466).

On March 1 the House Ways and Means Committee approved HR 3, the Economic Growth and Tax Relief Act, a bill cutting income taxes across the board, on a 23–15 party-line vote. The chairman's mark had been put together through a strictly partisan process, and the committee turned down two major Democratic amendments (one a substitute) on party votes. Bush had talked about bipartisanship, but Democrats claimed little was in evidence. "At no time were the Blue Dogs consulted about these things," said Charlie Stenholm of Texas, a senior leader of the group of conservative Democrats. "We weren't even consulted. What's bipartisan about that?" (*CQW,* March 10, 2001, 530).

On March 8 the House took up the bill, and debate was sharply partisan. The Republican leadership had brought up the bill under a rule that allowed only one Democratic substitute and no other amendments. In the debate on the rule, Republicans focused on the bill's substance, as a majority that knows it can pass its rule often does.

Democrats discussed their objections to the contents of the bill, but they focused more on the timing. It is against the rules—and worse, it is irresponsible—to pass a tax cut before agreeing on a budget resolution, they argued. A special rule can waive all points of order against the bill, including the relevant Budget Act provisions, as this one did, but that does not make it either right or sensible. A rule can be amended if (and only if) the motion to call the previous question is first defeated. The ranking Democrat on the Rules Committee, Joe Moakley from Massachusetts, explained, "Mr. Speaker, I urge defeat of the previous question so that I may offer an amendment to the rule. My amendment would require Congress to adopt the budget resolution before the House takes up the tax bill" (*Congressional Record,* March 8, 2001, H748).

The tactic failed, as everyone knew it would. The previous question was ordered, thus precluding any attempt to amend the rule, on a 220–204 vote; every Republican voted for the rule; only four Democrats did. The rule itself passed 220–204. To make their point as strongly as possible, Democrats in both cases forced recorded votes on motions to reconsider the vote.

In the hour of general debate and the additional hour of debate on the Democratic substitute that the rule allowed, Republicans continued to emphasize that the bill would stimulate a lagging economy and would lift the yoke of a cruelly and unnecessarily heavy tax burden off the backs of the American people. "Today we say to the American people, you earned it, you will get to keep more of it," a Republican declared (*CR*, March 8, 2001, H767). Democrats argued that the bill gave thousands to the well-off and very little or nothing to struggling working families; and they repeated that a budget resolution should be approved first. Charlie Rangel of New York, ranking Democrat on the Ways and Means Committee, offered the Democratic substitute, which was less costly and differently distributed, with much more going to the less-well-off. It was defeated on a 155–273 vote; all Republicans and fifty-three Democrats voted against it. Many of the Democratic opponents were simply unwilling to vote for any tax cut prior to a budget resolution being approved.

Democrats showed their disapproval of the Republicans' strategy one last time by the content of their motion to recommit with instructions. This is a motion that the minority can make that, if approved, essentially amends the bill. Charlie Stenholm moved "to recommit the bill to the House Ways and Means Committee with instructions not to report the bill back until April 15, 2001, unless Congress has completed action on the concurrent budget resolution for fiscal 2002" (*Roll Call*, April 15, 2001). The motion was defeated 204–221, with every Republican and two Democrats voting against it. Minority Leader Dick Gephardt of Missouri and Speaker Dennis Hastert of Illinois closed debate for the minority and the majority, respectively, signaling the importance both parties placed on the bill. HR 3 passed on a vote of 230–198. On the eight roll calls on the bill or the rule, not a single Republican defected, whereas only ten Democrats voted for the bill.

Although many conservative Republicans would have preferred an even bigger tax cut, all voted for the bill. The administration had by this point convinced the many Republican interest groups to support the Bush bill even if it did not include their favorite provisions. The groups worked in coalition with the Republican White House and the congressional leadership throughout the tax cut battles.

Passing a Budget Resolution

A much rockier road lay ahead in the Senate. Unless the tax cut was passed as part of the budget process, it could be filibustered. With the Senate split 50–50, the prospects of getting the sixty votes to end a filibuster seemed dim. Bush's campaigning for his tax plan in the states of electorally marginal Democratic senators had produced no results. Democrat Zell Miller of Georgia had come out in support of the tax cut early in the year, but no other Democrats followed. Republican Lincoln Chafee of Rhode Island was on record as opposed, and a number of other moderate Republicans were expressing anxiety about the size of the cut and proposing tying reductions to continuing budget surpluses, a notion Bush and most other

Republicans rejected. Passing the Bush plan in the Senate would certainly require the protections afforded a reconciliation bill, which cannot be filibustered. And that required passing a budget resolution.

On March 11, after a twelve-hour markup, the House Budget Committee approved a budget resolution on a 23–19 party-line vote. In his February 27 speech to Congress, Bush had called for holding the overall spending increase to 4 percent, in addition to proposing $1.6 billion in tax cuts; the budget resolution in general terms followed Bush's proposals. It did give the chair of the House Budget Committee unusual authority to raise the resolution's proposed ceilings on discretionary spending later in the year, with agriculture and the military mentioned as possible areas meriting more funding, and to accommodate a refundable tax credit if the Ways and Means Committee were to approve such legislation. The resolution also stated that the tax cuts could go higher than Bush's request if surplus projections improved during the year. Ways and Means was instructed to write four reconciliation bills cutting taxes with deadlines of May 2, May 23, June 20, and September 11. It called for a fifth reconciliation measure—to be reported by the Ways and Means and Energy and Commerce Committees by July 24—to alter Medicare and to add a limited prescription drug benefit.

Democrats complained about the unusual flexibility in the resolution and the consequent unprecedented power it gave the chair, and they objected that some important domestic priorities were shortchanged. Despite offering more than thirty amendments in committee, however, they were unable to alter the Republican-drafted resolution significantly.

The House began consideration of H.Con.Res. 83, the fiscal 2002 budget resolution, on March 27. The rule allowed votes on four comprehensive substitutes: a Blue Dog Democratic proposal that cut taxes less and increased defense spending more, a conservative Republican Study Committee version that increased the size of the tax cut and more strictly limited the growth in spending, a Progressive Caucus proposal that cut taxes less and increased domestic spending more, and a Democratic leadership version similar in thrust to—but more moderate in amounts than—the Progressive Caucus plan. All four were defeated, with the Blue Dog plan doing best, losing 204–221 on a largely party-line vote. On March 28, the House adopted the budget resolution 222–205, with only three Democrats and two Republicans defecting from their respective party's position.

Meanwhile, as the economy worsened, a proposal for an immediate tax rebate to stimulate the economy gained traction in the Senate. Budget Committee chair Pete Domenici, R-NM, suggested a $60 billion tax cut as an immediate stimulus, and Democrats endorsed the idea and began promoting it as a substitute for the Bush tax cut.

With the president unable to induce any Senate Democrats other than Miller to support his tax proposal, it became clear that the evenly split Senate Budget Committee would be unable to report a budget resolution. The 50–50 Senate split had forced Republicans to enter into a power-sharing agreement with Democrats that specified equal numbers of members on every committee. Republicans would, however, chair committees. (Because Dick Cheney as vice president was president of the Senate and cast the deciding vote, the Republicans were the nominal majority in the chamber; their leader was the majority leader.) Budget chair Domenici drafted a resolution that largely followed Bush's proposal, except for the $60 billion stimulus tax cut in 2001; Majority Leader Lott bypassed the committee and brought it directly to the floor.

Although Budget Act rules protect the budget resolution from a filibuster and from nongermane amendments, senators can and do offer germane amendments. On the second full day of debate, liberal Democrat Tom Harkin of Iowa offered an amendment reducing the tax cut by $488 billion and shifting the money to education and debt relief. When three Republican moderates—Chafee, Jim Jeffords of Vermont, and Arlen Specter of Pennsylvania—deserted their party, the amendment passed 53–47. Every Democrat except Zell Miller voted for the Harkin amendment. At the end of the roll call, Majority Leader Lott changed his vote from "nay" to "yea" because that would allow him to move to reconsider the vote later.

Vice President Dick Chaney, Office of Management and Budget (OMB) head Mitch Daniels, and other White House officials scurried around trying to figure out how to reverse the setback. However, the vote just broke the dam, and a number of other amendments altering the president's program also passed. The Senate took roll call votes on twenty-one amendments, and while Republicans defeated a number of Democratic amendments, in many cases they did so only by offering slightly less generous versions of those amendments themselves. The budget resolution as amended called for a tax cut of $1.18 trillion over ten years, an immediate $82 billion stimulus tax cut, and a cap on discretionarily spending of $678 billion, which was a 7 percent increase over fiscal 2001. Money had been shifted from tax cuts to spending on agriculture, education, the National Institutes of Health, defense, and veterans programs. The resolution passed the Senate 65–35, with all the Republicans and fifteen Democrats voting for it.

Republicans hoped to recoup some of their losses in conference with the House. When Democrats complained about being excluded from the negotiations, Domenici baldly replied, "We don't expect you to sign [the conference report], so we don't expect you to be needed" (*CQW*, April 28, 2001, 904). The administration focused on getting the support of just enough moderate Senate Democrats to pass the conference report in the Senate, so only they were included in the negotiations.

Maintaining the support of Senate moderates required not substantially increasing the Senate's tax cut figure but did allow other changes, including cutting the Senate's figure for discretionary spending back to Bush's requested 4 percent increase, which pleased conservative House Republicans. Conferees reached an agreement and filed the conference report calling for $1.35 trillion in tax cuts on May 3. In the rush, however, two very important pages were missing from the conference report as filed, so votes had to be put off until the next week.

Bush hailed the agreement as a bipartisan triumph, but most Democrats objected to that characterization. "When he gets up and talks about Democrats and Republicans working together, I'd like to know who the hell he's talking about," said John Spratt, South Carolina representative and the ranking Democrat on the House Budget Committee.

On May 9 the budget resolution conference report passed the House on a 221–207 vote, with six Democrats and three Republicans crossing party lines. The Senate vote the next day was 53–47. Whereas fifteen Democrats had supported the budget resolution as amended on the Senate floor, only five supported the conference report. This was enough, however, to offset the two Republican defections.

Reconciliation

With a budget resolution calling for tax cuts in place, the Senate could now proceed to write a tax bill, assured it would be protected by budget rules from a filibuster. The resolution called for one tax-cutting reconciliation bill; the Senate parliamentarian, a nonpartisan expert on Senate rules, had ruled that the Budget Act allowed only one.

The Senate Finance Committee has jurisdiction over tax legislation, and Chair Charles Grassley, R-IA, and ranking Democrat Max Baucus, D-MT, very much wanted the committee to take the lead role in drafting the tax bill. As the tax issue had become key in defining the difference between the parties during the 1990s, party leaders had increasingly usurped the committee's role. In addition to his desire to reestablish the committee's prestige, Baucus was concerned about his own upcoming reelection battle in a state that Bush had won handily. But Grassley and Baucus could maintain control over the legislation only if they worked together and crafted a plan with bipartisan support in the committee.

Grassley and Baucus began talking well before the budget resolution was approved, but once the conference report cleared, they were under pressure to produce a proposal. The budget resolution set a May 18 deadline for the committee to report. Senators in both parties looked on the collaboration with suspicion and were not shy about letting the committee leaders know: at a May 9 meeting of Republican Finance members, Grassley received "long lectures" from several of his more conservative colleagues, and when Baucus briefed the full Democratic membership, he "got an earful of dissent" (*CQW,* May 12, 2001, 1069). Lott attempted to talk Grassley out of drafting a bipartisan bill, and Daschle tried to discourage Baucus from working with Grassley. Both party leaders believed that reaching a bipartisan deal would require giving away too much. John Breaux, a moderate Democrat from Louisiana who supported the committee leaders' efforts, told Baucus not to worry about the heat. "The only good thing is they're jumping on Grassley just as much, so we must be headed in the right direction," Breaux quipped (*CQW,* May 12, 2001, 1069).

On May 11, Grassley and Baucus unveiled a rough draft of their compromise and set the markup for May 15. Their plan included the same components as Bush's proposal: a reduction in income tax rates, mitigation of the marriage penalty, a doubling of the $500-per-child tax credit, and a phasing out of the estate tax. To appeal to Democrats, the plan changed the distribution of tax benefits so that more went to lower- and middle-income people and less to the wealthy. It also made the $1,000-per-child tax credit available even to those who earned too little to owe income taxes. To abide by Senate budget rules, they were forced to include a provision that "sunsetted," or repealed, the entire bill after ten years, when the revenue set aside under the budget resolution would no longer be available. Without that provision, the bill would have lost the Budget Act protections and would have been subject to a point of order requiring an impossible-to-attain sixty votes to waive (*CQW,* May 19, 2001, 1145).

Led by Minority Leader Daschle, a member of the Finance Committee, dissatisfied Democrats attempted to alter the Grassley-Baucus draft during markup, but all their amendments failed. Many Finance Republicans also were unhappy with the draft, but they wanted to get a bill to the floor, so they held their fire. Grassley and Baucus steered their compromise through Finance without significant change, winning approval on a 14–6 vote, with all Republicans and four of the ten Democrats voting for it.

Before the budget resolution conference report passed, the House had already approved four different tax-cutting bills that contained all the components of the Bush request, although in somewhat rewritten form. Now, in order to give their tax legislation Budget Act protections, House Republicans repassed the income-tax rate cut. HR 1836 was identical to HR 3, but it was officially designated a reconciliation bill. Only a bill passed after the budget resolution is in effect and pursuant to reconciliation instructions can be so designated.

House Republicans were especially concerned that, were the conference to adopt the House's 33 percent top income tax rate rather than the Senate's 36 percent figure, the House figure would have reconciliation protection in the Senate and so not be subject to a sixty-vote requirement. As Ways and Means Democrat Ben Cardin of Maryland succinctly explained, the reason for repassing the bill in the House was "so we can pass a single tax bill in the other body, not by a bipartisan vote, but along very partisan lines. That is what this bill is allowing us to do. I urge my colleagues to vote against it" (*CR*, May 19, 2001, H2210).

The Republican leadership brought up HR 1836 under a modified closed rule that allowed one Democratic substitute—if offered by Ways and Means ranking Democrat Charlie Rangel—and one motion to recommit with or without instructions. The substitute amendment, which would provide a one-time, retroactive tax rebate; reduce the lowest income tax bracket rate to 12 percent; and increase the amount of income that one can earn and still qualify for the Earned Income Tax Credit, was defeated on a 188–239 vote, and the bill was passed by a 230–197 vote. All three recorded votes—these two and the vote on the rule—were highly partisan, with not a single Republican crossing party lines.

The Senate began floor debate on May 17 and continued it on May 21, 22, and 23. More than fifty amendments were offered and pushed to a roll call vote. Budget Act rules require that amendments to reconciliation bills be germane and specify that sixty votes are needed to waive that requirement. So in many cases the vote was not directly on the amendment itself but on a motion to waive the Budget Act with respect to a point of order against the amendment. Many of the Democratic amendments sought to shift money from top bracket tax cuts to Medicare, education, or other social programs and were killed by a point of order that they were not germane. Both Republicans and Democrats offered amendments, but Democrats seemed intent on delaying passage of the bill. Budget Act rules limit debate on reconciliation bills to twenty hours, but time spent in roll calls is not counted. Therefore, an almost unlimited number of amendments could be offered, "debated" for a minute or less, and then put to a vote, one after another in what is known as a "vote-a-rama."

On the evening of May 22, word that Jim Jeffords, R-VT, was considering leaving the Republican Party to caucus with the Democrats, thus shifting Senate control to the Democratic Party, began to leak out; the next day it was confirmed. Jeffords said he would leave the Republican Party the day the tax bill reached Bush's desk. Democrats no longer had an incentive to delay, and Republicans realized they had better settle for what they could get.

On May 23, twelve Senate Democrats joined all 50 Republicans to pass the legislation on a 62–38 vote. Despite the barrage of amendments on the floor, the bill passed largely intact. Grassley and Baucus had put together a package that could pass; neither liberal Democrats nor conservative Republicans had the votes to move the bill significantly in their preferred direction. To ease passage, Grassley and Baucus did put together a manager's amendment that made $65.7 billion worth of changes in the bill. The managers had negotiated behind the scenes with many senators who wanted changes; these senators agreed to refrain from offering their amendments on the floor in return for the managers including versions of their proposals in the manager's amendment.

The Senate had substituted its own bill for HR 1836, and as soon as it passed the bill, it insisted on its amendment, asked for a conference, and appointed conferees. The conferees were all from the Finance Committee and comprised Republicans Grassley, Phil Gramm of Texas, Orrin Hatch of Utah, Frank Murkowski of Alaska, and Don Nickles of Oklahoma, and Democrats Baucus, Breaux, Daschle, and Jay Rockefeller IV of West Virginia. On the evening of May 23, the House agreed to a conference, and the Speaker appointed as conferees Ways and Means chair Bill Thomas of California, Majority Leader Dick Armey, and Ways and Means ranking Democrat Charlie Rangel.

Bush publicly called on the conferees for a quick resolution; despite the complexity of the issues, the conference committee moved with unusual speed to approve a compromise bill. And as much as conservative House Republicans hated to admit it, the Republican leadership of both chambers, the experienced Republican conferees, and the Bush administration all recognized that the final legislation would have to largely track the Senate bill. The Grassley-Baucus bill had passed the Senate with a substantial vote, but the underlying coalition was fragile. Moderates, who were the key to victory, had to be kept on board. Fifteen Senate moderates, led by Democrat John Breaux and Republican Olympia Snowe, R-ME, signed a letter threatening to oppose any conference report that did not "closely reflect the delicate compromise that was reached in the Senate" (*CQW*, May 26, 2001, 1251).

After three days of negotiations, the conferees agreed on a bill that cut taxes by $1.35 trillion through 2011, considerably less than Bush's initial request and the House figure. It also distributed that tax cut somewhat differently, giving more to those in the lower income brackets, and it provided immediate tax rebates to act as a stimulus; finally, it sunsetted the entire bill at the end of 2010 (*CQW*, May 26, 2001, 1251–1254). In addition, it phased out the estate tax and alleviated the marriage penalty, both high Republican priorities. One possible reason for the fast wrap-up was the fact that the majority of the Democratic conferees were excluded from the negotiations; "as soon as I was appointed, I waited and I waited and I waited for an invitation to the meeting," Charlie Rangel recounted. "But the invitation never came" (*CR*, May 26, 2001, H2832).

The conference report was filed in the House at 5:17 a.m. on May 26. Because House members were eager to go home for the Memorial Day weekend, the Rules Committee reported the rule for consideration at 6:54 a.m. and consideration began at 8:24 a.m. The House adopted the conference report on the bill by a 240–154 vote shortly after 10:00 a.m. Every Republican voted for the conference report; Democrats split 153 to 28 against it. Republicans extolled the bill as fair and as delivering on a campaign promise:

> The real issue here today is who should spend the money. Do we believe that individuals and families make the best decisions about how to spend their money, or do we believe government is in the best position to do so? The special interests that we heard from the minority leader are in this bill. Want to hear what they are? People who are married, people who have children, people who are worried about the education of those kids, people who are worried about their small business and farms, and people who are worried about more and more money that goes to Washington that is not available to pay for higher energy bills, higher college costs and higher expenses. (*CR*, May 26, 2001, H2837)

The Senate cleared the measure, 58–33, later the same day; two Republicans—Chafee and John McCain of Arizona—voted against it; twelve Democrats supported the bill. Senator Gramm praised Bush's role in the passing of the legislation, "Elections have consequences. Leadership makes a difference." Enactment did indeed represent a big victory for President Bush and for congressional Republicans. The largest tax cut since Ronald Reagan's first year in office became law, and it included many of the provisions—across-the-board rate cuts, alleviation of the marriage penalty, and the eventual ending of the estate tax—that Bush had advocated and that the Republican base had long desired.

Once More with Feeling: The 2003 Tax Cut

The 2003 tax cuts again illustrate how crucial the budget process is to the enactment of major policy change in the contemporary Congress. It also shows the ability of the House as currently structured to pass important legislation quickly and with slim partisan majorities and the effects of the Senate's permissive rules, as currently employed by partisan minorities and individuals, on legislative outcomes.

The 2002 elections were a triumph for Bush. He had campaigned hard for Republicans in congressional elections and was rewarded with a highly unusual gain in seats by the president's party in midterm elections.

Republicans regained control of the Senate, albeit by the narrow margin of 51–49.

As a top priority, Bush asked Congress for a tax cut of $726 billion over eleven years, with an elimination of the tax on stock dividends as its centerpiece. He justified the tax cut as a necessary stimulus for an economy in the doldrums since the 9/11 attacks; throughout the process, Republicans labeled the proposal a jobs and economic growth plan. Most congressional Republicans strongly supported further big tax cuts, although their views on what form the cuts should take were diverse. Democratic opposition made it clear that the budget process would again have to be used so that the bill would be protected from a Senate filibuster.

Passing the Budget Resolution

After a "lengthy round of 'listening sessions' with rank-and-file Republicans," Budget Committee chair Jim Nussle of Iowa drafted a budget resolution that included the full $726 billion in tax cuts but otherwise was very austere, calling for spending cuts in Medicare, Medicaid, and most other entitlement programs (except Social Security)—for a total savings of $467 billion over ten years (*CQW,* January 3, 2004, 25). The Budget Committee approved Nussle's draft on a party-line vote, but it soon became clear that it could not pass the House. Republican moderates rebelled, forcing majority-party leaders to rewrite the measure significantly. The resolution that went to the floor did not include the tougher spending cuts, but did include the $726 billion for tax cuts. Even so, passing the resolution proved to be difficult and took a "full court press" by the leadership and Vice President Cheney. The resolution passed 215–212, with only one Democrat voting for it and twelve Republicans voting against.

As usual, the process was even more difficult in the Senate. Don Nickles, the new chair of the Budget Committee, produced a resolution that included the same tax cut figure but lacked the steep cuts in mandatory spending. The committee approved it on a 12–11 party-line vote. Floor debate was long and contentious. On March 19 the Senate adopted an amendment by Barbara Boxer, D-CA, to strike language that would have allowed oil drilling in the Arctic National Wildlife Refuge (ANWR) to be included in the reconciliation bill.

Much more troubling for the Republican leaders, on March 25, Democrat John Breaux offered an amendment that would limit the tax cut to $350 billion. A group of Senate centrists, which included Republicans George Voinovich of Ohio and Olympia Snowe, as well as Breaux, had been working on this alternative that they believed would be more defensible given the likely cost of the Iraq War and the soaring deficits. When the senators who opposed new tax cuts—most of the Democrats and Republican Lincoln Chafee—decided to vote for the Breaux proposal, it passed on a largely party-line vote of 51–48, with forty-seven Democrats, three Republicans, and independent Jeffords supporting it.

With most House Republicans passionately committed to big tax cuts, the adoption of the Breaux amendment assured that the conference would be excruciatingly difficult. When, after much cajoling and pressuring, Senate Republican leaders could not find more than forty-eight votes for a budget resolution with a tax cut of more than $350 billion, Majority Leader Bill Frist of Tennessee began advocating that the resolution contain different reconciliation instructions for the House and the Senate, something that had never been done before.

The first version of the strategy did not pass muster with the Senate parliamentarian, but a second version was cleared. The reconciliation instructions would allow the tax committees in both chambers to draft bills that cut taxes by up to $550 billion; however, any bill with more than a $350 billion tax cut would be subject to a sixty-vote point of order on the Senate floor that, everyone knew, proponents could not possibly waive. So, in effect, the Senate would not initially be able to pass a tax bill more expensive than $350 billion. The strategic element that made this approach attractive to proponents of a bigger tax cut was that a conference report that contained a tax cut as big as $550 billion would have reconciliation protections and so would only require a simple majority to pass the Senate.

The House passed the conference report on a tight 216–211 vote almost completely along party lines. The Senate moderates, however, refused to go along with the ploy. Voinovich and Snowe agreed to vote for the conference report only after extracting a promise from Majority Leader Frist and Finance Committee chair Grassley that the tax cut would not exceed $350 billion. The promise made possible the 51–50 approval of the budget resolution conference report, with Vice President Cheney casting the tie-breaking vote. Republicans Chafee and John McCain voted against it. Only one Democrat—Zell Miller—voted for it.

House Republicans were furious; Frist had reneged on an agreement, they contended. Tom DeLay (R-TX), House majority leader, insisted that $550 billion was the binding ceiling. "As far as we're concerned, that's the deal. We expect the Senate leadership to honor the deal," he said (*CQW*, April 12, 2003). Many Senate Republicans were themselves unhappy about the figure and hoped to increase it in the bill itself. "Obviously the House has expressed its feelings, and we have to respect that," said Rick Santorum of Pennsylvania, chair of the Senate Republican Conference. "We are going to do our best to repair it where it matters, and that is to get a bigger tax bill" (*NYT*, April 17, 2003).

Reconciliation

Ways and Means reported a $550 billion tax cut bill on May 6 on a 24–15 party-line vote. Committee chair Bill Thomas, after ascertaining that Bush's proposal could not garner sufficient Republican votes to pass, came up with a plan that would reduce but not eliminate tax rates on both dividends and capital gains; accelerate the 2001 tax cuts for individuals, as Bush had requested; and provide other tax cuts for business. The House considered the bill under a closed rule allowing no amendments. This meant that Democrats were forced to offer their substitute through a motion to recommit with instructions, the sort of procedural vote that is difficult to exploit electorally and, when Rangel did attempt to offer his substitute in the motion to recommit with instructions, the chair ruled it nongermane and the Democrats' appeal of the ruling of the chair was tabled (i.e., killed) on a party-line vote. The bill passed May 9 by a 222-203 vote, with only three Republicans and four Democrats crossing party lines.

Senate Finance Committee chair Grassley was faced with what proved to be an impossible task. He was under intense pressure from the administration and his leadership to include in his bill a version of Bush's proposal to eliminate the tax on dividends. Conservative Republicans wanted bigger tax breaks. Moderates were insisting that he not exceed $350 billion and that he make the cuts at least a bit more progressive. A number of senators also wanted him to include significant aid to the states, which were suffering because of the recession.

To get the crucial vote of moderate Snowe in the Finance Committee, Grassley reworked his original draft. To stay under $350 billion, Grassley had relied on manipulating the dates when the dividend tax cuts were to go into effect and expire, a method that Snowe considered a "gimmick" (*CQW,* March 10, 2003). Grassley replaced his initial plan with a dividend proposal that for each individual taxpayer would exclude the first $500 of dividend income from taxes and give a 10 percent exemption on dividend income over $500. In 2008 the additional exemption would go up to 20 percent.

Conservative Republicans disliked that plan, but it picked up Snowe's vote on the closely divided Finance Committee. Grassley added $20 billion in aid to the states, which helped him get the vote of Blanche Lincoln of Arkansas, the only Democrat he won. To keep the net cost of his plan down to $350 billion, Grassley also included nearly $90 billion in "offsets," primarily changes in tax law that would increase taxes on businesses. Finance approved the bill 12–9. Many committee Republicans voted for the bill only to get it out of committee.

The Republican leadership in both chambers; most Republicans, especially conservatives; and Republicans' business allies disliked the bill intensely and immediately vowed to change it on the floor. A Republican House member from Florida expressed the sentiment most colorfully:

> Some Republicans in the Senate are making it very difficult to abide by [President] Ronald Reagan's 11th Commandment [thou shalt not criticize fellow Republicans], because they're not acting like Republicans. I think the Capitol Police better check to see if someone's slipped something into the water over there. (*CQW,* May 10, 2003, 1087)

Senate consideration began on May 14. Over the course of the two days of debate, the Senate took recorded votes on thirty amendments.[2] Don Nickles, Budget Committee chair and a conservative member of the Finance Committee, proposed an amendment that would change the dividend provision in a direction more acceptable to the president and most Republicans. The amendment exempted 50 percent of dividend payments from taxation in 2003 and increased that to 100 percent from 2004 through 2006. Dividend tax rates would return to their previous levels in 2007.

To adhere to budget rules, offsets also were included to pay for the extra costs. The amendment passed on 51–50 vote, with Cheney casting the tie-breaking vote. Two Democrats voted for the amendment—Zell Miller, who had supported the Bush tax-cutting agenda since 2001, and Ben Nelson of Nebraska, won over by the lure of money for the states. Three Republicans opposed it—John McCain and Lincoln Chafee, who had opposed tax cuts all year because of concern about the deficit, and Olympia Snowe, who disliked the sunset gimmicks in the amendment. The vote on passage was almost identical, with only Evan Bayh, D-IN, switching to vote in favor. Although the Nickles amendment made the Senate bill more acceptable to many Republicans, it still included $101 billion in offsetting revenue increases, much of which would fall on businesses. Not only were business groups strongly opposed to these provisions, but also many House Republicans unalterably opposed tax increases of any sort.

Bush urged a quick resolution to the differences between the chambers' bills, and to effectuate that the administration threw its weight behind the Thomas plan on dividends. If, as seemed clear, the compromise could not exceed the Senate's figure of $350 billion, Ways and Means chair Bill Thomas asserted the House should have the greater say on how the tax cut was structured. Grassley objected but to no avail. The conference agreement included the Thomas provisions on dividends and capital

---

2. Some were not votes on the amendments directly but votes to waive the Budget Act to make the amendment in order.

gains; a number of other tax cuts, including acceleration of the individual income-tax rate cuts of 2001 and more generous first-year write-offs for business investment; and $20 billion in aid to the states. The offsets the Senate had included were dropped. To fit the total into the $350 billion total, conferees phased in some tax cuts and set early expiration dates for others. Majority Leader DeLay served as a conferee, but it was Vice President Cheney who played a crucial role in brokering the major deals that made an agreement possible (*CQW*, May 31, 2003, 1306).

On May 23, just before their Memorial Day recess, both the House and the Senate approved the conference report on largely party-line votes. In the House one Republican and seven Democrats crossed party lines. In the Senate, three Republicans—Chafee, McCain, and Snowe—voted against the final bill; two Democrats—Ben Nelson and Zell Miller—voted for it. Again, passage depended on Vice President Cheney's tie-breaking vote.

Cutting Taxes via Unorthodox Lawmaking

When Congress and the White House are controlled by the same party, the budget process offers an extremely useful tool for making sweeping policy change. This is even truer in the early twenty-first century than it was in the early 1990s because the parties have continued to become more ideologically homogeneous and more polarized. Thus Republicans were able to enact huge tax cuts in 2001 and 2003 over intense Democratic opposition and despite their narrow margins of control.

The budget process and some of the other tools of unorthodox lawmaking were indispensable to the majority Republicans' legislative success. Most crucial were the protections from filibusters and nongermane amendments that the budget process affords the reconciliation bill. Absent those protections, Senate passage without much more extensive compromise would have been unlikely. The Republican leadership in the House used the now ordinary tools of unorthodox lawmaking, such as highly restrictive rules, to facilitate passage. Republican leaders also extended the boundaries of unorthodox lawmaking, in this case by crafting a budget resolution in 2001 that formally gave the Budget Committee chair—and actually the leadership itself—extraordinary flexibility to adjust the resolution's contents after passage if necessary.

The design of the tax cut bills represents another form of unorthodox lawmaking. By adjusting the dates when tax provisions went into effect and when they expired, Republicans fit a much bigger tax cut into the amounts specified by the budget resolution than would otherwise have been allowed. The sunsets on a number of provisions would never go into effect, most Republicans believed; when they became imminent, political pressure would force extensions of the tax cuts (Hacker and Pierson 2005). Proponents of the tax cuts called the strategy clever; opponents labeled it dishonest and charged it was intended to fool the public. It does seem likely that the strategy could not have been successfully carried out without the tight majority-party leadership control over the process in the House and in conference that has become an integral part of unorthodox lawmaking in the twenty-first century.

TABLE 9.1   The George W. Bush Tax Cuts of 2001

	President George W. Bush formally sends Congress his tax cut proposal on February 8, 2001.				
Date	House action	Date	Senate action	Date	Postpassage action
2/13	Treasury Secretary Paul O'Neill testifies before the Ways and Means Committee				
2/28	HR 3 is introduced				
3/1	Ways and Means Committee marks up and approves HR 3, the Economic Growth and Tax Relief Act, a bill cutting income taxes across the board				
3/8	House approves restrictive rule, debates HR 3, and passes it				
3/11	Budget Committee approves budget resolution calling for four tax cut reconciliation bills				
3/27–3/28	House approves structured rule, debates and passes budget resolution, H.Con. Res. 83				

TABLE 9.1 (Continued)

Date	House action	Date	Senate action	Date	Postpassage action
		4/2	Budget Committee discharged. (Majority Leader Trent Lott bypasses Budget Committee and brings budget resolution directly to the floor.) Motion to proceed to consideration of measure agreed to by unanimous consent		
		4/3–4/6	Senate considers and passes budget resolution		
		4/4	Harkin amendment reducing the tax cut by $488 billion passes		
		5/11	*Finance Committee chair Grassley and Ranking Minority Member Baucus unveil a rough draft of their compromise tax bill*		
		5/15	Finance Committee marks up and approves Grassley-Baucus bill		

TABLE 9.1 (*Continued*)

Date	House action	Date	Senate action	Date	Postpassage action
5/15	HR 1836, the Economic Growth and Tax Relief Reconciliation Act, introduced. (HR 1836 includes major provisions from HR 3, the Economic Growth and Tax Relief Act; from HR 6, the Marriage Penalty and Family Tax Relief Act; from HR 8, the Death Tax Elimination Act; from HR 10, the Comprehensive Retirement Security and Pension Reform Act; from HR 622, the Adoption Tax Credits bill; and from S 896, the Senate budget reconciliation bill.) Bill is referred to Ways and Means. Rules Committee reports rule providing for consideration of HR 1836				
5/16	House approves rule; considers and passes HR 1836	5/17, 5/21–5/23	Senate debates tax bill		

TABLE 9.1 *(Continued)*

Date	House action	Date	Senate action	Date	Postpassage action
		5/23	Senate passes tax bill.	4/23	Senate asks for conference on budget resolution and names conferees
				4/24	House agrees to conference and names conferees
				4/25	Conference held
				5/3	Conference report filed
				5/9	House considers and agrees to conference report. Senate considers conference report

TABLE 9.1 (*Continued*)

Date	House action	Date	Senate action	Date	Postpassage action
				5/10, 5/23	Senate agrees to conference report. Senate asks for a conference on tax bill and appoints conferees. House agrees to conference and appoints conferees
				5/23–5/26	Conference meets
				5/26	Conference report filed. House approves conference report. Senate approves conference report
				6/7	President signs, and it becomes law

Note: Official actions are in roman type; behind-the-scenes, unofficial actions are in italics.

The Consequences of Unorthodox Lawmaking

UNORTHODOX LAWMAKING has become standard operating procedure in the U.S. Congress—in the strict definition of the term, it is unorthodox no more. Not only does the textbook model no longer describe how most major legislation becomes—or fails to become—law, but also no single model has replaced it. Some previously unusual practices, such as significant party leadership involvement at the prefloor stage, have become standard but, overall, variety, not uniformity, characterizes the contemporary legislative process.

After briefly reviewing the contours of unorthodox lawmaking, this chapter examines its consequences. Do the procedures and practices that constitute unorthodox lawmaking as here defined enhance or hinder a bill's chances of becoming law? Are there other, less measurable costs and benefits of unorthodox lawmaking? Overall, how should observers of Congress assess unorthodox lawmaking?

Lawmaking in the Contemporary Congress

Most major legislation used to follow a single, well-defined process; the question at each stage was simply whether the bill would survive (and in what form) to go on to the next. These days, bills and other important measures confront a series of decision points where more complex choices are at issue.

Will the bill be referred to more than one committee? In the House, rules of committee jurisdiction dictate which committees receive referral, but beyond that, the Speaker also has some discretion. Usually, the Speaker designates one lead committee; the other committees with jurisdiction may be given additional initial referrals, and the Speaker likely will impose time limits for action, which may be generous or tight. When a number of committees work on a bill, many perspectives and interests are represented in the bill-drafting process. If the committees come to an agreement among themselves, the supportive coalition for the bill becomes formidable. But the more committees involved, the longer the process is likely to take and the more difficult working out disagreements among the committees is likely to be.

In the Senate, committee leaders usually work out problems of conflicting jurisdiction among themselves, most often informally. Fairly frequently, several Senate committees work on different bills that deal with the same subject; such instances can raise many of the same questions and problems as multiple referral does in the House.

Although in both chambers most legislation is referred to committee, the option of bypassing the committee stage altogether does exist; most of the time it is one that only the party leaders can exercise. Bypassing committee can speed up the process significantly, especially if several committees have jurisdiction. For that reason committee leaders sometimes agree wholeheartedly with the strategy, particularly if the committee reported the bill or a very similar one in the previous Congress. Party leaders occasionally bypass committee and draft the legislation themselves or delegate the drafting to a special task force because they believe the committee will not do a satisfactory job. They fear that because of its membership or the political delicacy of the issue, the committee will not be able to come to an agreement in a reasonable period of time or that it will produce a bill that cannot pass the chamber or is unsatisfactory to significant numbers of majority-party members. Frequent bypassing of committees, however, can engender considerable hostility from the membership, majority as well as minority, and leaders who need their party members' votes for reelection to their positions have tended to be reluctant to take this action except under extraordinary circumstances. In recent Congresses, party leaders have perceived the circumstances to be "extraordinary" considerably more frequently than in the past, in part at least because the high partisan polarization makes the crafting of legislation that can pass the chamber a more delicate political task.

Once a bill has been reported from committee, the majority-party leadership must decide if the bill as reported is ready for floor consideration. That decision depends on the answers to a series of questions: If the bill has been reported from several committees, are there major outstanding differences between the committees' versions? Does the bill as reported command enough support to pass the chamber? Is it satisfactory to most majority-party members? If the answer to any of these questions is no, postcommittee changes to the legislation will have to be negotiated.

If the president is a fellow partisan, his views also are likely to be taken into account; provisions he opposes also may occasion postcommittee negotiations.

Once leaders decide postcommittee adjustments are necessary, they are faced with a host of choices about the form such changes should take. In the House the next decision centers on the type of special rule under which to bring the legislation to the floor. Are there special problems that confront the legislation as a result of multiple referral? Do special provisions have to be made for incorporating a postcommittee compromise into the bill? Are there amendments that members very much do or do not want to vote on? The majority-party leadership, in consultation with the Rules Committee majority, designs a rule intended to give the legislation its best chance on the floor. Whereas in the past most rules were simple open rules, and the rest were simple closed rules, now only leaders' creativity and the need for House approval limit the form of rules. More and more the choice is a highly restrictive rule. A majority of the House membership can defeat a rule, but because leaders are sensitive to their party members' preferences, this seldom happens.

In the Senate the majority leader has no such powerful tool at his command. He will often try to work out one or a series of unanimous consent agreements for expeditious and orderly consideration of the legislation on the floor; for success, however, he is dependent on the acquiescence of all senators.

The prerogatives individual senators and the minority party possess give them choices to make at this stage. If they dislike the legislation, should they try to block it from being brought to the floor by putting a hold on it? Should they explicitly threaten to filibuster it? Should they make known to the bill's supporters that they are willing to negotiate? Whatever their sentiments about the bill, if it does come to the floor, what amendments will they offer to the legislation? Should they offer measures not related to the bill's subject matter as nongermane amendments— either to load down the legislation and hurt its chances of enactment or to piggyback their own pet ideas on a popular bill? Should the minority party use the bill as a vehicle to get votes on its agenda? If a bill they strongly dislike passes the chamber, should they try to prevent it from going to conference or filibuster the conference report?

These are the sorts of choices confronting actors in the legislative process on more-or-less ordinary major bills. Legislative actors can also choose (or be faced with) complex types of legislation and processes that either did not exist at all or were rarely used several decades ago. For example, leaders can decide to package a broad array of provisions into an omnibus bill to raise the visibility of individually modest measures on a popular issue or to make possible the passing of unpalatable but necessary provisions by bundling them with more popular ones. The budget process makes omnibus measures a regular part of the legislative process and forces majority-party leaders regularly to deal with the problems passing such broad measures creates.

Central leaders—the majority-party leaders but also the president—can use the budget process as a mechanism for attempting to make comprehensive policy change, something that the legislative process as it functioned before the 1974 Congressional Budget and Impoundment Control Act made extremely difficult. When the president and the congressional majority cannot come to an agreement on major legislation through normal processes, they may decide to try a summit—formal negotiations between congressional leaders and high-level representatives of the president or even the president himself. Summits are unlikely to be required when the president and the congressional majority are fellow partisans, but high partisan polarization has made them increasingly necessary when the branches are controlled by different parties.

Congressional actors—especially congressional majority-party leaders but also individual senators and the Senate minority party—now have more choices, and the alternatives they choose lead to different legislative processes. Majority-party leaders make most of their choices with the aim of facilitating the passage of legislation; individual senators and the Senate minority party may have quite different aims in mind. When, as they often do, congressional actors make choices that produce a legislative process that is unorthodox by the standards of the old textbook model, what is the effect on whether the bill becomes a law?

Unorthodox Lawmaking and Legislative Outcomes

I have argued that changes in the legislative process can be seen as the responses of members to the problems and opportunities that the institutional structure and the political environment present as members individually or collectively pursue their goals of reelection, influence in the chamber, and good public policy. Specifically, I have contended that a number of the innovations and modifications were driven by the difficulties in legislating that internal reforms and a hostile political climate created for majority Democrats in the 1980s. When Republicans won control of Congress in the mid-1990s and a Republican president took office in 2001, Republicans adapted the process to the problem they faced: passing an ambitious agenda with narrow margins. And when Democrats regained control, they too made use of and, in some cases, further developed the processes and procedures of unorthodox lawmaking. If the aim was to facilitate successful lawmaking, does unorthodox lawmaking, in fact, do so?

TABLE 10.1   The Fate of Major Legislation, 1989–2010 (Selected Congresses)

	Percentage of major measures	Number of major measures
Total measures	100	511
Reached House floor	92	471
Reached Senate floor	82	419
Passed House	88	452
Passed Senate	72	366
Passed House and Senate	70	353
Became law*	62	318

*Or otherwise successfully completed the legislative process. This means approval of the conference report in both chambers in the case of budget resolutions and approval by two-thirds vote in each chamber in the case of constitutional amendments.

Source: Computed by the author.

Most bills do not become law. The House has been passing an average of 14 percent of the bills introduced by its members in recent Congresses (100th through 110th) and the Senate about 22 percent; and of course, passage in one chamber does not ensure enactment (Ornstein, Mann, and Malbin 2002, 146–147; Resume of Congressional Activity, various dates). Thousands of bills are introduced in each chamber during each Congress; neither chamber could possibly consider each one, so most are referred to committee and die there without any further action. Members introduce legislation for a variety of reasons, ranging from placating an interest group in their home state or district to publicizing a little-recognized problem or an innovative approach to an acknowledged problem. Members may not expect certain of their bills to pass and, sometimes, may not even want them to.

Major legislation is different; by definition, it is significant legislation that has made it onto the congressional agenda, where it is being seriously considered. As Table 10.1 shows, its prospects are considerably brighter than that of all legislation. Most major measures get to the floor of at least one chamber, and those that do usually pass—although the likelihood is considerably greater in the House than in the Senate.[1] About seven of ten major measures pass both chambers, and about six out of ten become law or otherwise successfully finish the process.[2] Thus measures that have

---

1. A bill on which the majority leader moves to proceed to consider but fails to invoke cloture is counted as having gotten to the floor.

2. Legislative success is defined as enactment in the case of bills, as approval of the conference report in both chambers in the case of budget resolutions, and as approval by two-thirds vote in each chamber in the case of constitutional amendments.

TABLE 10.2   The Effect of Unorthodox Lawmaking on Legislative Success, by
Chamber, 1987–2010 (Selected Congresses)

	Number of special procedures and practices*	All major measures	
		Percentage that passed chamber	Percentage enacted
House	0	68	50
	1	87	62
	2	95	63
	3 or more	98	71
Senate	0	62	54
	1	78	66
	2 or more	89	78

*The number of the following special procedures and practices that the legislation encountered as it worked its way through the chamber: for the House, multiple referral, omnibus legislation, legislation that was the result of a legislative-executive branch summit, the bypassing of committees, postcommittee adjustments, and consideration under a complex or closed rule; for the Senate, all of the above except consideration under a complex or closed rule.

Source: Computed by the author.

attained the status of being considered major legislation on the congressional agenda do tend to become law, but it is no sure thing.

How do the special procedures and practices that often characterize the legislative process on these major bills affect their probability of successful enactment? An examination of the relationship between the number of special procedures and practices used and legislative success provides at least a partial answer. The cumulative indexes introduced in Chapter 5 are used. For each of the major bills in the Congresses from 1987 through 2010 for which I have data, the House measure counts the number of the following special procedures and practices that the legislation encountered as it worked its way through that chamber: multiple referral, omnibus, the result of a summit, committee bypassed, postcommittee adjustments, and consideration under a restrictive rule. The Senate measure is identical, except that it does not include consideration under a restrictive rule

The likelihood that a bill will pass the House increases with the number of special procedures and practices employed, and the same is true for the Senate. When the legislative process on a bill in the House includes at least one special procedure or practice, that legislation is considerably more likely to become law than if it includes none, and if it includes two or more, it is still more likely to successfully complete the legislative process (see Table 10.2). Again, the relationship is similar for the Senate.

Because becoming law requires that both chambers pass the legislation, the combination of special procedures and practices in the two

TABLE 10.3   The Cumulative Effect of Unorthodox Lawmaking on Legislative
Success, 1987–2010 (Selected Congresses)

Number of special procedures and practices*	Percentage of major measures enacted
None in either chamber	53
None in one chamber, one in the other chamber, or one in each chamber	61
All other combinations except two or more in both chambers	62
Two or more in both chambers	78

*The number of the following special procedures and practices that the legislation encountered as it worked its way through the chamber: for the House, multiple referral, omnibus legislation, legislation that was the result of a legislative-executive branch summit, the bypassing of committees, postcommittee adjustments, and consideration under a complex or closed rule; for the Senate, all of the above except consideration under a complex or closed rule.

Source: Computed by the author.

chambers should make a difference. As Table 10.3 shows, it does. Of measures subject to two or more special procedures and practices in both chambers, 78 percent were successful; at the other extreme, if subject to none in either chamber, only 53 percent were successful.

Of course, other things being equal, leaders are more likely to use these procedures and practices on the most important legislation—legislation they believe really must pass for the good of country or party. Yet leaders are unlikely to employ the special procedures and practices under their control unless they expect passing the bill in satisfactory form will be problematic. Negotiating postcommittee adjustments and crafting and passing restrictive rules, not to mention bypassing committee, takes time and resources; if the legislation is going to pass without trouble, why expend either? Therefore, when the legislative process displays several special procedures and practices, the chances are that the bill was in some trouble and that, without intervention, its chances of legislative success were lower than those of other legislation. Since the data show a higher frequency of legislative success, these special procedures and practices do appear to accomplish their purpose.

The special practices stemming from the Senate's unique rules can be used by individual senators and by the minority party and may well be employed for different purposes and have different consequences than those that are primarily leadership tools. What impact do amending marathons and filibusters have on legislative outcomes? Amending marathons are associated with legislative success. Bills subject to ten or more Senate amendments decided by roll call votes are more likely to pass the Senate and more likely to become law than are other measures (see Table 10.4).

TABLE 10.4   Amending Marathons, Filibusters, and Legislative Outcomes for Major Measures, 1987–2010 (Selected Congresses)

Outcome	Amending marathon*		Filibuster problem	
	Yes	No	Yes	No
Percentage that passed Senate	87	78	71	79
Percentage enacted	76	65	61	67

*An amending marathon is defined as ten or more amendments offered and pushed to a roll call vote. Only measures that reached the Senate floor are included.

Source: Computed by the author.

The adoption of floor amendments may enhance a bill's chances of ultimate legislative success, since amendments may make a bill more broadly attractive or at least give the sponsors of successful amendments a greater stake in the legislation's enactment. However, the substantial differences in success rates between bills subject to high amending activity and those subject to low amending activity (regardless of whether the amendments that were offered passed) strongly suggest that senators engage in amending marathons on bills highly likely to become law. Senators sometimes use the Senate's permissive amending rules to try to kill legislation, but that is not their primary use; they primarily use such bills as vehicles for lawmaking. Of course, they also use them as vehicles for making political points.

The uses senators make of extended debate are much less benign in purpose and in effect, and extended debate has its most severe impact on legislative outputs when employed as a partisan tool. Legislation subject to a filibuster problem (a hold, a threatened filibuster, or a filibuster) is less likely to pass the Senate and less likely to become law than is other legislation (see Table 10.4). In recent Congresses 79 percent of major legislation that did not encounter any extended debate–related problem passed the Senate and 67 percent became law; in contrast, only 71 percent of major measures that ran into a filibuster-related problem passed the Senate and 61 percent became law. More than half of the major measures that failed to pass the Senate (56 percent) encountered a filibuster problem. Of all measures that failed to complete the entire process, 52 percent encountered a filibuster problem.

Of course, filibusters, actual or threatened, can influence outcomes without killing the legislation at issue. The perpetrators' aim, in fact, may be to extort substantive concessions from the bill's supporters rather than to kill the bill altogether. Those measures that became law despite a filibuster problem show a high incidence of postcommittee adjustments (47 percent for my selected Congresses from 1987 through 2010), suggesting that substantive alterations were required to overcome the filibuster problem.

Other Costs and Benefits

What effects does unorthodox lawmaking have beyond its impact on legislative outcomes? Scholars know that even planned changes in complex organizations and processes are likely to have unintended consequences; many of the changes examined here were not planned but evolved out of ad hoc responses to pressing problems.

Deliberation and Inclusion in the House

Congress has long done its serious substantive work on legislation in committees. A number of the procedures and practices that constitute unorthodox lawmaking were a response to the decline in the committees' autonomy and power; however, procedures and practices such as multiple referral, postcommittee adjustments, and the bypassing of committees have further eroded the committees' influence, at least to some extent. Has the result been less expertly crafted legislation and less deliberation at the prefloor stage of the process? If so, this would be a serious negative by-product of unorthodox lawmaking, since this is when real deliberation takes place, if it takes place at all.

The power of Congress, especially that of the House, in the political system depends on its specialized, expert committees. The issues and problems with which the federal government deals are too numerous, diverse, and complex for any one person to master. For a relatively small body such as Congress to hold its own vis-à-vis the executive branch and outside interests, it must divide labor and rely on its members' expertise in their areas of specialization. Has unorthodox lawmaking decreased the incentives for members to specialize and gain expertise?

At least before the mid-1990s, prefloor deliberation had not, by and large, been sacrificed. It is when committees are bypassed that the possibility that deliberation will be truncated is greatest. Yet in many cases, when a committee was bypassed in a particular Congress, the committee had, in fact, reported the legislation in a previous Congress. In those instances when Democratic House leaders used task forces rather than committees to draft legislation, they chose as task force leaders members who brought great substantive as well as political expertise to bear on the issue (Sinclair 1995, 188–192).

From the mid-1990s forward, a succession of seemingly special political circumstances led to less deference to committees and more centralization of decision making, including often substantive legislative decision making, in the party leadership. During the 104th Congress, the first Republican House majority in forty years had a lot it wanted to accomplish. The House Republican leaders put extraordinary pressure on committees to report legislation quickly. Hearings, if they were held at all, were perfunctory; markups often were hurried and were held before most members had had an opportunity to study the legislative language at issue; they were, in effect, pro forma. Party leaders and task forces on which inexperienced freshmen predominated exercised considerable influence on the substance of legislation in committee or through postcommittee adjustments; committees were frequently bypassed both to move legislation more quickly and for substantive reasons. In the 104th House, especially during 1995, substantive expertise and hard work on one's committee had relatively little payoff in influence. Deliberation and the quality of legislation did suffer. Many Republicans, members and staff alike, concede privately that the legislation brought to the floor was sloppy at best; the careful substantive work had not been done.

The modes of decision making prevalent during that Congress arose out of highly unusual circumstances—a new House majority after forty years and the attendant sense of mandate. Committees began to regain influence in 1996, and in the 105th and 106th Congresses, committee processes were in many ways similar to those before the Republican takeover. To be sure, the parties remained polarized, and the Republican seat margin was narrow, which led to the persistence of somewhat greater centralization. The difficulties of legislating under these circumstances forced the majority-party leadership to involve itself in all phases of the legislative process.

With the accession of George W. Bush to the presidency, however, the House Republican leadership, determined to deliver for their president, again dominated legislative decision making on top-priority legislation, effectively subordinating the committees. Committee chairs and other senior majority-party members usually played important roles, but most other committee members, majority as well as minority, were cut out of the action. And if they were not sufficiently responsive to White House wishes, even committee chairs could find themselves relegated to the sidelines, their committee bypassed or legislation reported by committee replaced with an administration-approved version.

Furthermore, the way in which the Republican leadership scheduled the House floor made it hard for committees to get much work done. The House typically considered only suspensions early in the week: either the House was not in session at all on Mondays or only suspensions were on the schedule. On Tuesdays, only suspensions were considered, and all recorded votes from both days were postponed until 6:30 p.m. At that time the votes were stacked; that is, they were taken in succession with no legislative business in between. The first was a fifteen-minute vote; the succeeding ones were shortened to five minutes. Most members arrived just in time for the recorded votes, which had been postponed until 6:30 p.m. on

Tuesday, and left after the last vote on Thursday. The House seldom had real legislative sessions on Friday. The 2006 House schedule, for example, called for votes during the day on only 71 days, with votes scheduled no earlier than 6:30 p.m. on an additional twenty-six days. In contrast, Congress was in session an average 140 days a year during the 1980s and 1990s (*Roll Call*, March 7, 2006).

This drastically truncated Washington workweek made it hard for committees and subcommittees to get much serious work done, particularly as work groups or collective entities. For members, meetings conflicted, and committees and subcommittees had difficulty getting quorums. Even if committees had been inclined toward serious oversight hearings, time pressure militated against such activity. Congress expert Norman Ornstein reports a steep drop in the number of committee and subcommittee meetings: "The average Congress in the 1960s and '70s had 5,372 committee and subcommittee meetings; in the 1980s and 1990s, the average was 4,793. In the last Congress, the 108th, the number was 2,135" (*RC*, March 7, 2006). Committees used to be forums in which representatives got to know members of the other party; that has become much less so in recent years.

When Democrats retook a House majority in 2006, committees again played a more active role but very much under the oversight and influence of the party leadership. Like the new Republican majority in the 104th, the new Democratic majority in the 110th had a big agenda and a conviction that both their policy and electoral goals required swift and decisive legislative action. With the election of a Democratic president in 2008, that conviction strengthened further. Passing the ambitious agenda required even more leadership engagement in all phrases of the legislative process; the committees continued to be highly active and the chairs of the committees that handled the major agenda items played central roles in working out necessary compromises, but the party leadership was clearly in charge. Certainly during the 110th and 111th Congresses, committees were sufficiently active decision-making arenas to make the development of expertise by their members worthwhile.

Speaker John Boehner (R-OH) has promised to exercise less central direction and restore committees to their dominant place in legislative decision making in the 112th Congress. The new House majority confronts pressures from its base and from many of its new members to make a sharp break with the direction of past policy; doing so will require making some very unpopular decisions, and the leadership's task of holding the membership together will not be easy. Consequently, Boehner is unlikely to be able to deliver fully on his promise. The return to a severely truncated Washington workweek announced by the new GOP leadership further complicates committee functioning.

Ensuring that the broadest possible range of interests is heard and considered is as important as expertise to an effective legislative process. What effect has unorthodox lawmaking had on the likelihood that the full range of views and interests will find a hearing? Since the mid-1990s the minority party has to a large extent been excluded from decision making at the prefloor—and often also at the postpassage—stage on the most highly visible major legislation in the House. To be sure, every Congress passes some quite significant legislation by large bipartisan majorities; policy matters that do not starkly divide the membership along party lines still are often decided in committee through bipartisan negotiations. However, the high partisan polarization that characterizes the contemporary Congress is based on deep differences between Democrats and Republicans, at the voter, activist, and member levels, in their notions of what constitutes good public policy. On many major issues a policy change that majorities of both Democrats and Republicans consider significantly better than the status quo does not exist, and, therefore, compromise is not in either party's interest. When the Democrats returned to the majority in 2007, several of the new committee chairmen made a sincere attempt to operate in a bipartisan fashion, but they found that on the highest priority legislation, bipartisanship and legislative productivity were mutually exclusive. Undoubtedly, the majority-party leadership and committee chairs sometimes unnecessarily use unorthodox processes that have the effect of excluding the minority from participation and thus exacerbate partisan polarization. More frequently, partisan polarization has made it necessary for the majority-party leaders to employ unorthodox processes and procedures at the prefloor and postpassage stages in order to legislate successfully.

Finally, in evaluating the effects of unorthodox lawmaking on the inclusiveness of the prefloor legislative process in the House, one must remember that the orthodox process often could be highly exclusionary. One committee had a monopoly on legislative action in a given area and was not necessarily responsive to the wishes of the chamber or of the majority party. Decisions were made behind closed doors, and the membership of many committees was biased in a way that favored some interests and excluded others. Diffuse interests—consumer and environmental interests in particular, which are seldom represented by wealthy and well-connected organizations—had little access.

Have specially tailored and usually restrictive special rules for House floor consideration of legislation degraded floor deliberation, as both Republican and Democratic minorities have claimed? It is unrealistic, I would argue, to expect deliberation, as a great many people use the term, to take place on the floor of either chamber and certainly not in the House. If *deliberation* is defined as the process by which a group of people gets together and talks through a complex problem, maps the problem's contours, defines the alternatives, and figures out where its members stand, it is unrealistic to expect all of that to occur on the chamber floors. Deliberation is a nonlinear, free-form process that depends on strict limits on the size of the group; subcommittees, other small groups, and, possibly, committees are the forums in which it might be fostered. Deliberation so defined certainly did not occur on the House floor before restrictive rules became prevalent.

What can and should be expected on the chamber floors are informed and informative debate and sound decision making. Restrictive rules can, in fact, contribute toward those goals. Rules can provide order and predictability to the floor consideration of complex and controversial legislation. They can be used to ensure that floor time is apportioned in a reasonably sensible way, both within a given bill and across legislation, and that debate focuses on the major alternatives, not on minor or side issues. In addition, through the use of restrictive rules, committee compromises can be protected from being picked apart on the floor.[3]

One's conclusions about the appropriate form of special rules depend on what sorts of decisions one believes can and cannot be made well on the House floor. The membership as a whole can and should make the big decisions; it can and should choose among the major alternatives that have been proposed. A body of 435 should not, I believe, get involved in a detailed rewriting of legislation on the floor via multitudes of individual amendments; the chamber is too large and unwieldy, the necessary expertise often is lacking, and the time almost always is too short for full consideration of the impact of proposed changes. Restrictive rules, in and of themselves, need not damage the quality of House floor consideration.

Yet when committee processes and other prefloor processes exclude the minority from meaningful participation, highly restrictive rules become much more problematic. Since the mid-1990s, the House minority party has become the majority three times. In all three cases, the party when in the minority had complained bitterly about how the majority used

---

3. Formal theorists have shown that, for any bill of more than minimal complexity (technically, any bill involving more than one dimension of choice), there exists an alternative that can defeat it (and, of course, there then exists an alternative that can defeat that one, ad infinitum). This result means that the legislators' preferences are not and cannot be the sole determinant of the legislative outcome because there is no single choice that a majority prefers to all others; the legislative outcome is also a function of the body's rules. For an accessible review of this literature, see Krehbiel (1988).

rules to limit floor participation and had promised to open up the process if it became the majority. In the first two cases, the new majority did not deliver on its promise. The Republicans in 1995 and the Democrats in 2007 quickly found that a more open floor process conflicted with their ability to deliver on their legislative promises. To be sure, both sometimes used overly restrictive rules simply for convenience. Yet in a period of high partisan polarization, expecting the minority to eschew maximally exploiting an open floor process for political gain and expecting the majority, in return, to refrain from employing the powerful tool of restrictive special rules is unrealistic.

In early 2011, Boehner received widespread praise for allowing the continuing resolution (CR) funding the government through the end of the fiscal year to come to the floor under a modified open rule, which only required preprinting of amendments. In fact, more than one hundred amendments were offered on the floor. Yet, while this process was more open than in the recent past, budget rules still protected the legislation the leadership had produced: amendments had to cut spending, or if an amendment added spending to one program, it had to cut at least as much elsewhere. Furthermore, such shifting among programs was tightly constrained; Democrats could not, for example, propose shifting spending for defense to domestic programs. Legislation on which an open amending process might well be more problematical has been brought to the floor under closed rules. The likelihood that the new Republican majority will deliver on its promise to open up floor proceedings significantly in the 112th Congress is low.

Decision Making in the Senate

In the Senate the most striking manifestation of unorthodox lawmaking is senators' increasingly frequent exploitation of extended debate and particularly, since the mid-1990s, its routine exploitation by the minority party. Does this trend in the Senate have consequences beyond the blocking of specific legislation? Are there benefits not otherwise attainable that outweigh the costs?

The habitual exploitation of extended debate by senators has a pervasive impact on the legislative process that extends far beyond its effect on specific legislation. By requiring a supermajority to pass legislation that is at all controversial, it makes the coalition-building process much more difficult and increases a status quo–oriented system's tendency toward gridlock. The costs of prolonged gridlock can be severe; a government that cannot act, that cannot respond satisfactorily to its citizens' demands, loses its legitimacy.

Supporters of the filibuster argue that it promotes deliberation; by slowing the legislative process, it provides an opportunity for second thoughts and perhaps for cooler heads to prevail. Furthermore, many argue, it gives extra weight to intensity in the process, allowing an intense minority to protect itself from a possibly tyrannical majority.

In reply one can argue that quite apart from extended debate in the Senate, the legislative process advantages intensity. For example, the committee assignment process (in which members' preferences are given substantial weight) and members' considerable freedom in both chambers to choose the issues to which they will devote their time result in greater influence being exercised by those with the more intense preferences on an issue (Shepsle 1978; Hall 1987). Deliberation is promoted by ensuring that a minority has time to attempt to raise public opposition to a proposal it believes unwise, but guaranteeing the minority an opportunity to publicize its views need not require such a difficult cloture procedure.

Individuals and small groups of senators frequently have used the Senate's permissive amending rules in combination with extended debate to highlight neglected issues and policy proposals. Their aim has been to get their issues on the public agenda, to push them to the center of debate, and perhaps to pressure the Senate into legislative action. Now the minority party regularly uses this strategy to force onto the agenda issues the majority party would rather not consider. The minority party's aim is to raise the visibility of the issues, to compel wide-ranging debate, and to pass legislation if possible. Yet within the current climate, the result more often than not is neither debate nor legislative action on either the minority's or the majority's agenda. The majority uses procedural devices to prevent debate and action on the minority's agenda, and the minority reciprocates by blocking the majority's agenda.

The 111th Congress's impressive legislative achievements—the stimulus bill, health care reform, financial services regulation, and the repeal of the "Don't Ask, Don't Tell" policy, as well as a number of less highly visible but significant bills—might be taken as proof that given the right circumstances the Senate can legislate, and so reform is unnecessary. In contraposition, one should remember that the Democratic majority was unusually large and still passing these bills was extraordinarily difficult. Increasingly the minority has been forcing the majority to go through the time-consuming process of imposing cloture on almost everything, with the result that the Senate is unable to consider even most of the appropriations bills. A great many bills that passed the House were never brought to the floor in the Senate for lack of time, which was of course the minority's aim. When Senate majorities are smaller, as they are likely to be most of the time, near gridlock is likely.

Assessing Unorthodox Lawmaking

Overall, then, how do we rate unorthodox lawmaking? A broader assessment requires some discussion of the appropriate criteria for judging Congress. Unless we are clear about what it is we want Congress to do, how are we to evaluate the impact of unorthodox lawmaking?

Certainly, we expect Congress to represent us; we expect members to bring into the legislative process the views, needs, and desires of their constituents, and we expect Congress as an institution to provide a forum in which the interests and demands of all segments of society are expressed. But beyond this, we also want Congress to make decisions—to pass laws.

This second criterion has sometimes been labeled lawmaking, but obviously not just any laws will do. In characterizing what sort of laws Congress is expected to enact, two criteria are frequently mentioned and often conflated. First, Congress should enact laws that reflect the will of the people; that is, Congress should be responsive to popular majorities. Second, Congress should enact laws that deal promptly and effectively with pressing national problems. These two criteria, which can be labeled responsiveness and responsibility, are distinct. Only in a perfect world would what the majority wants always accord with what policy experts deem most likely to be effective. Both responsiveness and responsibility are values we would like Congress to further in its lawmaking, yet at times they may come into conflict.

In popular and journalistic discourse, members of Congress are admonished to "do what's right, not what's popular." But do we really want Congress to regularly thwart popular majorities? Furthermore, and critically, uncertainty about the link between a specific policy choice and the societal outcome means that, in most major policy areas, legitimate differences of opinion as to what constitutes good public policy exist. Members of Congress are also told to pay attention to the people, not to special interests or out-of-touch experts; yet how should Congress respond when what the people want is based on faulty logic or incorrect information, a not infrequent occurrence given citizens' inattention to public policy problems? And what if the majority in question is a slim or relatively indifferent one and the minority passionately dissents?

Some tension among the values of representation, responsiveness, and responsibility is unavoidable. The institutional structures and processes most conducive to each are not necessarily the same. A decentralized, open, permeable body in which individual members have considerable resources and autonomy of action has great potential for representation—for articulating the broad variety of opinions and interests in our society. A more centralized, hierarchical body is more capable of expeditious decision making. Decision-making processes highly exposed to public scrutiny further responsiveness; those that are less visible may promote responsibility. Representation takes time, especially when there are a great variety of viewpoints; by definition, lawmaking requires closure, an end to debate, and, implicitly or explicitly, a choice among competing alternatives. Thus it is logically impossible to maximize all three values simultaneously. It would require an institution and a legislative process that make decisions quickly and slowly at the same time, ones that both expose members to the full force of public opinion and also provide some insulation.

If we expect a Congress that gives all interests a full and fair hearing on each issue and then, in every case, expeditiously passes legislation that both satisfies a majority, preferably a large one, and effectively addresses the problem in question, we are doomed to disappointment. Congress has never been able to live up to that standard, and the environment in which the contemporary Congress functions makes that even less feasible than in the past. The problems facing the country are highly complex. On many, there is little consensus among the experts about the appropriate governmental response; on others, the experts' prescriptions are unpalatable. Citizens are divided, unclear, and often ambivalent in their views as to what they want government to do. Political elites, including the representatives citizens elect, are sharply divided with regard to what they believe constitutes good public policy.

If, as I have argued, it is logically impossible for Congress to be perfectly representative, responsive, and responsible at the same time, and if the climate in which it currently functions is a difficult one, how should we evaluate unorthodox lawmaking? I argued in previous editions of this book that so long as unorthodox lawmaking facilitates Congress's ability to make decisions without sacrificing deliberation or restricting significantly the range of interests with access to the process, it performs an extremely important function. Since the mid-1990s the balance between inclusiveness and expeditious lawmaking has tilted too far toward expeditiousness in the House. The tools of unorthodox lawmaking have made that possible, but without them the House might not have been able to function at all. Given the high partisan polarization, significantly more open and inclusive processes—open rules for floor consideration on a routine basis, for example—might well render the House incapable of lawmaking.

In the Senate the minority party's exploitation of the chamber's permissive rules has made expeditious decision making nearly impossible and even slow decision making hard. A number of senators and numerous outside observers believe that state of affairs requires remedy if the Senate is to function adequately, and many reforms have been suggested. Making some motions or some types of legislation nondebatable—the motion to proceed to consider a bill, appropriation bills—has been proposed. Rule 22 could be altered so that the longer a measure is debated on the floor, the smaller the supermajority needed for cloture. Those opposed to cloture could be required to muster forty-one votes present and voting in opposition rather than the majority being forced to muster sixty in favor. (See Senate Rules and Administration Committee hearings on the filibuster at http://rules.senate.gov/public/index.cfm?p=CommitteeHearings.) The problem, of course, is that Senate rules are difficult to change. According to one interpretation, changing the rules always requires a two-thirds vote, an even bigger supermajority than that necessary to impose cloture on a bill. By another interpretation, the rules can be changed at the beginning of a Congress by a simple majority vote, but attempts to do so are likely to exacerbate interparty hostility.

Junior Democrats' efforts to make significant changes in rules largely fizzled at the beginning of the 112th Congress. A new rule attempts to ban secret holds, and another disallows senators from demanding the reading of an amendment so long as it has been available for seventy-two hours before it is brought up for floor consideration. Harry Reid and Mitch McConnell reached a "gentlemen's agreement" that the minority would be more restrained in filibustering motions to proceed and the majority more restrained in filling the amendment tree to prevent senators from offering amendments; what "more restrained" means was not specified.

If this assessment of congressional functioning seems a bit bleak, we need to remember there was no golden age in which Congress optimally balanced representation, responsiveness, and responsibility. If partisan polarization now seems to constitute a major barrier to a process that is both inclusive and capable of reaching decisions, ideologically heterogeneous and undisciplined parties were lamented as the barrier not so long ago. The Congress of the 1950s, now sometimes hailed for its "enlightened bipartisan" decision making and certainly a bastion of orthodox lawmaking, actually functioned as an oligarchy of senior and mostly conservative members who excluded junior members from meaningful participation and blocked liberal legislation (Bolling 1965; Matthews 1960).

The development of what I have called unorthodox lawmaking is the latest chapter in an ongoing story of congressional adaptation and change. Confronted by a political and institutional environment that made lawmaking difficult, congressional leaders modified and sometimes transformed existing procedures and practices as they attempted to do their job of facilitating lawmaking. The result, unorthodox lawmaking, is often not neat and not pretty, especially on those highly salient and contentious issues most likely to lead the news. It is, however, highly flexible and so can be tailored to the problems—political, substantive, and procedural—that a particular major measure raises. Unorthodox lawmaking tends to empower House majorities and Senate minorities, but so far, it has made it possible for our most representative branch to continue to perform its essential function of lawmaking in a time of popular division and ambiguity. It has thereby given us all the opportunity to work toward a political system in which the branch closest to the people better performs the tough tasks we assign to it.

References

Bach, Stanley. 1994. "Legislating: Floor and Conference Procedures in Congress." In *Encyclopedia of the American Legislative System,* vol. 2, ed. Joel Silbey. New York: Scribner's.

Bach, Stanley, and Steven S. Smith. 1988. *Managing Uncertainty in the House of Representatives.* Washington, D.C.: Brookings Institution.

Beth, Richard. 1994. "Control of the House Floor Agenda: Implications from the Use of the Discharge Rule, 1931–1994." Paper presented at the annual meeting of the American Political Science Association, New York, September 1–4.

———. 1995. "What We Don't Know about Filibusters." Paper presented at the meeting of the Western Political Science Association, Portland, Oregon, March 15–18.

———. 2003. "Motions to Proceed to Consider in the Senate: Who Offers Them?" Congressional Research Service Report RS21255.

———. 2005. "'Entrenchment' of Senate Procedure and the 'Nuclear Option' for Change: Possible Proceedings and the Implications." Congressional Research Service Report RL32843.

Beth, Richard, and Elizabeth Rybicki. 2003. "Sufficiency of Signatures on Conference Reports." Congressional Research Service Report RS21629.

Beth, Richard, Valerie Heitshusen, Bill Heniff, and Elizabeth Rybicki. 2009. "Leadership Tools for Managing the U.S. Senate." Paper presented at the annual meeting of the American Political Science Association, Toronto, Canada, September 1–4.

Binder, Sarah. 1996. "The Partisan Basis of Procedural Choice: Parliamentary Rights in the House, 1798–1990." *American Political Science Review* (March): 8–20.

———. 1997. *Minority Rights, Majority Rule: Partisanship and the Development of Congress.* New York: Cambridge University Press.

Binder, Sarah, and Steven S. Smith. 1997. *Politics or Principle? Filibustering in the United States Senate.* Washington, D.C.: Brookings Institution.

Bolling, Richard. 1965. *House Out of Order.* New York: Dutton.

Cohen, Richard E. 1992. *Washington at Work: Back Rooms and Clean Air.* New York: Macmillan.

Committee on Appropriations. 2010. Fact Sheet: Recent History of Earmark Reform. House of Representatives. March.

Committee on the Budget, United States Senate. 1998. The Congressional Budget Process: An Explanation. Committee Print. 105th Cong., 2nd sess.

Congress and the Nation. 1993. Washington, D.C.: CQ Press.

CongressDaily (now *National Journal Daily*).

Congress Today. www.cq.com.

Congressional Quarterly Almanac. Various years. Washington, D.C.: CQ Press.

Congressional Quarterly Weekly (before 1998, *Congressional Quarterly Weekly Reports*). Washington, D.C.: CQ Press. Online by subscription at http://library.cqpress.com/cqweekly.

Connelly, William, and John Pitney. 1994. *Congress' Permanent Minority? Republicans in the U.S. House.* Lanham, Md.: Rowman and Littlefield.

Cooper, Joseph. 1981. "Organization and Innovation in the House of Representatives." In *The House at Work,* ed. Joseph Cooper and G. Calvin Mackenzie. Austin: University of Texas Press.

Cooper, Joseph, and Cheryl D. Young. 1989. "Bill Introduction in the Nineteenth Century: A Study of Institutional Change." *Legislative Studies Quarterly* (February): 67–106.

Davidson, Roger H. 1981. "Two Avenues of Change: House and Senate Committee Reorganization." In *Congress Reconsidered,* ed. Lawrence C. Dodd and Bruce I. Oppenheimer, 2d ed. Washington, D.C.: CQ Press.

———. 1989. "Multiple Referral of Legislation in the U.S. Senate." *Legislative Studies Quarterly* (August): 375–392.

Davidson, Roger H., and Walter Oleszek. 1977. *Congress Against Itself.* Bloomington: Indiana University Press.

———. 1992. "From Monopoly to Management: Changing Patterns of Committee Deliberation." In *The Postreform Congress,* ed. Roger H. Davidson. New York: St. Martin's.

Dodd, Lawrence C., and Bruce I. Oppenheimer, eds. 1977. *Congress Reconsidered.* New York: Praeger.

DSG (Democratic Study Group). 1994. "A Look at the Senate Filibuster." *DSG Special Report,* June 13, 103–128, Appendix B (compiled by Congressional Research Service).

Ellwood, John W., and James A. Thurber. 1981. "The Politics of the Congressional Budget Process Re-examined." In *Congress Reconsidered,*

2d ed., ed. Lawrence C. Dodd and Bruce I. Oppenheimer. Washington, D.C.: CQ Press.

Epstein, Lee, and Jeffrey Segal. 2005. *Advice and Consent: The Politics of Judicial Appointments.* New York: Oxford University Press.

Evans, C. Lawrence, and Walter J. Oleszek. 1995. "Congressional Tsunami? Institutional Change in the 104th Congress." Paper presented at the annual meeting of the American Political Science Association, Chicago, August 31–September 3.

Fenno, Richard. 1973. *Congressmen in Committees.* Boston: Little, Brown.

Gallup Organization. 2011. "111th Congress Averaged 25% Approval, Among Recent Lowest." January. www.gallup.com.

Gamm, Gerald, and Kenneth Shepsle. 1989. "Emergence of Legislative Institutions: Standing Committees in the House and Senate, 1810–1825." *Legislative Studies Quarterly* (February): 39–66.

Gilmour, John B. 1990. *Reconcilable Differences?* Berkeley: University of California Press.

Gold, Martin. 2003. Interview by Donald Ritchie, Office of the Senate Historian. December 9.

———. 2004. *Senate Procedure and Practice.* New York: Rowman and Littlefield.

Gold, Martin, Michael Hugo, Hyde Murray, Peter Robinson, and A.-L. "Pete" Singleton. 1992. *The Book on Congress: Process, Procedure and Structure.* Washington, D.C.: Big Eagle Publishing. Supplements published biannually.

Hacker, Jacob, and Paul Pierson. 2005. *Off Center.* New Haven, Conn.: Yale University Press.

Hall, Richard L. 1987. "Participation and Purpose in Committee Decision Making." *American Political Science Review* (March): 105–127.

Hibbing, John, and Elizabeth Theiss-Morse. 1995. *Congress as Public Enemy.* New York: Cambridge University Press.

Jacobs, Lawrence, and Theda Skocpol. 2010. *Health Care Reform and American Politics.* New York: Oxford University Press.

King, David. 1994. "The Nature of Congressional Committee Jurisdictions." *American Political Science Review* (March): 48–62.

Koger, Gregory. 2002. "Obstructionism in the House and Senate: A Comparative Analysis of Institutional Choice." Dissertation, University of California–Los Angeles.

Krehbiel, Keith. 1988. "Spatial Models of Legislative Choice." *Legislative Studies Quarterly* 13, 259–320.

Lee, Frances. 2009. *Beyond Ideology: Politics, Principles and Partisanship in the U.S. Senate.* Chicago: University of Chicago Press.

———. 2010. "Individual and Partisan Activism in U.S. Senate Floor Politics, 1959–2008." Paper presented at the Dole Institute Symposium on Changing the Slow Institution. University of Kansas, March 25–26.

Lilly, Scott. 2005. "How Congress Is Spending the $.18 a Gallon You Pay in Gasoline Tax." Center for American Progress Report, October.

———. 2006. Statement before the Subcommittee on Federal Financial Management, Government Information, and International Security Committee on Homeland Security and Governmental Affairs, United States Senate, March 16.

———. 2010. From Deliberation to Dysfunction: It Is Time for Procedural Reform in the U.S. Senate. Center for American Progress, March 11.

Longley, Lawrence, and Walter Oleszek. 1989. *Bicameral Politics*. New Haven, Conn.: Yale University Press.

Mann, Thomas, and Norman Ornstein. 2006. *The Broken Branch*. New York: Oxford University Press.

Matthews, Donald E. 1960. *U.S. Senators and Their World*. New York: Vintage Books.

Office of Management and Budget. 2010. The President's Budget Historical Statistics.

Oleszek, Walter J. 2004. *Congressional Procedures and the Policy Process*, 6th ed. Washington, D.C.: CQ Press.

———. 2007. *Congressional Procedures and the Policy Process*, 7th ed. Washington, D.C.: CQ Press.

Oppenheimer, Bruce. 1994. "The Rules Committee: The House Traffic Cop." In *Encyclopedia of the American Legislative System*, vol. 2, ed. Joel Silbey. New York: Scribner's.

Ornstein, Norman, Thomas Mann, and Michael Malbin. 2002. *Vital Statistics on Congress 2001–2002*. Washington, D.C.: CQ Press.

Pearson, Kathryn, and Eric Schickler. 2009. "Discharge Petitions, Agenda Control and the Congressional Committee System 1929–1976." *Journal of Politics* 71, 1238–1256.

Politico. www.politico.com/.

Resume of Congressional Activity. *Congressional Record—Daily Digest.* Various dates.

Risjord, Norman K. 1994. "Congress in the Federalist-Republican Era." In *Encyclopedia of the American Legislative System*, vol. 1, ed. Joel Silbey. New York: Scribner's.

Rohde, David. 1991. *Parties and Leaders in the Postreform House*. Chicago: University of Chicago Press.

Roll Call. Online by subscription. www.rollcall.com/.

Roust, Kevin. 2005. "Special Rules and the Motion to Recommit." Manuscript.

Rybicki, Elizabeth. 2003. "Unresolved Differences: Bicameral Negotiations in Congress, 1877–2002." Paper delivered at the History of Congress Conference, University of California–San Diego, December 5–6.

Schick, Allen. 1980. *Congress and Money.* Washington, D.C.: Urban Institute.

Shepsle, Kenneth. 1978. *The Giant Jigsaw Puzzle: Democratic Committee Assignments in the Modern House.* Chicago: University of Chicago Press.

Sinclair, Barbara. 1983. *Majority Leadership in the U.S. House.* Baltimore: Johns Hopkins University Press.

———. 1989. *The Transformation of the U.S. Senate.* Baltimore: Johns Hopkins University Press.

———. 1991. "Governing Unheroically (and Sometimes Unappetizingly): Bush and the 101st Congress." In *The Bush Presidency: First Appraisals,* ed. Colin Campbell and Bert Rockman. Chatham, N.J.: Chatham House.

———. 1995. *Legislators, Leaders and Lawmaking.* Baltimore: Johns Hopkins University Press.

———. 1996. "Trying to Govern Positively in a Negative Era: Clinton and the 103rd Congress." In *The Clinton Presidency: First Appraisals,* ed. Colin Campbell and Bert Rockman. Chatham, N.J.: Chatham House.

———. 1997. *Unorthodox Lawmaking: New Legislative Processes in the U.S. Congress,* 1st ed. Washington, D.C.: CQ Press.

———. 2000. *Unorthodox Lawmaking: New Legislative Processes in the U.S. Congress,* 2nd ed. Washington, D.C.: CQ Press.

———. 2007. *Unorthodox Lawmaking: New Legislative Processes in the U.S. Congress,* 3rd ed. Washington, D.C.: CQ Press.

———. 2006. *Party Wars: Polarization and the Politics of the Policy Process.* Julian Rothbaum Lecture Series. Norman: University of Oklahoma Press.

Smith, Steven S. 1989. *Call to Order: Floor Politics in the House and Senate.* Washington, D.C.: The Brookings Institution.

———. 1995. *The American Congress.* Boston: Houghton Mifflin.

Smith, Steven S., and Marcus Flathman. 1989. "Managing the Senate Floor: Complex Unanimous Consent Agreements since the 1950s." *Legislative Studies Quarterly* (August): 349–374.

Stanton, John. 2009. "Three Days of Negotiations Delivered Nelson's Vote." *Roll Call,* December 19, 10:31 p.m.

Stockman, David Alan. 1986. *The Triumph of Politics.* London: Bodley Head.

Strom, Gerald, and Barry Rundquist. 1977. "A Revised Theory of Winning in House-Senate Conferences." *American Political Science Review* (June): 448–453.

The Hill. http://thehill.com/.

Thomas. thomas.loc.gov.

Thurber, James, and Samantha Durst. 1993. "The 1990 Budget Enforcement Act: The Decline of Congressional Accountability." In *Congress Reconsidered,* 5th ed., ed. Lawrence C. Dodd and Bruce I. Oppenheimer. Washington, D.C.: CQ Press.

Tiefer, Charles. 1989. *Congressional Practice and Procedure.* Westport, Conn.: Greenwood Press.

Wallner, James. 2010. "The Death of Deliberation: Public Opinion, Party and Policy in the Modern United States Senate." Paper presented at the annual meeting of the Midwest Political Science Association, Chicago, April 22–25.

Wolfensberger, Donald. 2002. "Suspended Partisanship in the House: How Most Laws Are Really Made." Paper delivered at the American Political Science Association meetings, August 29–September 1.

Wolfensberger, Donald. n.d. Information Sheets on Congress. The Congress Project.

Woodrow Wilson International Center for Scholars. www.wilsoncenter.org/congress.

Useful Web Sites
for Congress Watchers

Central Congressional Sites:

http://thomas.loc.gov/: Library of Congress site that includes bill chronologies, the *Congressional Record,* and links to other congressional and governmental sites.

www.house.gov/: Official House of Representatives site that includes information on operations and schedule and links to committee and member sites.

www.senate.gov: Official Senate site that includes information on operations and schedule and links to committee and member sites.

Congressional Party Sites:

www.dems.gov: House Democrats

www.gop.gov: House Republicans

www.democrats.senate.gov: Senate Democrats

www.republican.senate.gov: Senate Republicans

Capitol Hill Media:

www.c-span.org/

www.hillnews.com/

www.rollcall.com/

Abbreviations of Commonly Used In-text Citations

CD	*Congressional Digest*
CQA	*Congressional Quarterly Almanac*
CQW	*Congressional Quarterly (CQ) Weekly*
CR	*Congressional Record*
Daily	*CongressDaily*
LAT	*Los Angeles Times*
MR	*National Journal's Markup Reports*
NYT	*New York Times*
RC	*Roll Call*
Thomas	*Library of Congress site*
WP	*Washington Post*

Index